BEFORE THE LEMONS

A History of Bath Football Club RFU 1865-1965

BEFORE THE LEMONS

A History of Bath Football Club RFU 1865-1965

KEVIN COUGHLAN, PETER HALL AND COLIN GALE

This history is dedicated to all who have helped to establish and nurture the unique character of rugby at Bath, whether on the field, in the committee room or on the 'Flowerpots'

First published 2003

Tempus Publishing Ltd
The Mill, Brimscombe Port
Stroud, Gloucestershire GL5 2QG
www.tempus-publishing.com

British Library Cataloguing in Publication Data.
A catalogue record for this book is available from the British Library.

ISBN 0 7524 3109 9

Typesetting and origination by Tempus Publishing.
Printed and bound in Great Britain.

Contents

	Foreword	6
	Acknowledgements	7
	Introduction	8
	About the Authors	10
1	The Earliest Years	11
2	Buster	23
3	The First Derby Match	31
4	Nomads Again	45
5	Threepennies and Sixpennies	59
6	The First of the Lions	77
7	Gone North	95
8	Fields of Glory	107
9	They Played the Game – They Crossed the Line	127
10	Diamond Jubilee	147
11	Targeted by the Luftwaffe	175
12	Stormy Weather	195
13	Of Jockeys and Silks	215
14	Best of the First	243
	Bath Players	248
	Reference Notes	252
	Bibliography	256

Foreword

I AM DELIGHTED to have been asked to contribute a foreword to this first volume of an extraordinary production. And it is extraordinary – the result of more than five years of painstaking research, writing and editing by Peter Hall, Colin Gale and Kevin Coughlan. This trio deserve our gratitude and congratulations. Over several pints at their beloved Club, the originators committed themselves to researching the Club's history from its foundation year in 1865 (the year in which President Lincoln was assassinated) through to the end of the modern day. This first volume deals with the first 100 years.

Previous histories formed the starting point, but numerous public records, personal reminiscences and accumulated memorabilia were also studied. Then, in January 1999, came the discovery that has added so much to the finished product. For years it had been thought that several of the Club's Minute books had been lost during the Bath Blitz of 1942. Their discovery, at the home of the late Jack Simpkins, provided the real stimulus to make this the definitive record of the Club's proud history.

Of course it covers the low points, such as the death, in 1919, of Clifford Walwin following a collision on the Rec in a match against Cross Keys. But many high points are chronicled and rich anecdotal material included.

The Club's connections with the wider life of the city and beyond are also covered: from the role of team members in the Boer and both World Wars to the decision, in 1923, to ask the RAC to help with car parking on match days. And we gain insights behind the scenes; from the debate in 1903 about the size of the hoops on players' jerseys (the outcome was to increase their width from 4 to 6 inches) and the Management Committee's somewhat bizarre decision in 1923 to hold a Smoking Concert in aid of the Mayor's Fresh Air Fund!

The photographs tell powerful stories in their own right. The 1896 team photograph, for example, shows the Club's growing role within international rugby. In this one photograph can be seen Frank Soane (England 1893-94), Frederick Belson, who toured with a Great Britain side in 1899 in Australia (a precursor to the Lions), and J.B.S. D'Aguilar, son of Francis D'Aguilar who, when capped in 1872, was the first England player to be associated with the Bath club.)

Gathering all the information has not been easy and there are inevitable gaps. However, perhaps the hardest task of all has been in deciding what to leave out. But it does mean that, in addition to the work itself, there is now an impressive amount of material to add to the Club's bulging archives. Preparing this book has been a great achievement. The result is extraordinary. Enjoy it.

Don Foster,
House of Commons

Acknowledgements

THE ORIGINATORS OF this work wish to especially thank Mr. David Gledhill, Editor of *The Bath Chronicle* and his successive Librarians, Katie Lee and Theresa Ford, for allowing access to the *Chronicle* archives over a period of three years. Without them, this publication would not have been possible. By far the largest accumulation of information, in picture and in text, was discovered from within their resources. Our researchers uncovered not only a mass of match-related comment but also a wealth of stylish narrative by a long line of accomplished journalists

We are indebted to very many people who made a wide range of material available, and in many cases, volunteered practical help. We set out most of the names below and sincerely apologise if any individual has inadvertently been omitted.

HISTORICAL MATERIAL OR ASSISTANCE

John Roberts, Mrs. Florence Simpkins, Mrs. Phil Arnold, Mrs Joyce Weiss, Mrs Elizabeth Higgins, Geoff Pillinger, Ken Watts, Tony Guest, Freddie Hayman, Mick Hanna, Bob Orledge, Tom Martland, John Monahan, David Peters, Reg Monk (deceased), 'Patchy' Davies, Bill Donnelly (deceased), Malcolm Spark, Chris Perry, Brendan Perry, Tim Harris, Jed Smith (Curator, RFU Museum), Gerry Moore (deceased), Tommy Hicks, Geoff Hancock, Les Matthews, M. Hoskins (Bristol), Brian Henson, Dorrien Belson, Phil Hardy, Malcolm Henson, Ken Johnstone, Len Hughes, Peter Frankcom, John Downey, John Dolman, George Atchison (Avonvale RFC), Morton Evans, Mrs. Rosemary St John-Davies, Ben Hartley (Oldfield Old Boys RFC), Gerry Wheeler (Walcot RFC), Kevin Ford, Roy Farnham, John Palmer, John Brennan, Angus Meek, Peter Heindorff (deceased), N. Halse (deceased), Ted Arnold, Eric Hopton, Lyn Alvis, Mike Etheridge, Gordon Hall, Dr John Wroughton, Major John Quin, Nevil Field, Mrs Lorna Ebdon, The City Archivist, H.D. Rees, The Bath Library, John Edwards, Richard Mawditt, Steven and Louis Bush, Russell Gibbs, Jon Hall, Jerry Keeling, Michel van der Loos, Jacqui Fisher (NZ), The Royal Engineers Museum of Military Engineering, Chris Ducker, Andrew Hall and Bath Rugby PLC.

PHOTOGRAPHIC AND TECHNICAL ASSISTANCE

The Bath Chronicle; *Bristol Evening Post*; Bob Ascott; David Harrison; Val Cooper; Mr Paul Simes, of Caerprint, Cirencester – team photo scans (introduction facilitated courtesy of Roger Shute); Richard Seaman – long term digital camera provision and team photograph imaging.

Introduction

In days long past, players stopped for lemons. This dash of self-inflicted sharpness was evidently enough to revive spirits for the 'second moiety'. Thankfully for most taste buds, lemons generally gave way to a plateful of sliced oranges! Our title serves as a reminder that rugby is 'a game of two halves'. The 'lemons' interval was therefore a spell to rest and recuperate – and plan to come back with an even stronger game in the second half. This book is rich in anecdotal material – the way people were, the way people played. Bath FC's latter days of high achievement will be chronicled in a second volume. But let's go back a bit … On 1 March 1913, *The Bath Chronicle*'s rugby correspondent penned some 'serious' words of wisdom for a fellow spectator …

THE LEMON PEEL PROBLEM by 'An Old Player'

'The other afternoon I was seated in the grandstand of a certain football ground smoking indifferent tobacco (so a neighbour said), and watching with moody attention a somewhat forlorn rugby match. I called it "forlorn" for the players seemed somewhat lost, and there was a total absence of combination. But that's another story! Well, when the interval arrived a friend "spotted" me from afar, and came and gave me the pleasure of his company for a few minutes. As we sat and conversed on the waywardness of things in general, and the slackness of the halfway through match in particular, my friend suddenly waxed sarcastic in these terms: "Look at them," he vociforated, pointing at the players. "While the game was on they could not raise a gallop, and now see what they are doing." Naturally I did look. A few of the "resting" footballers were lying prone on the grass, some were kicking the leather about but the great majority were engaged in chucking segments of lemon peel at one another; certainly they were far more energetic than they were during the game. "And now observe another thing," he said, "look how all these slippery bits of peel are strewn on the field itself, as though the ground was not slippery enough." – "Yes!" I hazarded interrogatively, for I did not know what was coming. "Well," he replied, "why don't you kick up a shindy in the Press and get this sort of thing put a stop to?" I brought my sluggish brain to bear on the subject, then I said "I will give you a few suggestions on how to do away with the evil complained of if it will afford you any comfort. My remedies are as follows:-

Lemon sucking, 1933.

Football Herald & Chronicle

370 Registered at the General Post Office as a Newspaper SATURDAY, SEPTEMBER 3, 1938

f Bath led to the
toned, but he re-
because he can-
raining and to
committee meet-

drop players who
ldest move that I
y think it a bit
congratulate the
many players.
n right lines. It is
of the side if one
to train. On the
some men who do

the fact remains
would go stale if
r course of train-

to convey is that
in charge who
nside out and who
the training he
players are alike.
not agree with. It
ast resistance, but
ne. Much depends
self. He should
and the question

GETTING READY FOR NEXT WEEK: Pause during training for a picture of Bath rugby players who are getting fit for their opening match.

TIDIN

GOOD S
THE

SUPPORT
THEY'RE

BRISTOL

Bath City have
off well. They h
of a brace of poi
the back from B
no goals scored
this morning at
they were up am
Southern League
state of affairs to
a week's matche
Mr. Alex Raist
of heather from
near Glasgow. H
last Saturday. I
on Wednesday, a
well.
On Wednesday
to everybody
Wales. There w

Let's make a start!

(1) Abolish giving away lemons at half-time.
(2) Have the segments of the lemon peeled before distribution.
(3) Make the players take their mid-match refreshments off the playing area.
(4) Send a boy round with a basket into which the lemon-tasters could put such parts of the fruit they do not require.
(5) Command each player to bring his bit of peel and put it outside the playing field, flinging it at the spectators if he likes, off the pitch, or best of all
(6) Go and collect the debris off the ground yourself before the game is resumed.

"What do you think of that?" I concluded. Happily for me the game was continued at this point, and my friend left me, remarking: "go and pick them up yourself," and that's all the thanks I get for trying to solve the tough problem.'

About the Authors

KEVIN COUGHLAN: Kevin has reported on rugby on the Rec for two decades. He was educated at Prior Park College in Bath and trained as a journalist in Torquay before moving in 1979 to the sports desk of the *Evening Post* in Bristol; assignments included the 1984 Los Angeles Olympics and the 1991 Rugby World Cup. After a spell as Business Editor of the *Evening Post*, he moved into the world of PR with Strategy Communications in Bristol, where he is now Senior Editorial Consultant. Kevin has continued to contribute as a freelance rugby writer and broadcaster.

PETER HALL: Peter is immediate Past President of the Bath Club and a former player, having made his debut for the club in the early 1950s. Family associations with the club extend over nearly a century – married to Mollie, his father-in-law was Harry Vowles, a brilliant half-back immediately after the First World War, while their son, John, was at one time Bath's most capped England international. Now retired, Peter's career background in banking prepared him for the many months of meticulous research which prepared the ground for this definitive record.

COLIN GALE: Colin is a former Local Director of NatWest Bank and was the Bath club's Honorary Treasurer until the end of the amateur days. Educated at Bristol Grammar School, he has enjoyed a life-long interest in rugby and diligently researched this work together with Peter Hall over a period of five years.

-1-

The Earliest Years

IT WAS THE year in which Abraham Lincoln was assassinated and surviving veterans of Wellington's Army gathered to commemorate the 50th anniversary of the Battle of Waterloo. The year 1865 predates so much that has shaped the modern age – the internal combustion engine, global war, mass production, universal suffrage, air travel, instant communication. With the British Empire yet to reach its zenith, the subjects of Queen Victoria were to enjoy another half-century of unparalleled peace and prosperity.

Towards the end of that year a group of young men in Bath decided to form a football club, playing to the Rugby Code, under the name of Bath Zouaves. Facilities were rudimentary to the extent that the ball, a foul-smelling, misshapen pig's bladder, had to be inflated by mouth before each game; there was precious little by way of pitch markings and there were certainly no goalposts on the cricket ground they rented as their first home.

Needless to say, those involved could not possibly have imagined, even in their most optimistic flights of fancy, that they were laying the foundations for a club that was to set unmatched standards in the amateur game in these islands.

With warfare reduced to skirmishes in the outposts of the Empire, Englishmen's competitive instincts had quite recently turned to developing and codifying the variants of football that had been adopted as the winter sport in boarding and grammar schools around the country. It was only from 1863 that any distinction between association and rugby football had become evident, allowing enthusiasts of the respective codes to pursue their chosen games.

Etonians abhorred the tendency of Rugbeians to pick up the ball during a game and run with it. Hacking, tripping and mauling were subsequently outlawed by those who signed up to the 'Cambridge Rules' adopted by the Football Association. But eleven other London clubs and schools who favoured handling met in the same year, 1863, to draw up their own rules governing rugby football, as it was called. As a concession to those who had misgivings about the more violent aspects of the game, hacking, tripping and holding were permitted only to restrain the player with the ball – although there were mutterings of 'unmanliness' among the diehards at Blackheath. The argument was not settled for some years.

The names of the first Bath rugby players are known to us only through reminiscences recorded in 1921 by Thomas Gandy, a founder member and a central figure in the early history of the club. He recalled them as being The Reverend Robert Whittington, Mr H.G. Wood, Charles Hoare, the brothers John and Thomas Wilton, Charles Petgrave, Francis D'Aguilar, J.C. Matchem, Messrs Hulbert and Pearson, among others.

An indication of the fledgling nature of the club – and the sport of rugby football – is that Gandy, a forward then barely sixteen, was appointed Honorary Secretary and served in that post for the first three years of the club's existence. Sadly, no records appear to have survived from that time. What little is known about the Bath Zouaves comes from a 'special interview' given by Gandy to 'Bohemian' of the *Bath Herald* in 1921. Then in his early seventies, he recalled that they:

began playing on the field now used by the Bath Cricket Club, North Parade, and paid a licensee 2s 6d per match for the use of the ground. The football 'bladders' of those days were pigs' 'bladders' and these had to be blown up with the mouth, there being no bicycle pumps. The balls had a nasty knack of bursting and the only alternative was to get a new bladder, patching being out of the question.[1]

As for interest on the touchline, it must have been minimal. Indeed, at an annual general meeting of the club on 13 June 1895, reference was made to the fact that 'many of the old players of the Club were wont to disport themselves before some 20 spectators'. How different a game it was, as Bohemian noted in his interview with Gandy:

Their idea in those days was to get the ball through the scrum and follow it up with the forwards, just exactly the opposite to the present day practice. Mr Gandy is also of the opinion that the play is very much faster now than it used to be. There was none of that slinging of the ball about, he said. They used to kick the ball forward and the three-quarters would follow up. Passing back was never thought of.[2]

But why did they call themselves the Bath Zouaves? Originally the name of an elite light infantry corps of the French army drawn from the Berber tribes of Algeria, the Zouaves were renowned for their courage and fine physique. Zouaves' distinctive regimental dress consisted of a loose dark blue jacket and waistcoat, baggy Turkish trousers, yellow leather leggings, white gaiters, a sky blue sash and a red fez with yellow tassel.

According to Gandy, the first playing strip comprised blue jerseys and red caps, almost certainly an echo of the Zouaves' uniform. But, although the elite French infantrymen had distinguished themselves during the Crimean War a decade earlier, the role model for the young men of Bath may well have been American militia who adopted the same extravagant uniforms during the recently concluded Civil War.

Soon, however, the connection must have seemed less relevant and at some point in the early years they discarded the name for the less exotic Bath Rovers and then Bath Wanderers, doubtless intended to reflect their nomadic progress around the sports fields of the city. The playing strip of blue jerseys, white 'knicks', red stockings, and red

Zouave militia of the American Civil War (1861-1865). (Courtesy of artist Keith Rocco)

caps also gave way to the Blue and Black, reportedly brought down from Windsor by Gandy. Although they eventually settled on the title of Bath Football Club, the club crest still contains, coincidentally or not, the blue and red of the Zouaves' battle dress.

The first written record of a player roster originates from 1870 ('Club History', *The Bath Chronicle*, 25 November 1933) when the name of T.J. Gandy appeared along with those of E.B. Sugden, W. Sants, C.C. Baldwin, J. Baldwin, W. Baldwin, J.C. Matchem, W. Bond, F. Sainsbury, H.E. Richardson, E.A. Mercer, A.K.Cunninghame and G.O. Welch. Gandy had been succeeded as Honorary Secretary and Treasurer in 1868 by Walter Sants. Three years Gandy's junior, his involvement with the club as player, official and supporter was to span nearly 60 years.

Their respective contributions to the club are well documented but the absence of club records from those early years has cast a cloak of anonymity over others. Nevertheless, the census of 1881 reveals that, of the founder members, Reverend Whittington was by then Vicar of Swainswick, Charles Hoare was a banker and the Wilton brothers were solicitors, as was Charles Petgrave.

More interesting perhaps, given the public school origins of the game, is the number of artisans and labourers who found the energy to play rugby in these early days. Of those listed in the 1870 playing roster, the census eleven years later reveals their occupations as follows: 'Edward Mercer, Carpenter and Builder, from Walcot; William Bond, General Labourer, from Avon Street; Henry Richardson, "attendant on the insane" at the Somerset & Bath Asylum; Charles Baldwin, Labourer at Bathford Paper Mill; James Baldwin, Stone Miner from Bathford; Joseph Baldwin, Quarry Stone Labourer, from Canal Terrace, Bathampton.'

Although the name of Charles Petgrave, identified by Gandy among the founder members, does not reappear in the 1870 list, he was to become club captain in 1877/78.

One who had almost certainly left the club by 1870, when he was gazetted as a Lieutenant in the Royal Engineers, was Frank D'Aguilar, who holds the distinction of being the first member of the Bath club to earn international honours, although not as a Bath player. Francis Burton Grant D'Aguilar was born in the city on 11 December 1849, which would have made him fifteen years old at the formation of the club. He was educated at Cheltenham College and the Royal Military Academy (Woolwich), where his military education and training forced a switch of rugby allegiance to The Royal Engineers.

Commissioned on 1 December 1870, he completed his training at the School of Military Engineering at Chatham, where it was first as a cricketer that he made his mark on the sports field. The following summer he took four wickets against the Gentlemen

The England team of 1872, which included Bath's Frank D'Aguilar. The side was captained by Frederick Stokes, who later became second President of the RFU.

of MCC and five wickets in an innings on several occasions; his best performance was against the Civil Service when he took six wickets in an innings and ten in the match. In 1872 he also played Association Football, particularly distinguishing himself against Crystal Palace.

England and Scotland had inaugurated the international rugby football game in 1871, fielding 20 players a side at Raeburn Place, Edinburgh. Lieutenant D'Aguilar was capped in the England XX for the return match in front of 4,000 spectators at Kennington Oval on the Monday afternoon of 5 February 1872. On a pitch measuring 120 yards by 70 yards, England made the most of open spaces and won by a goal, a drop goal and two tries to a drop goal.

The second half of the match was principally remarkable for the grand forward play on the English side, and for a magnificent left foot drop by Freeman, who obtained a second goal for England. D'Aguilar and Finney also got in, but Isherwood's place-kicks failed...[3]

Both try scorers soon forsook rugby for Empire building. Finney, later to become Sir Stephen Finney CIE KB, had been educated at Clifton College, Bristol, and the Royal Indian Engineering College, and he continued his sport with the Calcutta club while working for the East Bengal State Railway.

Although D'Aguilar also scored a try on his debut, he never again wore an England shirt. On completing his studies at Chatham, he was posted to India and early in 1873 was to be found at Roorkee, the centre of military engineering in North India.

After seven years working in various locations in northern India, he was attached to General Primrose's Division of the Kandahar Field Force during the British expedition to Afghanistan. Extracts from a despatch during the withdrawal of military posts at Abdul Rayman, Mel Karez, Dabrai and Gattai by a Major W. Jacob make mention of D'Aguilar's contribution:

5. I had now the following troops with me at Gattai:- 190 rank and file, 19th N.I.; 97 sabres, Poona Horse; 25 Sappers and Miners under Lieut. D'Aguilar R.E. This officer was with me at Mel Karez, and has given me the most valuable advice and assistance throughout.

6. ...Throughout this long march of seventeen miles Lieut. D'Aguilar, R.E., was indefatigable in the assistance he gave me.

Promoted to Major on 1 April 1889, D'Aguilar rose to Senior Engineer 3rd Class in the Punjab and in February 1896 is listed as Senior Engineer of the Sirhind and Lahore Circle, Military Works Department, Meean Mear. Within four months, he was back in

England on leave, presumably because of ill health, because he died in Bath on 24 July aged forty-six. His son, John Burton Stockwell D'Aguilar, was a first-team regular with Bath and Somerset at the time of F.B.G.'s death.

Another early international with strong connections to the Bath club was Lennard Stokes who, along with his brother Frederick, had considerable influence on the development of rugby football. It was Frederick who earned a special place in rugby football history by proposing at a gathering of twenty-one clubs in the Pall Mall Restaurant on 26 January 1871 'that in the opinion of this Meeting the formation of a Football Society is desirable; that such a society be formed forthwith and that the co-operation of all clubs be invited'. The Rugby Football Union was born, although with no representative from the Bath club. Two months later, Frederick Stokes became the first captain of England and in 1874/75, at the age of just twenty-four, he was appointed the second president of the RFU.

While Frederick was educated at Rugby School and played for the celebrated Blackheath club, Lennard's alma mater was Sydney College, which operated as Bath College from 1877 to 1909. *The Bath Chronicle* of 17 November 1881, reporting on a match between Bath and Bath College through the eyes of 'one interested in the Bath club', suggested that 'Sydney College…has turned out one, if not two, men who had played for England. I refer to the Stokes [brothers].'

Gandy, in bemoaning many years later that 'drop-kicking had fallen away altogether, and that no one can drop-kick like they used to in the olden days,' recalled that 'Stokes, who used to play for Sydney College, and who turned out for Bath on vacations, had the credit of dropping a goal from beyond the halfway line.'

Lennard was described by *Guy's Gazette* (1873) as 'a faultless catch and field, and a very quick starter, and with his speed of foot, wonderful dodging powers, and clever "shoving off", [he] was an extremely difficult man to tackle'. He amassed 40 points for England between 1875 and 1881, the season in which he is reckoned to have dropped a goal from some 80 yards against Scotland! He would have earned rather more than 12 caps had he not retired to concentrate on his medical career. Lennard served on the RFU committee for over fifty years, remaining a trustee until 1929, and by the time of his death on 3 May 1933, aged seventy-seven, he had outlived his brother by five years.

An even more famous doctor turned out for Bedminster against Bath on the North Parade Ground in 1871. W.G. Grace would have been twenty-three years old at this time, and was already a hugely accomplished cricketer but very much an all-round athlete. An early report (*The Bath Chronicle,* 16 March 1871) records 'time called at 5pm when Bath had scored four rouges and Bedminster one goal, seven rouges and one try. (Goal kicked by W.G. Grace).'

From the city of Bristol there soon arose more formidable opponents in the shape of Clifton, established in 1872 under the motto 'Dum Ludimus Ludamus' (While we play, we learn). On 9 November that year, *The Bath Chronicle* reported:

The England team to play Ireland in 1875 included Lennard Stokes (back row, fourth from right), who was educated at Bath's Sydney College. (Courtesy of the RFU Museum)

A football match was played on Saturday, on the Association ground, between the Bath Wanderers and the Clifton Club. The match was a very spirited one, and resulted in a victory for the Cliftonians, who made one goal and five rouges against the Wanderers' nil.

Within two seasons, Clifton were strong enough to complete the 'double' over their West Country neighbours – by four goals, five tries and 12 'touches' to nil in the first match and by four goals, nine tries and 15 'touches' to nil in the return at Bath.

The first published fixture list appears the following season, spanning just four and a half months of the winter and spring of 1875/76:

Nov 4 v. Redland (at Clifton); Nov 11 v. Ashley (Bath); Nov 22 v. Somerset College; Nov 25 v. Cheltenham White Cross; Dec 2 v. Sydney College; Dec 6 v. Wells (away); Dec 9 v. Swindon Rangers (away); Dec 13 v. Stanton Druids (Bath); Jan 10 v. Wells; Jan 13 v. Cheltenham White Cross; Jan 27 v. Ashley Down (at Redland); Feb 19 v. Clifton (at Bath); March 17 v. Swindon Rangers (Swindon); March 21 v. Stanton Druids (away).

The captain in that season was a nineteen-year-old, London-born forward, Herbert George Fuller. Destined to become the first player to be capped from the Bath club, he led the side for two seasons before going up to Peterhouse, Cambridge, where he earned a record six Blues between 1878 and 1883. Clearly, this was 'too much of a good thing' because the university subsequently passed a rule which prevented fifth-year students playing in the Varsity match.

Fuller, instantly recognisable for his prematurely bald pate and reputed to have invented the scrum cap, won the first of six England caps in a drawn game in Dublin on 6 February 1882 and ended his international career in the victory over Wales at Leeds in 1884. He was also a Bath committeeman and captain of Somerset during that period but then moved overseas for two years before returning to be elected president of Cambridge University RFC. He was to die at Streatham in south London, aged only thirty-nine.

At some point around 1877, the club had found a new home on Claverton Down, where, as Gandy recalled in his 1921 interview with the *Bath Herald*, 'they first used tall goal posts', adding that 'the players either had to walk or drive up to the playing field, which was previously used by the one-time famous Claverton Cricket Club'. By this time more names had been added to the original roster: Essex, Digby, F. Pinch, A.J.D. Moger, Walter Sants, Bush-Salmon, Robertson, the three Williamses, Brymer, the brothers Sainsbury, J. Baldwin, and Everitt.

Match reports from this era are very rare and it was not until the 1880s that publications such as *The Bath Chronicle*, *The Bath Argus*, *The Bath Herald* and *Keene's Bath Journal* began to acknowledge fully the growing interest among readers in organised team sports. Constant reminders were published exhorting clubs to send in results and match reports but detail was often scant and in recording a Bath defeat at Devizes, *The Bath Chronicle* of 22 February 1877, gave the line-up as 'Marsh and Sants three-quarter backs, Matthews and Petgrave half-backs, Moger (captain), Norman, Butcher, Peach, Gandy and Fletcher – forwards'. This implies that Bath fielded only ten men or, as is more likely, the reporter forgot to mention the other five! The report continued:

This match was played at Devizes on Saturday last, and resulted in a victory for the Devizes club by four tries (one disputed) and three touches against three touches scored by Bath. The touch downs for Devizes were made by – two by Rose and two by Cooper, who both played exceedingly well.

Petgrave took over the captaincy from A.J.D. Moger for the following season and the only surviving match report is of another heavy defeat at the hands of Clifton, by three goals, two tries and seven touches to nothing. The team was as follows: A. Petgrave (captain) and A. Von Donop (half backs), H.C. McTyre (three-quarter back), C.G. Matthews and E.B. Dunsterville (backs), G. Brooke, H.A. Carlton, P.A. Ogilvie, A. Lysaght, A. Robertson, H. Jones, G. Pile, R. Carpenter, J. Matcham and J.S. D'Aguilar (forwards). Fuller is listed as appearing for Clifton, presumably as a guest player.

With rugby football very much in its infancy and clubs still occasionally fielding more than fifteen-a-side, there appeared to be a degree of conflict over the way the game should be scored. A letter to the *Bath Argus* on 17 December 1878 summed up the frustration felt by more progressive thinkers:

GENTLEMEN – Bath may lay claim, I should think, to being a 'football' city. At any rate, Bath has no reason to be ashamed of the players to be seen here from week to week. But why should some of our clubs – notably that of the new Bath College – continue to make themselves ridiculous and despicable in their neighbours' sight by innocently proclaiming their ignorance of the rules. Again and again we see in your paper accounts of matches 'won by a rouge,' 'drawn in A's favour by a try,' &c., &c. Now, more than two years ago 'rouges' were banished from the Rugby Union Rules, and 'tries' were declared to be decisive in the game. Those who undertake the task of composing an account for the public might as well make themselves acquainted with the meaning of the terms they employ.
Yours truly, TOUCH-IN-GOAL

Contrary to what people might believe of the Victorian sportsman, he often had little or no respect for the referee, whose involvement in the game had been a fairly recent innovation. Gandy's recollections were that, originally, 'there were two flag men and a referee on the field, and unless the two flag men put up their flags the referee was supposed not to whistle. That system took too long…and they soon got tired of it.'

And that was if they had the luxury of a referee at all. When Frank Soane joined the club as a fifteen-year-old in the early 1880s, there was often no official, as he recalled in an after dinner speech at the Diamond Jubilee celebrations forty-five years later:

'…they usually picked up an umpire on the ground, and if they did not like his decision they did not take any notice of him! [Laughter]'

The scoring system was a constant source of frustration – and sometimes salvation – as Soane, then the grand old man of Bath rugby, pointed out to his twentieth century audience: 'In those days it was necessary to kick a goal to win a match. He remembered one occasion when their opponents scored six tries and Bath kicked a goal towards the end and won! [Laughter]'

Lambridge Meadows became the home of the club from 1880/81 but rough pitches, inadequate markings and unruly spectators all contributed to the unpredictability of late nineteenth-century rugby. This was the first season in which records appear to have been kept, albeit haphazardly, with the campaign further disrupted by the Great Blizzard of January 1881. The following season was notable for 'an unpleasant game' at Devizes on 21 January 1882 'when a dispute took place and the game terminated rather abruptly' as *The Chronicle* reported:

The Bath Captain [E. Digby] *withdrew his men from the field ten minutes before the expiration of time, saying he had come to play football and not to fight. At the termination of this unpleasant game the Bath team had scored one goal and three tries to nothing.* [4]

The peculiarities of the scoring system meant that the next match, against Salisbury, was 'drawn in favour of Bath by two touches in goal and three or four touch downs to nil', presumably because neither side managed to kick a goal as required by the laws at that time. Three days later, on 4 February, Bath drew with GWR Swindon at Lambridge in what was reckoned to be one of the games of the season.

The ball was carried down to the opponents' quarters by a good run and pass from Reid to Digby, who although collared on the touch-line by two men, succeeded in placing the ball behind the Swindon goal line. The try was not allowed, Swindon objecting on the grounds that Reid was offside when he took the ball. The Bath umpire, Mr W Jones, decided it was not offside, but to avoid any ill-feeling, gave in. There was no further score.[5]

Such gentlemanly good will was not always in evidence. Boxing Day 1882 saw a home fixture with Kensington 'spoilt by bad weather and a flooded pitch', according to *The Bath Chronicle*, which also reported:

Result was disputed – Kensington claimed a win by one goal, one try to one try. Kensington were originally given a try although the umpires were unsighted, due to encroachment on to the pitch. At 'no-side' the match was declared as drawn. Fuller, Lysaght, Ogilvie and Cunninghame played well [6].

An indication of the passions which the game of rugby aroused, even at that early stage of the sport's development, can be gauged by the correspondence which ensued.

Letters: To the EDITOR of THE BATH CHRONICLE.

"SIR – I have seen a report of our match with Bath on Boxing Day, in your paper in which the result is incorrectly given as a draw. It was a win for us by one goal and one try, to one try. This result has been admitted by all the members of the Bath team that I have spoken to since and during the match, notably H G Fuller, E McLorg."
R James, Hon Sec K. F. C., 5 Harley-gardens, South Kensington; Jan. 2nd, 1883.

"SIR – Allow me to call attention to the report of this important match which appeared in your issue of 28th.ult. You seem to have been misled by the patrons of the home team inasmuch as the report says, 'then the Kensington forwards … rushed the ball down the ground and claimed a try close to the Bath goal, which was disputed by Bath; the umpires being unable to give a decision as they were not able to see owing to the spectators encroaching, Kensington kicked the goal successfully under protest. If the umpires were unable to give a decision, Bath were unable legally to dispute the try, therefore the visitors were clearly the winners by one goal and one try, to one try."
Jan. 2nd, 1883 AN ONLOOKER

Clearly, the game could only thrive if there was agreement on how it was to be officiated – and the same went for efficient administration. For continuity's sake at least, Bath must have been fortunate that the combined post of Honorary Secretary and Honorary Treasurer had been shared by just two individuals for the first two decades of the club's existence: Thomas Gandy and Walter Sants. Gandy played in the team until after he married, and was Treasurer for twenty-five years, being presented with a handsome salver and framed photo of the team upon his resignation.

Management Committee meetings were frequently occupied by discussion of matters financial and there is evidence of the need for fund-raising by the presence in the fixture list of the annual 'Fancy Dress' match. First recorded as having taken place on 27 December 1879, it served a dual purpose – first and foremost to raise funds for the club but also to foster team spirit and companionship. A club tradition was born, one that was to persist for many years. By New Year's Day 1881, it was an annual event. Despite being postponed from the previous Monday and the wet weather persisting, 'there were more than four hundred people on the ground, a great number of them being ladies'. Note the reappearance of a Zouave:

*The Rhine String Band was present and played a selection of music. At 3.15 Mr and Mrs Caudle were deputed to pick sides. Just then, the Clown (C. Everett) and Harlequin (C. Nash) drove on to the ground in a donkey tandem. The ball was started by Mrs Caudle (W F Ommaney) it being quickly returned by Polly (W. Williams) and Charles (Edwards) getting hold of it made a good run but was safely held by a Zouave (G B Hodson). After some quick play Mr Caudle (C.F. Luckman) obtained a try, a goal resulting. Soon after another try was gained by ***** Minstrel (A. Williams) but the kick failed. About five minutes before half-time another goal was kicked for Mr Caudle's side from a try gained by a Guard (E. Sants).*

On half-time being called Mrs Caudle's side rallied and aided by some fine runs by an Executioner (C. Daubeny), Mephistopheles (L.A. O'Donoghue) soon after kicked a goal, this however proved only an effort, for a Sprite (W. Sants) presently gained a try and a goal was kicked. Another try was obtained by Mainwaring, but the kick failed; soon after this darkness put an end to the enjoyable game. For Mr Caudle's side, besides those mentioned above, Hodson and C Williams made some good runs while for Mrs Caudle's, Stuart, McLorg, Fosberry and Daubeny tried hard to avert defeat. Victory rested with Mr Caudle's side by three goals and two tries to one goal. [7]

Waiting in the wings at this formative period in the club's history was a 'larger than life' character who was to dominate activities on and off the field for the rest of that century and well into the next.

-2-

Buster

THE SOANES' PIANO and sheet music shop in Old Bond Street was the Virgin Megastore of late Victorian Bath.

Music provided such a strong social focus that few middle-class families would have been without an upright piano on which to entertain themselves and their guests. It is one of the most evocative images of life from that time, although quickly consigned to history by the breakneck pace of technology.

When Frank Soane was brought into the family business as a teenager in the early 1880s, Thomas Edison was struggling to perfect his phonograph and Emile Berliner's gramophone had yet to revolutionise home entertainment. By the time of Soane's death in 1932, the world was thrilling to radio and the 'talkie' film and eagerly awaiting the first BBC television service.

The quiet gentility of a piano and music shop could not be further removed from the violence and mayhem of a Victorian rugby match but such contrasts and contradictions were to provide much of the sport's folklore and interest over the next century or more until professionalism began to eradicate occupational and professional distinctions.

For someone who loved the sheer physical intensity of the game of rugby, it is somehow typical of the amateur game that Soane earned his living selling pianos and sheet music to the middle-class denizens of his native city.

Before the days of weight training and strict dietary regimes, the archetypal rugby forward was an individual whose occupation kept him naturally fit and relatively well nourished. Farmers, miners, industrial workers and fishermen established the muscular character of rugby in the West Country and Wales.

It is not too fanciful to assume that Soane's prowess on the rugby field owed more to an ability to shift his wares than play fancy tunes on them. Perhaps he could tickle the ivories – but his preference was to rattle a few teeth on Saturday afternoons!

Only the second player to be capped from the club after Herbert Fuller, Soane was very much a 'local boy' whose reputation was enhanced by his unstinting commitment to club and county long after he had won his fourth and last cap in 1894. The *Bath Herald* of 1 November 1919, paying tribute on the occasion of his retirement from the Somerset RFU committee, recorded that: 'he had remarkable strength and staying power, was keen on the ball, efficient as a dribbler and a deadly tackler'.

Frank Soane, capped by England in 1893.

More than 100 years later, the Edwardian studio portrait of Soane in his England playing strip attracts barely a glance from twenty-first century rugby followers in the Recreation Ground clubhouse, although he was one of the prime movers in establishing the 'Rec' as the home of Bath rugby from 1894.

He was not an especially big man in the physical sense – 5ft 9in tall and weighing in at 13 stones in his prime, yet he was remembered as 'a player of the vigorous type' and he soon earned the sobriquet 'Buster' in recognition of his fearless and fearsome tackling. Certainly, he was a forceful personality, engendering tremendous loyalty and affection among his team-mates. In any era, he would have been a powerful influence and may well have been the most charismatic captain the club has ever known.

Although born in Bath, at South Hayes House on 12 September 1866, Soane was educated at Clifton House School, Eastbourne, where soccer was the winter sport. On returning to his home city, he took up rugby with the Oldfield Park Club before making the impromptu debut that was to begin a fifty-year association with the Bath Football Club. At the time of the 1881 census, Soane was a 'scholar' aged fifteen, living with his family at South Hayes House on the Wells Road, his father, J.W. Soane, being a 'piano and music seller'. It must have been in the following season, 1881/82, that young Frank made the first of more than 300 appearances for the club.

Some forty-five years later he rose at the Diamond Jubilee dinner to relate the then well-worn story of how he went to see a Rugger match at Lambridge. Bath were a man short and they asked him to play. He played in his trousers and shirt, and the club were so pleased with his 'robust' play that they asked him to play again! [Laughter and applause] He remembered on that occasion that the players had an enormous 'blow-out' of suet pudding. Perhaps that is why he 'caught the eye' of the club! [Laughter]

Soane did not become a regular until the 1884/85 season but at nineteen he was already a member of the Bath committee and within four years had earned selection in the Somerset pack against Devon. 'Honours thenceforth fell thick upon the sturdy leader of the Bathonians,' as the Somerset RFU noted in 1894:

He has appeared five times for the Western Counties, on three occasions for the South, and twice for the Rest of England against Yorkshire. His remarkable strength and staying power as a forward, his keenness on the ball, efficiency as a dribbler and certainly in tackling, in 1893 won for him the proud distinction of representing his country, for last year the Rugby Union gave him a place in the team against Scotland.

So delighted were his many friends in Bath at the honour which their captain had obtained that he was entertained to a complimentary banquet at Fortt's, where he was the hero of the evening. Those who read the laudatory allusions to Soane's play in the Scottish engagement anticipated that his International career would not be restricted to this match, and these opinions were verified, for this season saw Soane among the Englishmen who defeated Wales so signally at Birkenhead, at Blackheath facing the sons of Erin, who to the surprise of all, gained the day, and at Edinburgh. [1]

Representative rugby outside internationals was a recent phenomenon. It had been only as recently as 7 September 1882 that Bath officials and representatives of other clubs had met at the Clarence Hotel, Bridgwater, to form a Somerset Football Union. It was resolved that club membership fee should be one guinea and that the selection committee should include the Bath club captain, H.E. Jacob, along with H. Fox (Wellington), F.E. Hancock (Wiveliscombe), and the Honorary Secretary, A. Abmuty-Mitchell, also from Bath. The captain was to be elected on the field 'before each match' and the playing colours of scarlet, black and white stripes were adopted.

For the 1883/84 season, the club captaincy passed from Jacob to A.K. Cunninghame at the annual general meeting, which also approved a reduction in subscriptions from 10s to 5s forthwith. A deputation was also to be sent to Mr Dyer 'with a view to getting the annual rent of Dyer's field reduced from the present £10 per annum'.

Playing records are almost non-existent from that season, just five results, including heavy defeats by Weston-super-Mare and an ignominious 'double' suffered against Gloucester. Events elsewhere, however, were to have a significant effect on the evolution of the game, which had up to that point involved nine forwards, two half-backs, three three-quarters and a full-back. Coventry then fielded four three-quarters in a game at Stratford-on-Avon, a ploy quickly taken up by Cardiff at Gloucester on 23 February 1884 in order to accommodate the same Frank Hancock, from Wiveliscombe, who had been elected on to the Somerset county selection panel.

Records for 1884/85 are just as threadbare – three results from eight fixtures – and Soane's name is documented for the first time in a heavy defeat by Bristol Arabs on Durdham Down. A fortnight later he played on the losing side again, at home to Volunteers, alongside the brothers Tom and Fred Blanchard. Tom was the first Avonvale player to represent Bath and with his brother played a large part in the founding of the local village club. Tom's playing talent developed first as a fly-half and then as a three-quarter and he represented Bath on many occasions in the 1880s.

The final result on record for 1884/85 is a comprehensive defeat at home to Clifton, who scored two goals and five touchdowns playing three men short!

The following season witnessed a remarkable transformation in fortunes as Bath settled into their new surroundings at Kensington Meadows. They lost only one of their 20 matches, drawing 2 and winning 17 with a playing squad which included F. Hill, J. Stringfield, F. Soane, T. Blanchard, H. Lavis, A.N. Farwell, A. Hill, J. Crowden, C.A. Knight, H.T. Foord, M. Swabey, A. Parham, G.C. Helps (capt), L.A. O'Donoghue, W.B. Severs and W.A. Walker.

Gloucester, as physically intimidating in those days as they are today, were held to draws at home and away. The drawn return match on 9 January 1886 was described by *The Bath Chronicle* as 'one of the best games ever witnessed'.

As the successful season continued, there was some concern that the standard of rugby was not attracting the attendances it appeared to merit. The *Chronicle* commented after another victory over Volunteers:

In a recent letter to the local Press, it was stated that the Bathonian lends not his interest to matters intellectual, neither, it is manifest, does he effect matters athletic, but Gallic-like, prefers general indifference. The attendance was of quite average meagreness. The Bath club won their 15th victory by five tries and five touchdowns to two touches. T. Blanchard, playing in splendid form, obtained two tries.

...the number of spectators was again ridiculously small considering the brilliant form displayed this season ... they have lost only one match in seventeen. The utter lack of interest in their doings by Bath people is, to say the least, disappointing to the members of the club.[2]

The harsher side of Victorian life was emphasised in the final match of the season when Bath travelled to Bristol to play Fishponds. Victory was duly achieved but on a sombre note as all gate takings went to the Easton Colliery Relief Fund, raised for the victims and families of the mining disaster in neighbouring Easton on 18 February 1886.

At a well-attended annual meeting of the Bath club at the Christopher Hotel on 25 March, 'the Honorary Secretary, E.W. Mitchell, outlined a very successful playing season, during which the number of subscribers had increased to 64. Nevertheless gate receipts were down, largely due to bad weather. Two players had represented the County. Regrettably, the Club had been unable to fulfil one of the fixtures. The Treasurer, Mr Gandy, submitted a statement of accounts, and was pleased to report a balance of £1 2s 0d. He also stated that this was the Club's most successful season. He was then presented with a salver and framed photograph as a token of the members' appreciation of his unfailing zeal and efficiency.'

The 1886/87 season brought a reform of the scoring system after RFU members determined that 'a match shall be decided by a majority of points: a goal shall equal three points and a try one point. If the number of points be equal, or no goal be kicked or try obtained, the match shall be drawn. When a goal is kicked from a try the goal only is scored.'

With S. Swabey scoring three tries and A. Porter kicking eight goals, Bath, captained by G.C. Helps, swept past Frome 27-3 in the opening game before stumbling against Clifton (0-7). There was then an 8-4 victory over Redland Park before they encountered tougher opposition in Gloucester (1-4) and Bridgwater (3-4). The fixture against Redland Park, one of many clubs whose existence is only a yellowed memory, is notable for the debut of T.N.M. Parham, who scored two tries, the first 'with a dodgy run'. The half-back kept his place for the Gloucester game, again scoring a try under the posts.

Tommy Parham became a prolific try-scorer over the next seven seasons and, according to reminiscences by the *Bath Sports Herald* thirty-five years later, 'a dominating personality in Bath and Somerset football circles for many years'.

No better half-back has ever been associated with local rugby than this thick-set diminutive player. Wonderfully strong on his legs, with a daring pair of hands and an active mind to direct them, he was a rare problem for all his opponents. I don't think I ever saw a player with a more remarkable swerve than he possessed. He could mystify the deadliest tackler and leave him utterly dumbfounded.[3]

Tommy was paired with his brother, A. Parham, at half-back for the return fixture with Clifton on 4 December 1886 – and a rare away win over what was then the neighbouring city's premier club. Soon after half-time, one of the three-quarters, E.M. Rowland, 'secured the ball at the half-way flag and, after a grand run through the Clifton men, obtained a try.' Much of the praise, however, went to the Bath forwards who more than held their own in securing a 1-0 victory, the try going unconverted. The Bath correspondent also noted 'the prosperous condition of the Club, which this year is playing two teams and has a very fair record for both'.

Just as prized a scalp was taken a week later in a 4-0 win at Swindon Rangers, the first in four years of fixtures. The effort could not be sustained, however, and Bath lost 6-0 at home to Weston-super-Mare the following weekend, the forwards playing uncharacteristically poorly. Tommy Parham 'put in some good tackles', it was noted. That match had had to be switched to Mr Browning's field at the other Weston on the north-western side of Bath because Kensington Meadows were under water. Weather was to dominate conversation for the next month.

The Christmas of 1886 will be memorable for the great snowstorm associated with it. The wintry tempest was not only remarkable for the suddenness with which it burst upon the land, but for the sustained force. A gale from the north-east apparently brought the snow and maintained itself at a tolerable uniform pressure for about eight hours. There were none of the lucid intervals which characterised the hurricane of a fortnight since. Forcibly and determinedly the wind blew, damaging property, rooting up trees or lopping their branches, while many of the evergreens, unable to sustain the weight of snow gathered upon their foliage, were roughly pruned by the tempest. The drifts have been in places almost as deep as during the great snowstorm of January 1881, and although there has not been the same interruption of railway traffic, the delays in arrival and departure of trains have been numerous and the dangers of travelling augmented by the telegraph poles blown across the lines. The storm, like that of 1881, appears to have been scarcely felt in the northern counties, but the Midlands, with the west, south, and east, everywhere bear traces of its fury. The rain, with high temperature prevailing, is causing a rapid thaw, which the slush in the thoroughfares and the rising of the river make disagreeably plain.[4]

Flooding prevented any rugby being played until the third week of January 1887 but the club remained unbeaten through to the end of the season. Results included a 1-1 draw at home to Swindon Rangers and 10-0 win over local side Widcombe Institute to round off the campaign. Reverend B. Burton was referee but 'in Bank Holiday weather, the conditions were far too tropical for devotees of the leather'. Frank Soane (2), his brother Victor, Tommy Parham ('with a capital dodgy run') and F. Hill scored tries while Tom Blanchard converted two.

Soane, still only twenty years old, was elected deputy to the club captain, G.C. Helps, for the following season when members met for the annual meeting at the Christopher Hotel. C.J. Moneypenny and F.W. Anderson shared the Honorary Secretary's duties and Thomas Gandy continued to oversee the finances. Helps, Anderson, Moneypenny, Soane and S. Swabey formed the Match Committee while the General Committee comprised A. Hill, H.G. Lavis, J. Stringfield, W. Sutton, W.A. Walker, E.W. Mitchell, Tommy Parham and Walter Sants, still serving the club more than twenty years after its formation.

Pocket-sized and pugnacious, Parham appears to have been as doughty a competitor in the committee room as he was on the field, as the *Bath Sports Herald* correspondent recalled in 1922:

On the Committee too, he did splendid work and more than once, with a few commonsense remarks, I have heard him put in proper perspective foolish suggestions. Once or twice I crossed swords with him, but I learned to appreciate his rapier-like thrust. Altogether I never knew a player who more deserved his popularity than he did.[5]

In those days Freshford Ale was advertised for sale in *The Bath Chronicle* at 1s 2d gallon – 1s 4d for XXX Mild. There must have been plenty of it sunk in the 1887/88 season, when Bath continued to build their reputation by losing only two of the nine fixtures recorded – at Bridgwater (5-0) and at home to Gloucester (0-14). The victories were achieved against Bristol Medicals (16-0), Redland Park (3-0), Bath College (11-0), Bridgwater (7-0), Weston-super-Mare (16-4), Westbury Park (13-1) and Widcombe (13-0).

A Boxing Day fixture with Carlton Bristol attracted a large crowd only to be cancelled at the last minute after a telegram from Carlton advising that they could not raise a team. The archive lists early season games at home to Westbury Park and Batcombe Rectory but no results are recorded, although the report of the return match against Westbury carries reference to a 'second crushing defeat' and also paints a comical picture of Victorian crowd involvement:

Very soon after the start, one of the Westbury's three-quarters getting the ball, ran behind the Bath backs, being utterly unable to stop him owing to the crowd of spectators who were all over the field.[6]

Among the more consistent performers for Bath during that season, in addition to Soane and Parham, were the brothers C.J.B. and C.B. Moneypenny.

Early in the following season, C.J.B. Moneypenny offered a cup for place and drop-kicking. There were also cups for those players who took part in most 'runs,' an early attempt to build collective fitness.

C.J.B. later earned the distinction of becoming one of the first Bath players to be honoured by the Barbarians when he was selected on the wing in a festival against Corinthians, of FA Cup fame, held at Queens Club in 1892. The fixture included not only a rugby match but also contests at soccer, cricket and athletics. A history of the Barbarian club records that:

Bath's C.J.B. Moneypenny won the 100 yards in 10.2 seconds. He also won the Quarter mile in 50.2 seconds.[7]

Bath players continued their 'runs' throughout the autumn and into December. In these early days they were believed to have started from the 'Castle' in Forester Avenue and later the 'Crown' at Bathwick. The players ran out as far as the former 'Dry Arch' on the Warminster Road and made their way back, naturally enough, to the pub.

-3-

The First Derby Match

FRANK WHITE HOLDS a special place in the annals of the Bath club as the man who scored the opening try in the very first derby match against Bristol – minus his shorts! It was all of fifty years after the event that White wrote to the Bath club with his recollections of that historic day, even down to the playing strip he and his team-mates wore – black and white jerseys, with a blue cap and silver tassel. 'Anything in the shape of shorts "did" but it was not done in those days to show too much knee,' he recalled in his letter dated 17 January 1939. Yet his own try was achieved without his shorts, which were left in the hands of the Bristol full back. 'As, however, I wore bathing drawers underneath, Bristol was not unduly horrified.'

By the start of the 1888/89 season, interest in rugby football was burgeoning and the formation of a Bristol Football Club to rival those of Bath and Gloucester was only natural. The new club had been born in April of 1888 when representatives of Bristol Carlton, who had cried off the Boxing Day fixture at Bath at such short notice only four months previously, met their counterparts from Redland Park at the Montpelier Hotel to make a new start under combined colours, a fetching slate grey, yellow and white.

While Clifton continued to be the premier club in the city for a number of years, Bristol's emergence was eventually to establish a formidable triumvirate with their rivals from Gloucester and Bath. The first meeting between Bristol and Bath was set for Saturday 27 October 1888, at the recently opened Gloucestershire County cricket ground in Nevil Road, Horfield.

Bath, under the leadership of W.A. Walker, had already accounted for Clifton (2-1), Swindon (11-10) and Widcombe Institute (17-0) but the skipper was absent for the first away match. The more practised observers in a crowd estimated at 'between 700 and 800' noted with some interest that Bath were fielding four three-quarters for the first time, finally following the lead set by Coventry four years previously. With Mr W.J. Crosby as referee and Mr W.C. Chandler and Mr Davis as umpires, the teams lined up as follows:

Bristol: Derham (Back); Rev J.M. Bastard, V.W. Davies, I. Huxtable and H.B. Turner; (Three-Quarters); R.D. Cruickshank and E.T.S. Badger (Half Backs);

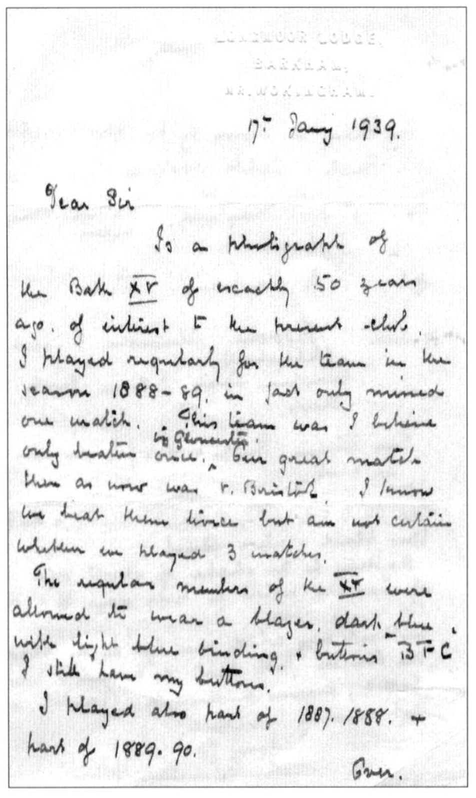
17th Jany 1939.

Dear Sir

This is a photograph of the Bath XV of exactly 50 years ago. of interest to the present club. I played regularly for the team in the season 1888-89. in fact only missed one match. This team was I believe only beaten once, by Gloucester. Our great match then as now was v. Bristol. I know we beat them twice but am not certain whether we played 3 matches.

The regular members of the XV were allowed to wear a blazer, dark blue, with light blue binding & buttons "BFC". I still have my buttons.

I played also part of 1887. 1888. & part of 1889. 90.

Over.

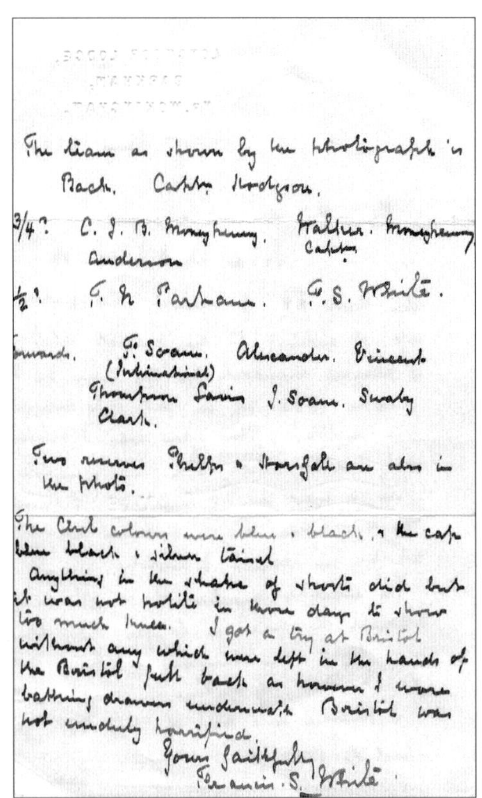
The team as shown by the photograph is

Back. Captn Hodgson.

3/4s. C. J. B. Moneypenny. Walker. Moneypenny. Capt. Anderson

½s. T. N. Parham. F. S. White.

Forwards. F. Soane. Alexander. Vincent (International) Thompson Lewis J. Soane. Swaby Clark.

Two reserves Phelps & Horsfall are also in the photo.

The Club colours were blue & black, & the cap blue black & silver tassel

Anything in the shape of shorts did but it was not polite in those days to show too much knee. I got a try at Bristol without any which were left in the hands of the Bristol full back as however I wore bathing drawers underneath Bristol was not unduly horrified.

Yours faithfully

Francis S. White.

Francis White's memory of the first Bristol *v.* Bath fixture on 27 October 1888.

A. Gee (Captain), B. Gee, S.W. Brown, M. Thompson, W. Cogan, C. Giles, R. Bryan and P. Loxley (Forwards).

Bath: G. Horsford (Back); C.J.B. Moneypenny, F.W. Anderson, F.S. White and H.T. Vincent (Three-Quarters); T.N.M. Parham and B.C. Helps (Half Backs); R.J. Hare, T. Alexander, A.S. Clerk, T.R. Thompson, F. Soane (Captain), V. Soane, G. Bailey and H.A. Spencer (Forwards).

The *Bath Sports Herald* recorded events as follows:

These teams met on the Gloucestershire County Ground on Saturday, and attracted a fair number of spectators, estimated roughly between 700 and 800. The Bristol men still want more combination before they will be seen to advantage, but they improve weekly, and will doubtless continue to do so. The Bath men are certainly stronger this season than they have been for some time. Walker, the captain, was absent, but F. Soane, who took his place, exercised capital control over his men, who really play with a wonderful combination.

Moneypenny and Anderson at three-quarters, Parham at half, and F. Soane, Clerk and Alexander forward, did excellent work. Special mention must be made of Parham. Gee won the toss, and elected to play with the wind, and at 3.45 p.m. Bath started the ball; Derham returned and play commenced in neutral ground. Bath had a free kick soon after the start, but nothing resulted from it. White at length got away, and scored the first point for Bath. Moneypenny failed at goal. The leather was restarted, and Brown scored a try for Bristol, which Derham by a capital kick converted into the converted three points. After half-time Gee kicked off, and after some good passing behind, Anderson by a good run notched the second try for Bath. Moneypenny tried the place, which was again a failure. Both sides then played up with spirit, and Bastard got away with a dashing run, made a good deal of ground but was collared, and passed blindly, enabling Moneypenny, who was on the spot, to get clean away and score a third try for Bath, which he managed to convert into a goal. Gee started the oval once more, and directly after Vincent kicked into touch-in-goal. The remainder of the play was of a give-and-take description, and when 'no side' was called the score stood:- Bath, one goal, two tries, and one minor; Bristol, one goal. Bath thus winning one of the fastest games we have seen by five points to three.[1]

The *Western Daily Press* also reported on the game, describing how White 'succeeded in getting the ball over the line very close to touch', leaving Moneypenny with too difficult a kick at goal.

Easy victories followed for Bath against Batcombe Rectory and the Royal Agricultural College, Cirencester, before the perennially testing trip to Bridgwater. Neither side managed to score although Bath claimed a victory of sorts by 'three minors to two.' An interesting footnote to this game was that Tommy Parham declined a call from Somerset to play a Scottish XV, leaving no doubt who had first claim on his loyalties.

It was 1 December before the unbeaten record was surrendered, the team going down 5-0 at Gloucester. However, the team's consistent progress did not go unrecognised and Frank Soane and Tommy Parham were first to be awarded Distinction Badges by the club, followed in succeeding weeks by A.E. Clerk, I. Thompson and C.J.B. Moneypenny. After away victories during December over Clifton and East Gloucestershire, Soane, Moneypenny and Parham were selected for inter-county matches, and were then joined by another Bath forward, C.W. Hayward, in the Somerset XV to face the touring Maoris at Wellington on 26 January 1889. The New Zealanders won heavily but Moneypenny had the satisfaction of running in two spectacular tries.

A week later the trio were back in Bath colours for the return match with Bristol at Kensington Meadows. Within moments of the kick-off, Moneypenny interpassed with Parham to score the first try, and further scores from Anderson (try and goal) and Pattinson (try) secured a 5-0 victory. The *Western Daily Press* reported:

Cruickshank, Lockey, Thompson, Bastard, Brown and Winter were most conspicuous for the visitors, while Parham played splendidly for the local team for whom White, Pattinson, the Soanes, Moneypenny and Strachan also rendered capital service.

Bath: H.T. Vincent (back); F. Anderson, F.S. White, C.J.B. Moneypenny and W. Pattinson (three-quarters); R.P.J. Gunn and T. Parham (half-backs); F. Soane (Captain), V. Soane, B.H. Vincent, G.L. Strachan, T. Alexander, J.W. Hosper, G. Bailey and A.L.M. Swabey (forwards).

Bristol: Derham, (back): Rev J.M. Bastard, V.W. Davies, Thomas and P. Lockey (three-quarters); R.D. Cruickshank and F. Hill (half-backs); A. Gee (Captain), W.J. Davies, Winter, Luffman, Bryan, Vosper and Thompson (forwards).[2]

Bath's ascendancy over their near neighbours was fairly short-lived, however, and as the century drew to a close, victories over Bristol were rare events.

With the emergence of Bristol and the introduction of a 'Cardiff XV' in the fixture list, longstanding relationships were beginning to be forged between clubs on either side of the Severn. Bath were defeated by an unknown margin at home to Cardiff but a sequence of victories in the early months of 1889 over Bristol, RAC Cirencester (away, 7-2), Weston-super-Mare (away, 4-0) and Bridgwater (home, 5-0) restored morale.

There should have been an away fixture on 16 March with Widcombe Institute but according to a Management Committee report on the October fixture, Bath's full-back, Horsford, had 'got badly hurt…putting out his shoulder. One of the Widcombe men broke his collar bone and a small boy that got in the way got hurt.' The return was cancelled at a late stage by the match committee, owing to 'disagreeable wrangling and general unfairness'.

A week later they had another difficult decision to make ahead of the return match with Cardiff, just four days hence. Only four committee members were present – W.A. Walker, Frank Soane, A.L.M. Swabey and C.J.B. Moneypenny – and their deliberations were minuted as follows:

It was decided not to play the return match with Cardiff because neither Moneypenny nor Pattinson could get away owing to illness. W.A. Walker also was unable to get away. At the committee meeting on Thursday it was discovered that through a blunder of the Hon. Sec., Cardiff still expected us. It was decided that the Capt. should write a letter to Cardiff explaining how it was we couldn't raise a team.

On Friday morning the Capt. received a Telegram as follows: 'Received a letter on Thursday morning saying you were coming, on strength of this have put off match with Newport. You must come or will report to the Union, with reply.[3]

That evening another committee meeting was hastily arranged at which it was decided, by a majority of three to one, to go to Cardiff after all, 'so as to avoid any unpleasantness'. It is not recorded who was the dissenter but Bath were 'wiped up' 3-10 by the margin of two goals and four tries to one goal.

The 1888/89 season had been notable for the introduction of the County Championship, providing a competitive structure for the growing number of county fixtures. Somerset played 20 matches in that year, winning 8, drawing 4 and losing 8 – points for 147, points against 83.

Frank Soane and C.J.B. Moneypenny were retained by Somerset for the latter stages of the championship but their hopes of honours evaporated in a 9-1 defeat by Yorkshire in front of 10,000 spectators at Bradford in mid-February. Yorkshire, unbeaten after scoring 18 goals and 17 tries to one goal and three tries in the competition, were duly declared champions by the RFU.

When members gathered at the Christopher Hotel in April for the Bath club's half-yearly meeting, Thomas Gandy 'was pleased to report a balance of £15 at hand. This was a favourable advance, as the Club had started the season with a surplus of £5.' Hosting the Somerset *v.* Gloucestershire fixture the following season was an attractive prospect, not least for the financial returns, so Frank Soane and C.J. Moneypenny 'were to go to Mr Dunn (Headmaster) and try to get use of College field for the match on Dec.21st 1889'.

There were rumblings of dissent on selection policy however, as evident from a proposal that some non-playing members should be on the match committee 'as it was thought the teams might be chosen more on their merits. Mr Soane pointed out that no criticism on selection had been received and that subject was irrelevant as the officers were elected at the autumn meeting, and the matter could be brought up then.' Even then, in his early twenties, Soane brooked no argument.

The Christopher Hotel was also the venue for an historic gathering on 17 July, arranged for the purpose of founding a soccer club to represent the city. Significantly, it involved a good number of Bath rugby players and administrators and briefly raised the prospect of close co-operation between the codes.

Lord Weymouth MP, (a rugby Patron), was the first Association Football Club President, with the following, also rugby Patrons, being appointed as 'Association Club' Vice Presidents: Colonel Laurie CB MP, E.R. Woodhouse MP, the Mayor (Mr H.W. Freeman), R.B. Cater, A.G.D. Moger, and R.S. Blaine (Rugby President). The Provisional Committee included rugby men R.B. Cater, T.N. Parham (player) and J.E. Henshaw (rugby Chairman), according to *The Bath Chronicle*:

J.E. Henshaw proposed Mr. Boyce as Captain W. Sants, who was spoken of as a successful Rugby player, was unanimously chosen as vice-captain on the proposition of Mr Boyce, seconded by Mr Pinch.

In his address, Chairman R.B. Cater, observed that Bath was singular in not possessing an Association Football Club ... Bath was getting rather famous for sports, and he thought there was plenty of room to edge in this Club [applause]. He proposed that a Club be formed, to be called the Bath Association Football Club... He saw a good many football men present, and he should like it to be known that this proposal was in no way antagonistic to the Bath Rugby Football Club [hear, hear], and he was sure they would pull together harmoniously.

Similar attempts had been made a few years previously, but there had been difficulty in arranging fixtures. Since then, several Somerset and Wiltshire clubs had been set up and were prospering. There was a further pledge of support from Mr A.N.C. Treadgold, of Bath College. Mr Walter Sants seconded and expressed belief that there was plenty of room for the Club in Bath, though he knew a few years ago two or three unsuccessful attempts were made to start one.[4]

A little over two years later, on Friday 18 September, 1891, *The Bath Chronicle* reported on a joint meeting of the rugby and soccer clubs, with Frank Soane in the chair. On the agenda was a proposal for amalgamation but the first item was a statement of accounts from the treasurer, Thomas Gandy, showing a rugby club deficit of £23 19s 1d, partially offset by later receipt of £6 in subscriptions.

Several thought it would be best to start the alliance with a clean sheet, and the Association men would not bring any debt if that were done. These remarks gave rise to considerable discussion, during which the CHAIRMAN remarked that really there was no amalgamation. The Rugby club had agreed if sufficient Association players joined it, to play an Association team. He candidly admitted that he never was in favour of the amalgamation, and he did not see the benefit the Bath Football Club would gain by it. MR CLARK said they wished in the interest of sport that the alliance should be as amicable and thorough as possible, and personally he was willing to join the Bath F.C. regardless of debt [hear, hear].

MR PEACOCK mentioned that last year the Association Club had subscriptions amounting to £33 odd. MR. MELSOME proposed that the debt be placed to a separate account to be wiped off by special efforts, and that the combined Club should start clear. MR WALKER seconded as he wished to see urgent steps taken to wipe off the deficiency. MR HOOPER proposed an amendment, that the debts on the two Clubs remain in the general account, and this was seconded by MR

This, the earliest Bath team photograph was taken at Kensington Meadows in 1888. The group includes: Capt. Hodgson, C.J.P. Moneypenny, Walker (captain), C.B. Moneypenny, Andrews, Parham, F.S. White, F. Soane, T. Alexander, Vincent, Thompson, Lavis, V. Soane, Swabey, Clark, and two reserves, Phelps and Horsgale.

PATTINSON, who said he should like to see the Association game continue in Bath and some match played here every Saturday. The amendment was carried by a considerable majority. The election of officers was then proceeded with.

> *Sir R.S. Blaine was elected president. Mr Frank Soane was again elected captain of the Rugby Club, with Mr Pattinson as deputy-captain. Mr J. Peacock was elected captain of the Association team, and Mr F.J. Butt vice captain. Mr T.J. Piper and Mr C.H. Clark were appointed co-secretaries. Mr T.J. Gandy resigned the office of Hon. Treasurer, which was filled, with the election of Mr White. Messrs G.H. Noke, W. Sants, C.H. Melsome, J.E. Henshaw, J. Miller, J. Hooper, Gilby, E. Rogerson, W.A. Mackay, V. Soane and T.J. Gandy were elected on the General Committee and Messrs F. Soane, Hooper, Rogerson, Gilby and Mackay were appointed as Match Committee for the Rugby game. The meeting closed with a vote of thanks to Mr Gandy for his past services, and a similar compliment to the Chairman.*[5]

A set of club rules were to be instituted in 1893, specifying in particular:

1 *That the Club shall be called the Bath Football Club and shall consist of Honorary and playing members.*
2 *That both Rugby and Association games may be played.*[6]

At a time when written records of the rugby club's existence were becoming more reliable, 1889 was notable for the earliest recorded team photograph, taken at Kensington Meadows. The line-up was Captain Hodgson, C.J. Moneypenny, W.A. Walker (captain), C.B. Moneypenny, Andrews, Parham, F.S. White, F. Soane, T. Alexander, Vincent, Thompson, Lavis, V. Soane, Swabey, Clark, with two reserves, Phelps and Horsgale.

Behind the scenes, the club had begun to assemble an impressive line-up of Patrons, the 'great and the good' who reflected the public school origins of rugby football. At the half-yearly meeting, held at the Christopher Hotel, on 26 July 1889, R.S. Blaine, of Summerhill, Lansdown, presided, with General Benson, of Lansdown Crescent, as vice president. The patrons were listed as:

Lord Weymouth MP, Longleat, Warminster,
E.R. Wodehouse, Minley Grange Farnborough, Hants,
Colonel Laurie C.B. M.P., Mystoke, Canterbury,
Revd T M Bromley,
General Burn, 19 Lansdown Crescent,
Capt. Lysaght, R.M., The Whins, Sion Hill,
Capt. T P Fitzgerald, Johnstone Street,
A.G.D. Moger, Waines,
E.W. Mitchell Esq.,Tohmian Club, Piccadilly,
C. Hensley, The Circus,
R.B. Cater Esq., St Margaret's Buildings,
W. Pratt Esq., Gay's House, Camden Place,
C.W. Radway Esq., Grand Pump Room Hotel,
Rev. L Fish, 5 Camden Crescent,
A.K. Cunninghame Esq.,
The Mayor of Bath.

A general meeting was held the following month at George Street at which distinction badges were awarded to W.A. Walker, C.J.B. Moneypenny, F.S. White, T.N. Parham, C.B. Moneypenny, F. Soane, V. Soane, W. Alexander, H.T. Vincent, I.T. Thompson, A. Clerk, C.W. Hayward. Thompson and Clerk 'left for India after Christmas'. A more significant gathering was held at the Clarence Hotel, Bridgwater on 18 September, when the Somerset Referees Society was founded. Before the club season had begun, Somerset held a County Trial at Bridgwater on 5 October at which the Bath club was represented by D.G. Astley, T. Alexander, C.J.B. Moneypenny, T.N. Parham, F. Soane and H.T. Vincent.

The opening fixture of the 1889/90 season brought a 43-0 victory over the students of Batcombe Rectory, coached by Revd Baker. The scoreline – from 11 goals and 10 tries – was not surpassed until the early years of the following century, and all this was achieved without C.J.B. Moneypenny, playing at three-quarter in the Cambridge Varsity Trial, and S. Swabey, appearing for Blackheath.

There followed a mixed bag of results – defeat at home to Weston-super-Mare, then victory over the Royal Agricultural College (Cirencester), followed by a 0-0 draw at Bristol on 9 November, when Frank Soane, C.J.B. Moneypenny and Tommy Parham were absent on duty for Somerset at Blackheath. If Bath found any consolation, it was in the fact that they scored three Minors to none. The tie only heightened anticipation of the return match, just a month later, during which time Bath achieved a 15-0 win over Bath College, witnessed by 'several hundred spectators', and suffered the customary defeat by Gloucester (9-0) before gaining a 5-2 home victory against Bridgwater. Snowfall, a far from rare occurrence in Victorian England, ushered in the month of December, leaving Kensington Meadows 'in a filthy condition, and only suitable for a forward game', but Bath regained their ascendancy against Bristol, scoring a goal and a try to a try (4-1).

Bristol's fly-half that day was W.T. Pearce who, forty years later, became president of the RFU. Invited to attend the 1929 annual general meeting of the Bath club, he entertained the gathering with recollections of the early days, including his experiences of changing in a cowshed before the derby match on Kensington Meadows. Back in those days, however, the outcome – or, more accurately, a newspaper report of the match – brought a wintry chill between the clubs and was considered serious enough to be raised at a meeting of Bath's general committee three days later.

Committee was informed that the Bath Captain had written to his opposite number in Bristol: '... asking him whether the report of the match Bath v. *Bristol which appeared in the* Bristol Mercury *of Dec 9th and which was possibly incorrect and misleading, had been published with his cognisance and approval, but he had not yet received a reply.' On the motion of Mr. F Soane seconded by Dr. Hardyman it was resolved that 'If Mr Brown's explanation were not perfectly satisfactory, no matches should be arranged with Bristol FC for the season 1890-91.'* [7]

Fortunately, it is on record that Mr Brown did eventually give a satisfactory reply – but exactly what he said to pacify the Bath players and to resolve the first 'tiff' between the clubs is not known. In any case, there were other matters for the committee to deal with:

Three sandwich men to be employed to advertise home matches, instead of one as heretofore.

Resolved that at County matches, not more than six members should be provided with Committee badges to walk between the ropes and touch-lines on

The Somerset team of 1889, which included Bath's Frank Soane (standing, second from right) and Tommy Parham (seated, first left), and also two of the celebrated Hancock brothers from Wiveliscombe. (Courtesy of Somerset Rugby)

either side of the ground in order to keep spectators from pressing the ropes forward, was passed 'nem. con.'.[8]

Season 1889/90 marked the first county game played at Bath, with gate takings totalling £20 as 800 people crowded on to Kensington Meadows to see Gloucestershire defeat Somerset by a try to nil on 21 December 1889. It was one of five matches lost by the county that season, two more being drawn. Tommy Parham made four appearances, with D.G. Astley and B.H. Vincent also earning selection, along with C.J.B. Moneypenny, in his last season of county rugby.

Only two club fixtures were won after Christmas in that 1889/90 season, and the club's account of defeat by a single try at Bridgwater betrayed more than a hint of frustration.

The game was very fast and stubbornly contested throughout and should have ended in a draw, the try gained by Bridgwater being palpably a most unfair one, the man who gained it falling on the ball fully two yards from the goal line (thereby rendering the ball dead) and coolly wriggling over the line with the ball underneath him.[9]

To add to the general air of depression, Tommy Parham received an injury that was to rule the influential half-back out for the rest of the season. Gloucester won 16-0 at Kensington Meadows and although spirits were lifted by a 5-5 draw against Cardiff Seconds, the team then 'displayed wretched form' in losing at home to Swindon Rangers. A match at Cirencester was then scratched, '...the service of trains being so inconvenient as to render it impossible for us to send a representative team'.

Just twenty-four hours after a 13-3 Good Friday victory over Wiltshire Wanderers at Chippenham, Bath rounded off a season of mixed fortunes with the fifth in the series of derby matches and the first to be won by Bristol, by three tries and four minors to two minors.

The two teams met as early as 18 October the following season. W.A. Walker had handed over the captaincy to Frank Soane but the twenty-four-year-old's stirring brand of leadership was unable to carry the day as Bristol won by a goal and a try to a try (4-1) at the County Ground.

An experiment with M.W. Dixon as 'flying half', an innovation borrowed from the Maori tourists' recent tour to England, had been judged to be successful after an easy win at Widcombe Institute, but defeat at Taunton forced a return to a more conventional line-up against Bristol. 'Parham was very conspicuous and had a hand in almost everything that happened,' according to a contemporary report by a Bristol newspaper, but the home side were able to celebrate a second successive victory over their neighbours with tries by Lowther and Thomson to a 'somewhat doubtful try' by Pattinson, despite the Bristol captain appealing for a touch-in-goal.

There then followed a run of eight straight victories, one of them 'an absurdly easy win' over Vauxhall at Kensington Meadows in which Pattinson crossed the line five times. The sequence included a return with Bristol, the seventh derby match between the clubs kicking off forty minutes late, most probably to accommodate the large number of spectators who saw Bath win 9-0 with two goals and three tries.

The home fifteen played a grand game, the passing by the halves and threequarters being especially good, and although individual pieces of good play were noticeable, especially by F. Soane, Parham, Pattinson and Vincent, the success of the team was principally due to the unselfish play, the good passing, and the hard work done by them as a whole.[10]

The remarkable sequence continued with victories over Swindon Rangers, Bath College and Weston-super-Mare as the season moved into December. Then the weather intervened, a heavy frost wiping out all fixtures until the third week of January when another trip to Bristol ended in a 10-3 defeat on the County Ground, which 'was almost completely covered in water'. The turnaround in fortunes could not have been more pronounced as the team failed entirely to regain their early season form and could muster only one more victory, against Weston-super-Mare.

The Bath team that lost 2-7 to Taunton at Kensington Meadows on 21 March 1891. From left to right, back row: T. Alexander, E.C. Rogerson, J.T. Piper (Honorary Secretary), F. China, H.T. Vincent, A. Ward, J. Miller, L.J. Fry, J.W. Hooper, W.T. Vincent, J. McTier. Front row: G.L. Strachan, A.D. Ford, A.L.M. Swabey, F. Soane (captain), W. Mackay, W. Pattinson, J.V. Soane, M.W. Dixon.

Players enjoyed no better fortune in Somerset colours, failing to top the South Western group as had been confidently expected.

With Frank Soane continuing as captain for the 1891/92 season, Bath began to achieve some consistency, ending the campaign with 14 wins from 18 matches. The only defeats were against Cardiff Second XV in a quagmire at the Arms Park and Bristol (twice).

Even if Soane had been available for the first derby match on 19 December – he was picked for the South against the North in the England trial – it is doubtful if Bath would have made much impression on 'a particularly strong Bristol side' who were said to have provided 'the finest exhibition of three-quarter play seen in the West of England' in winning 27-0 at Kensington Meadows. The return match a little over a month later at Kingswood was a much closer affair, Bath losing 10-7 to a score in time added on. Their protests that the final pass to the try scorer, Ashford, was forward, went unheeded.

A new name appeared on the fixture list on 28 January, with the visit of Cheltenham, beginning an association between the clubs that lasted very nearly 100 years, only to be ended by the onset of league rugby.

With their home ground again unfit, Bath borrowed Henrietta Park to stage the game. The love affair with Kensington Meadows was showing signs of strain.

-4-

Nomads Again

IN THE SUMMER of 1892, some twenty-seven years after first kicking a pig's bladder around North Parade, Bath's rugby players were again getting itchy feet. Known as Bath Rovers and Bath Wanderers during their comparatively brief stays at Claverton Down and Lambridge Meadows, the club had regarded Kensington Meadows very much as home during the seven years they occupied the ground. It was clear however that the Meadows, which had so often resembled a boating lake during winter months, could not be considered as a permanent solution. Fortuitously, Henrietta Park, 'more central and less liable to swamping', according to the *Chronicle*, had just become available, owing to the demise of the United Banks soccer club. The newspaper added portentously:

The Association game is dead as far as the Club under notice is concerned, the miserable attendance at the few contests played last winter showing that this department of football does not find much favour among Bathonians.[1]

The *Bath Herald* was in more lyrical mood when it reported on the forthcoming rugby season on 12 September 1892:

We shall soon have the footballers among us again, for the cricket season is practically at an end, and the various football clubs are actively preparing for their turn, although the season seems to come upon us somewhat as a surprise this year, seeing that summer appears only to have been with us a few weeks. However the fact remains that we must say goodbye to cricket for the next seven or eight months, and –

> *With many a merry shout,*
> *In riot, revelry, or rout,*
> *Pursue the football play.*[2]

On a more prosaic level, it welcomed the Bath club's move to Henrietta Park and suggested that matches would be played out in more a more civilised manner: 'The ground will be properly roped round, canvas erected etc., and thus it is hoped a stop will be put to the system which has hitherto been in evidence, that of the crowd following the players all round the field.'

Sadly, the new surroundings did not prompt a change in the weather and after November deluges and a rain-soaked scoreless draw against Bristol, *The Bath Herald* suggested that the committee be advised 'to set about constructing an ark for the rescue of well soaked football men and their enthusiastic followers'. On better days, however, Henrietta Park must have provided very agreeable surroundings. For the visit of Exeter in December 1892, for example, spectators were entertained by the Somerset and Dorset Railway Band.

On the playing front, the call of Empire occasionally demanded sacrifices. Bath were deprived of the services of a three-quarter, Roberts, who departed for work in Ceylon after spending barely three months with the club – 'brief but brilliant' was the verdict from the Management Committee minutes. G.L. Strachan also left at this time, for the rather less temperate climate of Nova Scotia, the former Hermitage pupil meriting more fulsome tributes:

He has figured in many a glorious victory for the club, and by his brilliant achievements has gained not only a lasting fame among local footballers, but has, without doubt, established himself in the memory of many of the fraternity in other towns.[3]

Four matches were arranged with Bristol that season, the last being on 14 January 1893. The wonder was that the match was played at all, since six inches of snow had fallen in a snowstorm over Bath and 'conditions were near impossible' as the home team ran out with 13 men to Bristol's 14. Remarkably, some 200 to 300 spectators stuck it out to the bitter end to see the visitors triumph 13-5, but 'the game had been little better than a farce', according to club records.

Rugby football was not all hardship and self-denial at this time, as the Bath press reported at around this time, with a note of southern disapproval:

The Yorkshire committee are of opinion that a lot of dead-heads get admission to the dinners which follow county matches. The county treasurer was presented with a bill for 70 dinners in connection with the recent Yorkshire v Somerset match. These banquets are very costly affairs at times, and we remember that at one Lancashire and Yorkshire dinner at Manchester 125 bottles of champagne were charged for.[4]

Bath's rugby champion, Frank Soane, had as strong an appetite as any and no doubt availed himself fully of northern hospitality when he represented the Rest of England against the Champion County, Yorkshire. Before a month was out – 4 March 1893 to be exact – Soane had even more to celebrate, as he was awarded his first cap against Scotland at Leeds.

'Buster' played in a national side that truly reflected the strength of rugby throughout England, although discontent in the north over broken time payments was to

England *v.* Wales, 1894. Frank Soane is seated, far right.

precipitate the Northern Union's breakaway within two years. For the time being, however, the England pack could embrace such diverse personalities as Reverend Lancelot Jefferson Percival, later KCVO, and the humble railwayman William Yiend, captain of Hartlepool Rovers.

Making his final appearance was Andrew Stoddart, the only man to captain his country at both rugby and cricket. After the 1887/88 cricket tour of Australia, he had stayed on to rendezvous with the visiting British rugby team, taking over as captain after R.L. Seddon was drowned in the Hunter River. Stoddart also played in 16 cricket Tests for England, leading his country to victory over the Australians in 1894/955. A complex character, he blew his brains out in 1915.

Although the Scots won 8-0, Soane's club-mates wasted no time in organising a celebratory dinner at Fortt's Restaurant in Milsom Street, just yards from the family music shop.

The toast was drunk most enthusiastically with musical honours. In reply, Mr Soane thanked the company for its hearty manner. He was sure he did not deserve half of what had been said about him. He was proud of the Bath Club and also for the first time in its history, it was out of debt – that sort of thing had never occurred before [laughter]. That state of affairs was due to the splendid exertions of Mr. Tommy Parham [applause], who was not only the most brilliant half back who ever played for Bath, but a most able Treasurer. It was very strange but football seemed to run through families like gout [laughter], and they had many instances in their own club – Parhams, the Vincents, and the Helps. Football was a splendid game, not only on account of the physical training, but the moral good that it did. It taught men to control their tempers and kept them from public houses [applause]. Having alluded to the valuable help he experienced from his old friend and deputy captain, Pattinson, [applause], Mr Soane again thanked those present for the honour they had done him; when he looked round and saw so many familiar faces he thought he had few enemies and many friends [cheers].

He was to make further appearances the following season, firstly against Wales at Birkenhead on 6 January 1894, when England fielded four three-quarters for the first time, winning 24-3. Unfortunately, that was the only occasion on which he finished on the winning side because Ireland triumphed 7-5 at Blackheath and Scotland won 6-0 at Raeburn Place, Edinburgh, on 17 March. England contemporaries in that season included Alf Allport, of Blackheath, famous for his repertoire of comic songs, and at least three players lost to Rugby Union after the breakaway – 'Little Dicky' Lockwood (Heckmondwike), John Toothill (Bradford), and Bob Wood (Liversedge).

The game of rugby football was proving exceptionally popular in the north where games attracted large crowds and factory owners were encouraged to release workers from Saturday afternoon shifts to play. Those players had to forego wages and their clubs sought to compensate for this 'broken time', much to the disapproval of those clubs, mainly in the south, who championed the ethic of amateurism.

The disagreement was fundamental. One side believed that any suggestion of payment for playing would destroy for ever the ideals of a noble pastime, while the other dismissed their protestations as public school cant, a hypocritical attempt to protect the 'shamateurism' that enabled the monied, leisured classes to dominate the sport.

The die had been cast at a general meeting of the Rugby Football Union, held at the Westminster Palace Hotel on 20 September 1893, when a motion was tabled, proposing that 'players be compensated for *bona fide* loss of time'. Against the proposal, the Establishment tabled the following amendment: 'that this meeting, believing that the above principle is contrary to the true interest of the game and its spirit, declines to sanction the same.' The amendment was carried by 282 votes to 136.

Given the entrenched positions, the breakaway of twenty-two clubs from Lancashire and Yorkshire was inevitable, with the Northern Union, as it was called, being established on 29 August 1895. The name was not changed to the Rugby Football League until 1922.

The Northern Union did not sanction professionalism for another three years and even then it required that players should also pursue some other employment. But the schism, in men's minds as much as in the rulebook, was total and set the scene for a long and bitter struggle for possession of the game and its talent. The RFU, being utterly convinced of the rightness of its position while shaken to its core by these seismic events, made immediate law revisions to protect the principles of amateurism.

As early as spring 1894, the RFU took peremptory action against Gloucester, suspending the club from 5 to 24 March on a charge of professionalism after deciding that a Stroud player, Shewell, had been improperly approached. The Gloucester captain was suspended for the remainder of the season and his club was ordered to pay the entire costs of the inquiry. The bastion of amateurism stood for very nearly a century. Bath, like every other Rugby Union club, was affected by the split as over the years covert approaches were made to players from Northern clubs. Some defected – but one of the biggest dangers was in merely being seen talking to a League scout.

Back home, however, an article in the *Bath Herald* reflected concern that young men were jeopardising rather more than their amateur status:

AN INJURY BLACK LIST
A correspondent of the Westminster Gazette has just sent in to that journal a truly appalling document, which he has been pleased to call the Football 'Butcher's Bill,' 1890-3. The compiler of this remarkable production has kept a mercilessly vigilant eye upon the newspaper reports of matches, and from them has collected in three years' play a grand (!) total of deaths and damages (reported) of 437. This big number is thus made up:- Deaths 71; legs, etc., broken, 121; broken arms, etc., 33; broken collar bones, 54; other injuries, not included in the foregoing, 158. After reading this it would seem rather superfluous to ask whether the game of football is dangerous or not. The writer of this sad chronicle gives chapter and verse, as it were, for every casualty in his list, quoting name of place, club, victim, and date.[6]

Later in the year, the Bath committee met to discuss the advisability of insuring playing members against injury. In the meantime, however, they had more parochial matters to attend to, a general committee meeting at 9 George Street on 9 April 1893 resolving that 'Henrietta Park be taken for the season 1893 at £10, to include Ground and Pavilion'. This decision was notwithstanding the fact that the ground had not been available from 1 March. Prior claim by Bloomfield Cricket Club forced the rugby club to play out the rest of the season at Claverton Down but it finished with a creditable record of 22 games played, 14 won, 7 lost and 1 drawn.

It was also suggested that a local Challenge Cup be instituted, to be contested by clubs within five miles of Bath. There was still time for a vote to remove Widcombe, Bristol Hornets, Oakfield and Swindon Rangers from the following season's fixture list.

Another committee meeting towards the end of the month agreed that 'all members of the 1st XV wear the City Arms on their Jersey and Blazers, any member who has played in not less than six 1st XV matches being eligible to wear the badge, but a written order from Hon Secretary to procure it'.

With a fully-fledged England international as captain, spirits could not have been higher at the start of the 1893/94 season, as recorded in the minutes of the club's AGM on 15 September:

Upon re-election as captain, Soane called for serious training and a stronger fixture card. Players needed to practise passing and kicking etc. Re-elected as Vice captain, Pattinson mentioned the advantage of having an international forward to lead them, and he hoped the Club would soon have an international back. He detected an enthusiasm for the coming season and players were impatient to 'get at 'em'.
The Chairman was pleased that the Club affairs were in order, and there was a balance in hand of £10. Mr Parham urged every member to recruit three other members. Regrettably, he could not continue as Honorary Treasurer, and in the absence of a ready successor, Mr Parham and Mr J.W. Hooper were nominated to find a replacement.

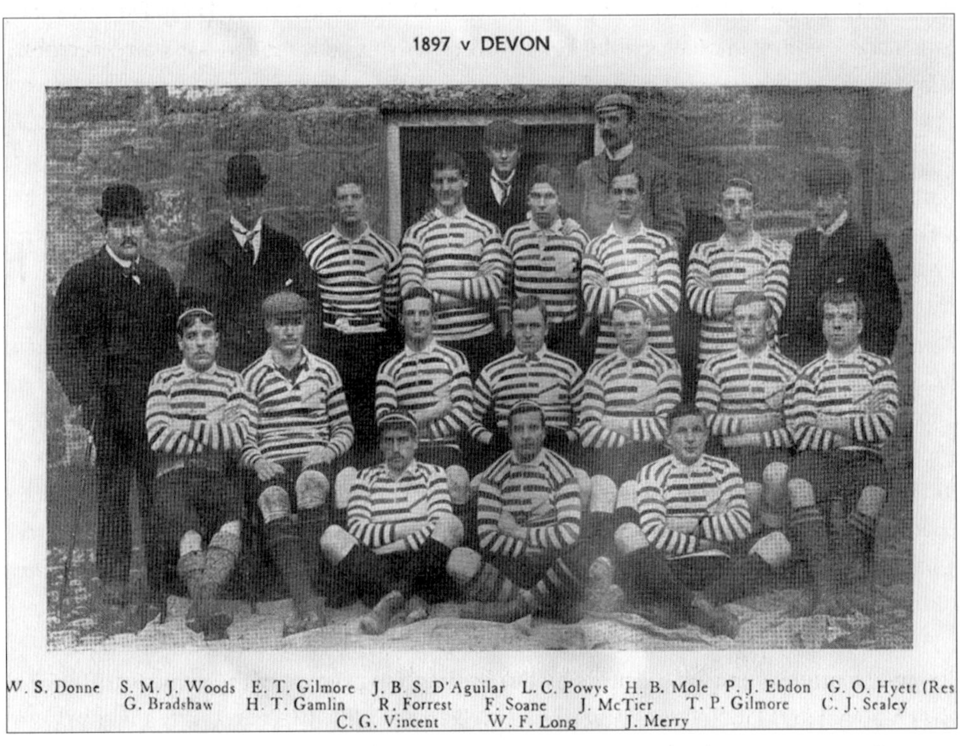

The Somerset team of 1897, which included Bath representatives J.B.S. D'Aguilar, F. Soane, J. McTier, C.G. Vincent and W.F. Long. (Courtesy of Somerset Rugby).

It was decided that a uniform charge of 3d admission at the gate and 3d extra for the reserved side should be made at all matches with the exception of the Bank Holiday games, and it was agreed that a match for the benefit of the Hospital should be played if possible. Over 30 new members were elected.

A special general meeting of the RFU was also held at around this time and it was decided to incorporate into the Laws of the Game 'that the referee shall have sole control of the game, and may blow his whistle without waiting for any appeal'.

This reinforcement of the notion that the referee was the sole arbiter of events on the field was tested in Bath's very first game, against Clifton at Horfield. Bingham scored for the home side early in the second half as Bath protested that the official had previously blown for an infringement. The matter of the disputed try was put before the RFU for a decision but the 5-3 scoreline to Clifton recorded in the Bath archive suggests that the appeal was, not surprisingly, turned down.

A distinctive and familiar name reappeared on the Bath team sheet at this time. John Burton Stockton D'Aguilar was the son of Bath's first international player, Francis Burton Grant D'Aguilar, capped against Scotland a quarter of a century earlier. J.B.S. proved himself an able performer alongside seasoned campaigners such as Soane, Parham, Pattinson, T.C. Rogerson, W. Coles and A.E. Hayward Pinch. D'Aguilar was soon established as first-choice goal-kicker and finished his first season with a respectable tally of 22 conversions and a penalty goal in addition to five tries.

Wins over Weston-super-Mare (6-0) and Bath College (45-3) would have provided encouraging rehearsals for the first meeting with Bristol on 28 October, except that Bath had to travel without Soane, Rogerson, Parham and Coles, who were required for a Somerset county trial. Appeals to Bristol to scratch the fixture were turned down, prompting the following observation from the Bath press:

Whilst admiring the courage of the Bath Club in facing certain defeat rather than disappoint the Bristol public, we cannot help recognising the un-sportsmanlike conduct of Bristol in refusing to release their neighbours from the engagement. The motive was, we hear, purely a financial one – if this is so it is greatly to be regretted that so popular a club as Bristol should be guilty of such mercenary behaviour. It is our proud boast that rugby football is purely an amateur sport, but when we are confronted with a similar case to the Bristol v. Bath fiasco we prefer to remain silent on this point.[7]

To make matters worse, the visitors had to play a good portion of the game with 13 men after Walwyn and Pinch were injured in a collision. Bath actually led with a first-half try by Coles until just before the end when Bristol gained the upper hand and created a try for Turner, converted from a difficult angle by Thompson. This must have been the game referred to in a nostalgic article in *The Bath Chronicle* of 23 October 1909, even though it dates the match in 1892 rather than 1893.

Among the spectators at the Bath and Wellington match today was Dr A.E. Hayward Pinch, who was a prominent player for Bath several years ago. He was secretary of the Club from 1889 to 1892, and played as full back from 1889-1894. When he was in the team Tommy Parham and B.C. Helps were the half-backs, while the three-quarter line was generally composed of Pattinson, Strachan, H.B. Rowlands (afterwards an International), and C.J.B. Moneypenny. Dr Pinch, like many others, was disappointed to see that a victory was snatched from Bath at Bristol last week, and recalls to my memory how history repeats itself. For in 1892 Bath were leading at the close of the game, but the referee, by mistake, (like Mr Able at Bristol last week), allowed extra time, and in those additional minutes Bristol won the game. Dr Pinch had vivid memories of the match, as he was knocked out and carried off the field in an unconscious state.

Back at Henrietta Park a week later, Bath defeated Clifton 9-0 in front of 500 spectators with tries by Soane, Parham and D'Aguilar, the latter failing with all three conversion attempts. Notwithstanding the committee decision a few months before, Swindon Rangers reappeared on the fixture list only to be defeated 14-0. A scoreless draw was played out in a snowstorm at Stroud and a visit to Cardiff Harlequins resulted in a 9-0 defeat, although 'Soane stood out head and shoulders above his fellows'.

A crowd of 600, including 'a large number of ladies', saw the home team win 28-0 against Cheltenham and there were further victories over Stroud (9-0) and at Clifton (6-0) before a Bath side weakened by 'business, illness and other causes' lost 14-3 at Weston-super-Mare. The unbeaten home record was surrendered on Boxing Day 1893 in front of 1,500 at Henrietta Park against Jesus College Wanderers, the Cambridge students winning 3-0 with an unconverted try. The following day, while Frank Soane played for the Barbarians at Cardiff, his club-mates took on the Rest of Bath, drawing 3-3.

Another crowd of 1,000-plus saw Bath beat Wellington 5-0 on 30 December and there were further successes against Swindon Rangers (7-0) and Taunton (27-0) before Bristol again broke the spell with a 6-0 victory at Henrietta Park and Wellington exacted their own revenge with a 23-0 win. Clifton then pulled off a 6-0 victory in Bath, a controversial one at that after the home forwards apparently dribbled the ball over the Clifton line only for the referee, Mr D'Asth, of Yeovil, to whistle play back to halfway.

Contemporary newspaper reports recorded that, after the game, the official was followed back to the Angel Hotel by 'a howling crowd, who expressed their resentment at his decisions by loud hooting'. The correspondent continued:

Such conduct cannot be too strongly condemned. A referee may make mistakes, but it is a thankless office at the best, and insults of this kind do the cause of football much harm.[8]

An 8-0 home win over Exeter was distinguished by a fine display from Pattinson, once passing through four or five of the opposition and later providing the scoring pass to Middleton for the only try.

Defeat at Cheltenham (11-3) was followed by a win at Taunton and then a meeting with the Civil Service at the College Ground on a hot late March afternoon attracting 'an exceedingly heavy gate, with the fair sex well represented'. D'Aguilar, laying claim to be Bath's first specialist goal-kicker, landed six of the seven conversion attempts.

The annual dinner a week previously had honoured the soon-to-be-wed Tommy Parham for his meritorious service to the club, not only as 'an admirable Bath and Somerset half-back' but also as the club's Honorary Treasurer. The player accepted the gift of a handsome French timepiece, made of soft red and black marble with bronze mountings. Supplied by Messrs Jackman & Son, it was on display at their Milsom Street premises for several days.

As champions of the South West, Somerset published their own booklet – *A Record of Past Seasons, with particular reference to 1893/94*, printed at the Chronicle and Pictorial offices, Bath, and priced 6d. Among the tributes in the publication, compiled by Bath official George E. Roberts, was this paean to Parham:

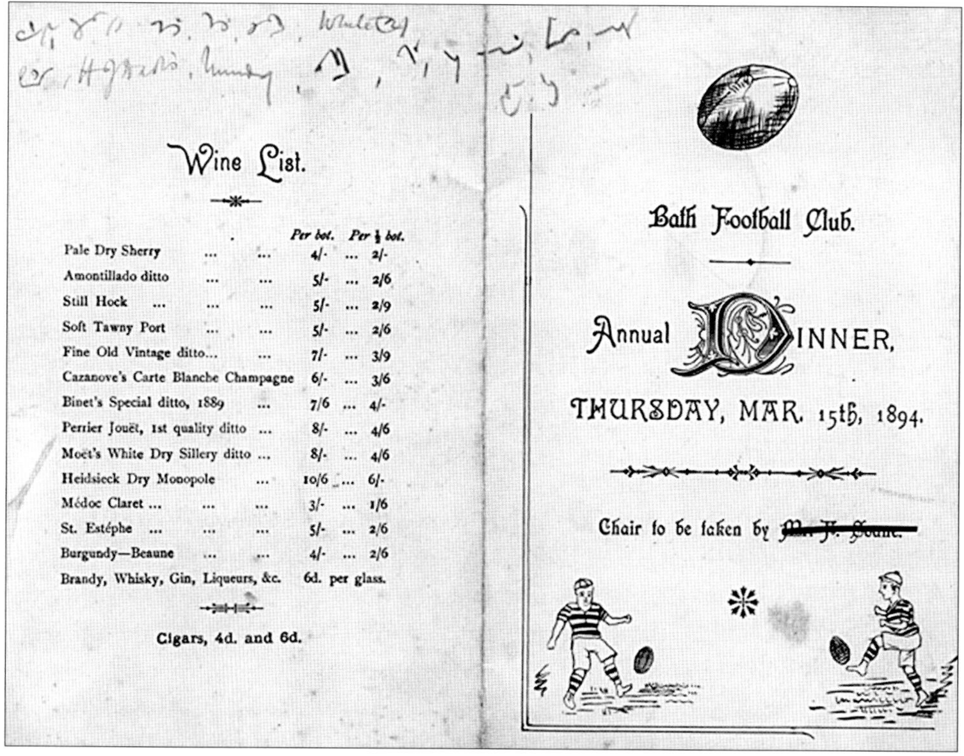

Wine List.

	Per bot.	Per ½ bot.
Pale Dry Sherry	4/-	2/-
Amontillado ditto	5/-	2/6
Still Hock	5/-	2/9
Soft Tawny Port	5/-	2/6
Fine Old Vintage ditto...	7/-	3/9
Cazanove's Carte Blanche Champagne	6/-	3/6
Binet's Special ditto, 1889	7/6	4/-
Perrier Jouët, 1st quality ditto	8/-	4/6
Moët's White Dry Sillery ditto	8/-	4/6
Heidsieck Dry Monopole	10/6	6/-
Médoc Claret	3/-	1/6
St. Estéphe	5/-	2/6
Burgundy—Beaune	4/-	2/6
Brandy, Whisky, Gin, Liqueurs, &c.	6d. per glass.	

Cigars, 4d. and 6d.

Bath Football Club.

Annual DINNER,

THURSDAY, MAR. 15th, 1894.

Chair to be taken by

The annual dinner of 1894, at which Tommy Parham was honoured.

Menu

SOUPS.
Clear Spring. Ox Tail.

FISH.
Salmon and Cucumber.
Fried Smelts.

JOINTS.
Roast Lamb. Sirloin Beef.

POULTRY.
Roast Chicken and Sausages.
Ox Tongues. Black Cock.

SWEETS.
Muffin Pudding. Jellies. Creams.
Tipsy Cakes.

Cheese.

Dessert.

Toast List

The Queen and Royal Family.
Proposed by the Chairman.

Army, Navy, and Reserve Forces.
Proposed by the Chairman.
Responded to by Capt. E. Lewis.

The Guest.
Proposed by the Chairman.

Bath Football Club.
Proposed by Mr. N. Parham.
Responded to by Mr. F. Soane and Mr. W. Pattinson.

The Visitors.
Proposed by Mr. C. Chivers.
Responded to by

The Press.
Proposed by Mr. W. Pattinson.
Responded to by Mr. Roberts.

The Chairman.
Proposed by Mr. A. J. Freeman.

Curtis. Bath.

Note the toast to Army, Royal Navy and Reserve Forces, but not the Royal Air Force – there were no aeroplanes at this time!

Bath can claim the distinction of having produced one of the cleverest scoring half-backs the county has ever seen. Born on the 13th November, 1869, Thomas Nevil Maskelyne Parham went to school at the age of ten to All Hallows, Honiton, where the brothers Syd and Harry Smith were also educated. During the six years of his school life he gave great promise as a Rugby player, and in the year 1885 captained the School XV. At the time he left Honiton (1886) he was captain of the cricket club, and although he has never particularly excelled at the summer game, is a capital cover point and a useful batsman. Directly after leaving school he was articled to a solicitor at Bristol, and has regularly appeared in the Bath Football Club team ever since, with the exception of the season 1890-91, when he was in London, reading for his final. There is probably no more popular man in Bath than 'Tommy' Parham, and to his wonderful play in the field, and his sterling hard work in football finance is due in no small degree the present healthy and affluent state of his club. Parham's first appearance in the County XV was in the match against Blackheath in 1888, when he did so well as to win the praises of both the committee and the Press. Since then he has donned the crimson black and white jersey a great number of times, always with the happiest results, his performances in the field being most consistent. We think the zenith of Parham's popularity was attained in the present season (1893-4) in his native city, when playing for the home county v Gloucestershire, he scored, with sensational runs, the only two tries obtained by his side. With his marvellous dodging ability he will score where many a three-quarter would fail to get through. In club matches he has achieved a high standard of success, for besides being brilliant in attack he is a safe defensive player, kicking well with his left foot and being a certain tackler. Unlike the majority of modern halves Parham is rarely penalised for offside play. Just before Christmas, Parham received a nasty injury at Weston-super-Mare, whilst captaining a weak team of Bathonians. In stopping a fierce rush of the home forwards he was stepped upon and severely bruised about the muscles of the back. Although now almost completely recovered, his medical man advises him to give up the game of which he is such an admirable exponent. He stands 5ft 4in in height, and weighs 10st 10lb. At the annual dinner of his Club Parham was presented with a handsome wedding present as a token of esteem.

Not only was Parham forced to retire but Bath's annual general meeting on 14 September 1894 was told that A.E. Hayward Pinch had also had to give up the game on medical advice.

Three nights later club officials met again in committee to discuss a proposal which offered a longer-term solution to the perennial problem of finding a permanent home for the Bath Football Club. Henrietta Park, although an improvement on Kensington Meadows, was cramped and provided too many opportunities for gate-crashers. More importantly, 'Captain Forester, owner of Bathwick Estates, was seeking an Act of Parliament to enable him to develop the park into extensive gardens and a pleasure area'.

However, the committee heard that 'the newly formed Bath and County Recreation Ground Company had acquired the 17 acres "green sward" of Pulteney Meadows and was desirous of developing the area for the athletic pursuits of the citizens of Bath'. The company had appealed for capital of £3,000 to render the area fit for first-class cricket and other sports but initially only £1,000 was raised and the rugby club was showing some reluctance to accept on the rental and revenue sharing terms suggested.

A long discussion then took place with regard to negotiations between the Club and the Syndicate in possession of the Pulteney Meadows. The area could be made available for the coming season, and the Company would erect a grandstand in time for the first match. The chief concern was a raise in rent. The Company would additionally take 20% on the gate money and 20% of the takings at the Grandstand. Nevertheless, the Chairman thought it too good an opportunity to miss, but there were dissenters. Mr Sants did not like the terms offered and thought there would be difficulty in gate taking if there were other events in progress. However, it would appear the Club would be given exclusive rights on certain days. Mr Henshaw counselled that the interests of the Club and Company were too much in common to allow insuperable difficulties to arise. He was sorry the Company had not raised more money, but suggested that if one hundred Club members took up £10 each the problem would be solved. He thought that all sportsmen in the city could contribute to its success.

The CHAIRMAN repeated that Henrietta-park was inadequate, and if they could not get a good ground like the one about which they had been talking, it would be 'Good bye' to county football in Bath. On the other hand, if proper accommodation were provided there would be county football here and probably it would lead to county cricket in Bath. They must try and get the ground if possible.

Discussion was adjourned, and it was decided that a sub committee meet the Syndicate on the matter.

According to *The Bath Chronicle*, the deputation of Frank Soane (captain), C. Gilby, J.E. Henshaw and W. Sants met the company chairman C. Radway and the company secretary L.C. Mundy at The Grand Pump Room Hotel on Tuesday 18 September.

The terms suggested were that the Company should receive 20 per cent of the takings at the gates, and half the receipts at the grand-stand which they would erect, and that no fixed rent, or only a small nominal rent, should be paid by the Club. The Chairman said he would recommend the directors to accept these terms, and the deputation from the Club will place them before a general meeting to be convened on Monday next. There is every prospect of a satisfactory settlement, the only question which now remains being as to the erection of a barricade.[9]

There was a large attendance at the adjourned general meeting, held at the Angel Hotel to consider the terms offered by the company, and subsequently reported by *The Chronicle* as follows:

The CHAIRMAN [of the meeting – Mr Frank Soane] read the draft of the proposed agreement with the Company. This provided that the Club should occupy that portion of the ground on which the Somerset county matches were played; last season from September 15th 1894 to 31st March 1895, and from September 15th 1895, to March 31st 1896. The Club should have the exclusive use of the ground during these periods for the purpose of football provided that on any day not fixed for a football match the Company should have the use of the ground free of charge. The Club to have the sole right to charge for admission to that portion of the ground on match days, all persons (other than subscribing members of the Club and ladies) to pay for admission at the gate. The charges for admission to be fixed by the Club and the Company to take one-fifth of the receipts at the gate. The Company undertook to erect proper barriers around the ground, to keep it in proper order for football, and to erect a suitable grandstand. All persons, whether members of the Club or not, to pay the charge for admission to the grandstand fixed by the Company, one half of the money taken at the stand to be handed to the Club, who should pay the necessary gatemen and police and also money taker at the stand on match days. With regard to county football matches, the Company agree that on not more than two days in each season the ground could be used for county matches, the County executive to take all the receipts and to pay all expenses.[10]

In little more than a week of meetings and negotiations driven by the forceful Soane, the club had negotiated terms for a permanent home – so permanent, in fact, that its tenure was to span three separate centuries and six monarchs.

-5-

Threepennies and Sixpennies

THE FIXTURE LIST of 1894/95 determined that Bath's opponents for the historic first match on what was to become known as the Recreation Ground would be Exeter, on Saturday 6 October. Once negotiations had been concluded with the company, arrangements were hastily made to make the ground fit for spectators. Excitement over the new ground was quickly translated into urgent action to build a grandstand and erect a 'stout wooded barrier' around the pitch, situated away from the river on the other side of the cricket square rather than on the site of the current Bath Rugby facilities. The home side had warmed up with an 8-0 reverse at Clifton the previous weekend, one of the try scorers being W.G. Grace Jnr, whose father had been an opponent in the 1870s.

More than 500 spectators paid £13 4s to witness Bath's first-ever fixture on the Recreation Ground, although there was much muttering and grumbling over the 6d charge for admission. The *Chronicle* correspondent was one of many who said he 'would sooner see a thousand at 3d rather than 500 at 6d, and it is the best policy'. In line with the tenancy agreement, the club collected four-fifths of the gate. A meeting of the General Committee was convened for the following Thursday evening, ostensibly to let the 'threepennies and the sixpennies' fight it out

The honour of scoring the first of many Bath tries on the Recreation Ground – they won 22-nil – fell to eighteen-year-old wing W.F. Long, as recorded by *The Bath Chronicle*:

It was after four ere the match commenced before a fairly large crowd of spectators, considering the sixpenny gate. Soane started for Bath and the leather was weakly returned. A scrum was formed and the onlookers soon had the satisfaction of seeing a splendid piece of work by the home three-quarters. Vincent getting hold from the scrum handed out to Soane, the captain transferred to MacTier, who after a brief hold passed to Long on the left wing. The last named with a beautifully smart dodgy run, got through the Exonians, and landed a try.[1]

The inaugural meeting of the Recreation Ground Company was held the following Wednesday. Plans were outlined to shareholders to provide for five asphalt tennis courts, a croquet area, a revival of Lawn Tennis week, an area for flooding for ice skating and sooner or later to get county cricket on the ground. It was recorded that a few problems

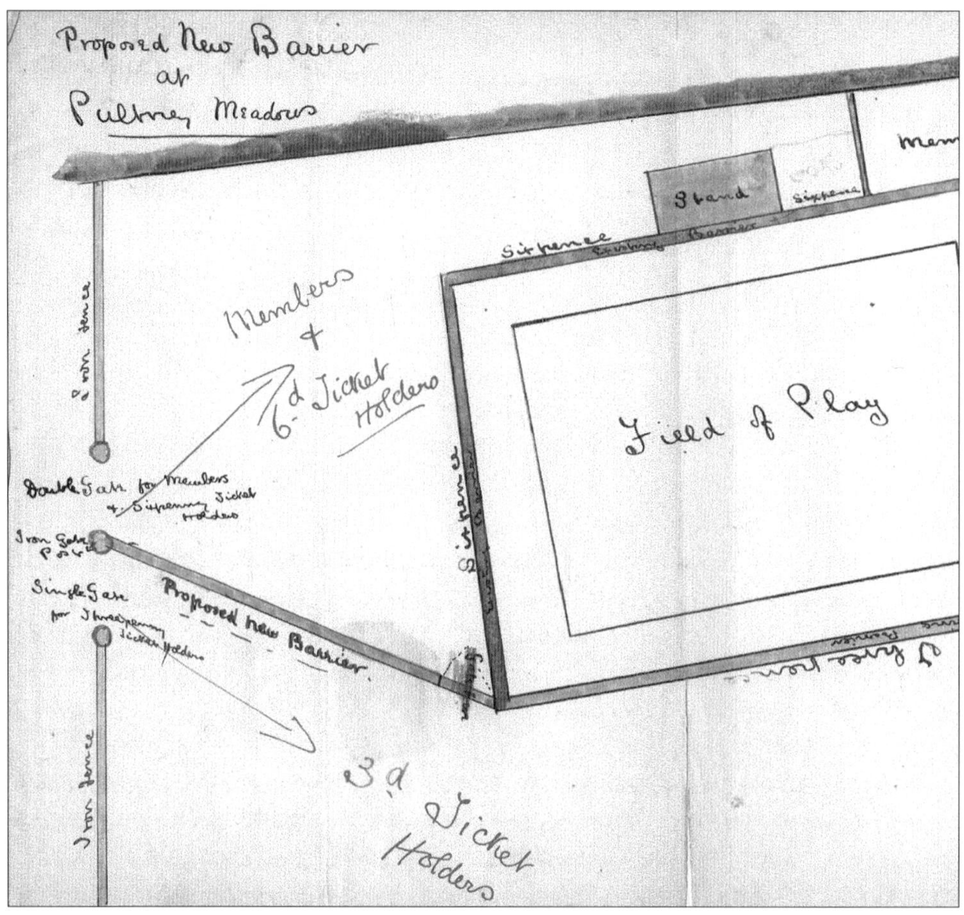

Bath move to the eastern side of the Recreation Ground, 1894.

had cropped up in relation to the Bath Football Club leasing arrangements but, with goodwill on both sides, most matters were quickly sorted out.

A new 150 foot grandstand would be built having its back to William Street, and this would be quite distinct from the temporary football stand. There was a problem with this last named, in that according to the tenancy, the football stand should have been five yards back from the fence surround. It was to be left for the present, with an adjustment next season.[2]

The preoccupation with gatecrashers also surfaced again:

To obstruct the gaze of the hundreds who took an outside ticket on Saturday a rank of evergreens is being planted, on a raised bank, by the Company inside the railings near the entrance to the field. The Johnstone-street view is also to be blocked.[3]

With the brothers F.C. and B.H. Belson having been recruited from Clifton, Weston-super-Mare were defeated 8-4, but Bath then suffered a 3-0 reverse against Edwardians on a badly flooded pitch in Birmingham. Victory over Stroud (5-3) and a 0-0 draw against Taunton, in which committee-man Tommy Parham was pressed into an impromptu and short-lived comeback, should have been followed by a bumper home gate against Gloucester.

On the afternoon of Monday 12 November 1894, Bath was struck by a downpour of biblical proportions. 'The Great Flood' as the *Chronicle* described it two days later, left in its wake 'Whole Districts Submerged – Houses Flooded – Scores of Families Homeless – Great Distress'. On the Recreation Ground it started with large puddles on the rugby and cricket pitches but a few hours later 'each field was several feet deep in a seething, swirling mass of water'.

The Recreation Ground was like a large lake and much damage was done there. The new grand stand was stormed by the irresistible flood, and was at last toppled over on its back. The water seemed to enjoy bringing a quantity of planks left on the ground against the hoarding, and several of the small trees freshly planted near North Parade-bridge were torn out by the roots. A large roller of considerable weight was completely overturned and the College Pavilion was soon surrounded…till the new earth bank in the Recreation ground disappeared. It had not broken, but fears are entertained whether it will suffer by its submersion.

The sight from the end of Johnstone Street on Tuesday morning was so unusual that it is worth while witnessing. From this point of view a huge expanse of water met the eye, the Pulteney Meadows being totally flooded. Of the Pavilion used by the Grammar School boys, only the roof was visible, while the large grand-stand recently erected by the Company on the football ground had been lifted up and thrown bodily on its back. The crossbar of the goal posts could be distinguished, and there was evidently six or seven feet of water in the centre of the field.[4]

Enthusiasm for Bath Football Club's move to Pulteney Meadows was seemingly not shared by Bath College who, having secured agreement to use the ground at a rent of £100 per year (provided their activities were adjusted to avoid any clash with the primary tenants), preferred to use their Warminster Road ground for the meeting between the teams on 24 November. The college authorities were alleged to have blocked the students' use of the Recreation Ground because 'they could not be seen playing in a field to which a charge for admission was made' but *The Chronicle* dismissed this stance as 'only too palpably a piece of petty spite against the Recreation Grounds Company, whom they regard as having ousted them from their former playing ground. Those who know the facts are aware that the most reasonable proposals were made to the College Council and they were declined. Now they have to endure a hilly bit of country from which no one can be excluded as there is a public right of way across the ground.' Playing on a pitch like 'a lean-to roof' on the Warminster Road, Bath won 29-3.

Back on home territory for a match with Cheltenham on 1 December, the fog covered the Meadows so completely that one side of the pitch could not be seen from the other and the referee ruled play 'impossible'. However, the sides agreed to an exhibition game which continued in earnest, the visitors winning 5-0.

After trouncing Swindon Rangers 61-0, Bath met Clifton on 22 December, winning a stubbornly and evenly contested game 3-0. Unfortunately, the headlines were again captured by the weather, displaying a *fin-de-siècle* vehemence as one of the worst gales of the century accounted for more than 100 lives, 'with losses among shipping and fishing vessels still awaited'.

Spirits were quickly lifted in Bath by the first visit on Christmas Eve of the Barbarians club, with such luminaries as the Irish international fullback L.H. Gwynn, a young C.B. Fry and the recently capped Philip Maud, a veteran of the North West Frontier and destined to rise to the rank of Brigadier General. Also in their ranks was Norman Biggs of Cardiff and Wales, soon to be a familiar face at Bath.

With five internationals in their line-up, they were too strong for Bath, scoring tries through M. Toller of Blackheath (2) and the Oxford University students W.J. Carey and E.M. Baker, with Biggs adding a conversion. 'Twur like schoolboys against grown men,' observed the *Chronicle*, while commending the local players on their efforts. The Barbarians shared the gate of £52 from the crowd of over 2,000 and went on to beat Cardiff a few days later by three tries to two.

A hectic programme of five games in eight days continued with an 11-6 win over the Jesus College, Cambridge students on Boxing Day, followed twenty-four hours later by the first visit by Bristol to the 'Rec'. With a thousand of their 'townies' to cheer them on, Bristol scored two soft tries early on and the *Chronicle* recorded with some dismay that fouling and unsportsmanlike tactics were 'a blot on the escutcheon of Bristol'. Even Soane was stretched out, winded. 'It is the first time I have known it happen to the sturdy Bath captain, but a thrust from a head like Davies's under the fifth rib is enough to pump the stoutest reservoir. Fenner received a severe caution from the referee on the same score.' Bath were not disgraced by the final 11-8 scoreline, both their tries coming from F.R. Rowett, with D'Aguilar converting the first.

By the fifth fixture of the holiday, Bath were able to muster only 14 players for the trip to Wellington, losing 11-0, and they also went down 5-18 at Penarth a week later. Wins over Cheltenham (13-0) and Taunton (3-0) restored morale, but snow was already in the air and four fixtures were then lost to frost.

The cancellation of the Weston-super-Mare fixture on the last weekend of February was attributed to the fact that the Recreation Ground Company did not feel justified in allowing the ground to be 'Leicestered', as their representative so graphically put it. This appeared to be a reference to the East Midlands club's practice of burning coke fires to thaw out the pitch.

It was 2 March 1895 before rugby resumed and Bath won only one more game, 9-8 against Clifton while drawing 0-0 at Stroud and losing to Bristol (0-3), Penarth (0-6) and

Bridgwater (0-13). It meant that they finished the season in deficit with 10 wins, 11 defeats and 2 draws.

Nevertheless it was a largely cheerful annual general meeting on 13 June which heard the treasurer, A.J. Freeman, report healthy finances with a balance in hand of £132 4s 2½d. Frank Soane, from the chair, re-stated the Club's aim in the advancement of rugby football, and stressed that in order to do so they must continue in their endeavours to popularise the Club.

How far we have succeeded in doing so is evident by the fact of our having been elected by that champion touring team, the Barbarians, as one of the very few clubs who opposed them during the season [applause]. Many of the old players of the Club who recollect the time when they had to pay their own expenses to out matches are somewhat inclined to cry out against so much attention being paid to the convenience of our teams, but they should reflect that whereas they were wont to disport themselves before some 20 spectators our XV, have once this year played before a £70 gate, and I think the present team should receive proportionate respect [hear hear]. In conclusion gentlemen, I feel sure that with plenty of money, plenty of patrons, and plenty of merit amongst our players the Bath Football Club will continue that quick march of progress which has characterised its movement in recent years [applause].[5]

However, the subsequent season, 1895/96, proved even less successful, the club playing 33 fixtures and winning only 11, losing 14 and drawing 8. Both meetings with Bristol were lost 6-3 and absenteeism accounted for a number of other narrow defeats.

Continuing resistance to the 6d charge was blamed for meagre attendances as when Bath fielded a 'wretchedly weak' side against Cheltenham on 30 November 1895 and lost an ugly match 11-8. There was outrage in the home camp after B.H. Belson was seen to have been 'struck a deliberate blow in the face late in the game', the culprit later being identified as Craddock. The *Bath Herald* and *Daily Chronicle* correspondent, 'The Spy', declared: 'The game was a veritable prize fight in miniature and the way in which the visitors followed up their tactics of tripping, scragging, fouling and hacking really took the biscuit.'

A 3-3 draw at home to Gloucester which packed out the grandstand for the first time raised spirits, Soane working 'like a horse' and being well backed up by Belson, Derrick and Heath among others.

Christmas 1895 was greeted by spells of rain, sleet and snow and a Christmas Eve fixture against Burton-on-Trent failed to attract enough paying spectators to cover the match guarantee. On Boxing Day morning the 'A' team's match raised £6, and the afternoon First XV game against Kensington only £20. The A game on 28 December raised £2 on the gate and 30 shillings for the stand.

Meanwhile the Recreation Ground Company reported a loss of some £148 on the first year's trading, with Tennis Week responsible for £108 of that figure. The accounts indicated that the Company derived a net £53 13s 5d from the rugby club, nearly one-third of the total income, and this encouraged the club to take a tough stance when it came to negotiating new renting terms, as the *Chronicle* reported on 2 January:

Mr. Henshaw must have gained the thanks of all members of Bath F.C. for the determined manner in which he championed their case at the meeting of the Recreation Grounds Company. It is quite time the Board settled the negotiations and were made acquainted with the fact that the Club will not advance on the terms it has offered. The statement of one of the directors, who all along has been known not to be friendly towards the Club, that its terms will not be accepted to the extent the committee desires, was the only clue to the position taken up by the Board. It would be a source of general regret to see the Club take its departure from the Pulteney Meadows, and that is not at all a remote contingency for the management of the Club will resent any suggestion of tightening the screw.

The difference between the Company and the Club now is practically this. For every member the Company ask one shilling allowance, and the Club is only willing to pay sixpence a head. The Board has waived its claim to 25 per cent instead of 20 per cent of the gate money, and consents to the free admission of two ladies accompanied by a member. This, I understand, is the ultimatum which will be laid before the Club Committee next Monday. I sincerely hope a satisfactory result may be arrived at.[6]

Eight days later the newspaper thought there was little prospect of a settlement between landlord and tenant and suggested that the club would return to Kensington Meadows for the 1896/97 season at a rent of £8.

Meanwhile a scratch team, deprived of a host of first-teamers – A.E. Fry, G.G. Vincent, F.S.B. Taggart, W.J. Williams, F. Soane, F.C. Belson, J.B.S. D'Aguilar, B.H. Belson, L.J. Fry and J. Ruddick – achieved Bath's first victory in Wales, a totally unexpected 8-6 victory at Penarth. Less than a month later, however, they were so short of players for a trip to Wellington that they press-ganged two youngsters at the station: 'they proved mere passengers, worse than useless ... the club had much better have saved their fares.' Aside from the continuing difficulties with the Recreation Ground Company, the committee also had to field a stiff letter from B.H. Belson and D'Aguilar protesting at the lack of training facilities and threatening to call a general meeting of the club. Arrangements were hastily made to rent a gym in Broad Street on two nights each week.

By 3 February 1896, draft rental terms had been thrashed out with the Company on the understanding that the rugby pitch be moved to the river side of the Recreation Grounds for the following season (although this was subsequently deferred for another year). The Directors impressed upon the Football Committee 'the great desirability on behalf of both interests the discontinuance of the 3d gate.'

Interestingly, a request for use of the Rec by a ladies' football club was rejected by the committee only a month or so later.

The visit of Bristol on 8 February attracted 4,000 spectators, a record for a derby game, and at the final whistle 'the Bristolians gave way to a frenzy of joy, hats, umbrellas and handkerchiefs being frantically waved'. The first visit to Gloucester for ten years was made in the grip of a smallpox epidemic and, although one of the five married men in the team declined to travel, Bath achieved a creditable scoreless draw and enjoyed the post-match hospitality.

After keeping up Bath's reputation for feeding, the interval before the return train started was devoted to harmony and, with Rowse present, the piano was kept going merrily.[7]

Among the many inconclusive results that season, Bath drew 14-14 with the Barbarians on 2 April but the doubling of prices and the holiday season made for a comparatively small attendance. Only £14 was taken, including stand transfers, of which the visitors took 40 per cent and even this would have paid only a small proportion of their expenses.

On the pitch, F.C. Belson scored two tries and J.B.F. Derrick another as the honours went to the home forwards who 'were clever in the scrum, broke up quickly and in the loose were quick and clever, both with their feet and in passing'.

Bath *v.* Bristol, 8 February 1896. From left to right, back row: A. Billett, J. Ruddick, M. Cole, M.S. Bigwood, Mr Hooper, W.F. Long, G.G. Vincent, F. Derrick, E.H. Seers, A.E. Fry. Front row: J.B.S. D'Aguilar, F.C. Belson, F. Soane (captain), G. Middleton, R.A. Bartlett, L.J. Fry.

During the spring the committee was involved, no doubt wearily, in a long-running saga of the lost Carlton walking stick, which had disappeared from the Bristol junior club's dressing room after an 'A' XV away fixture on 8 February. Carlton had written a letter and two postcards, regarded as 'unjustifiable and ungentlemanly' by the Bath club, and it was nearly two months before the issue was resolved after various meetings and letters on both sides. Exhaustive inquiries eventually revealed that it had been mistaken for a 'fascimilar stick' belonging to W.T. Davis and lent to Gooding, who had hurt his ankle and who used it to assist his journey home.

Unfortunately, there was no satisfactory answer to another exchange of correspondence with Mr Berryman, proprietor of the Angel Hotel, after Club officials requested sufficient baths for visiting teams. The hard-working committeemen were doubtless relieved to finalise a three-year rental agreement on the Rec at the end of the season, although subscriptions had to be raised from 5s to 6s. This was to compensate for the loss of an equivalent shilling, surcharged by the Company for each member who would otherwise have paid nothing to watch home matches.

Management committee minutes reveal that there were some 400 memberships to be collected for the 1896/97 season with admission fees for First XV matches finally set at 6d and 1s for the reserve side. All 'A' team matches were to be charged at 6d and 3d.

To facilitate the smooth running of the Club, a room at No. 4 Bath Street was taken for use by the Honorary Secretaries and Honorary Treasurers, posts held respectively by J.W. Hooper with J.T. Piper and W. Stockwell with T.N. Parham. The Angel Hotel agreed to become the club's headquarters, 'it being a condition that no private room be provided for playing members changing'.

On the playing side, Old Merchant Taylors and London Lennox were dropped from the fixture list, which now placed greater emphasis on contests with Welsh opposition – notably Penarth, Llanelly[8], Neath and Llywnypia. To meet this challenge, Frank Soane, who had been keeping 'exceedingly fit' with a summer of rowing for Bath Avon, was re-elected captain, assisted by the 'hard working, good tempered' J.B.S. D'Aguilar as his deputy. Enthusiasm throughout the club merited the setting up of a third or extra XV.

Most of the talk however was of F.C. Belson, another keen oarsman, who had been posted to Abergavenny by his employers, The National Provincial Bank. The story went that he had requested a transfer from Bristol, hoping that the move would be eastwards! Belson's reluctant exile lasted from September 1896 through to February 1897, during which time he appeared for the District XV in a Newport trial match, for Abergavenny *v.* Newport and twice for Bristol, against Wellington and Newport.

With so much pride and interest being invested in the outcome of matches, the Bath club recognised the need for consistent performances from officials and made a proposal that certainly met the approval of *The Chronicle*:

Gentlemen with a thorough knowledge of the Rugby Code, sound in mind and limb, are asked to communicate with the hon. Sec. of Bath F.C., at 4 Bath Street, with a view of founding a referee's association for Bath. This is a step in the right direction, and I hope it will succeed. Who is to be the examiner?[9]

With J. McTier making a welcome return from a sojourn in Florida and Titch Fry in sparkling early season form, Bath kicked off with wins over Old Edwardians (11-0), Rosslyn Park (20-8) and Cheltenham (3-0), where Craddock made his apologies to B.H. Belson and shook hands to end any ill feeling over their 'severe contretemps' the previous November. Now for the Welsh challenge. Penarth set the tone by winning 3-0 at The Rec to herald the first-ever meeting between Bath and Llanelly on 19 October 1896, a fixture that over the next century became redolent of rugby's virtues – fierce rivalry on the field and enduring friendships off it. On this first occasion, however, the visitors seemed like men from another world to *The Chronicle*:

Welshmen, Welshmen, and still they come, and if Bath football goers cannot fathom the curious lingo which has mingled with the Queen's English on the Recreation Grounds, they have had a fair insight into football as she is played in the Principality; while it is safe to say the Bath team bear bruises they will carry many a week as a result of the Welsh invasion.[10]

Norman Biggs, six times capped for Wales, pictured in his Cardiff strip. (Courtesy of *History of Cardiff RFC 1876-1939*)

Selwyn Biggs (Cardiff, Richmond and Bath), holder of nine Welsh caps.
(Courtesy of Yore Publications)

With the financial pressures on the club, the Press was a key ally in drumming up interest and attracting people through the turnstiles. So successful were they, however, that the management committee (2 November 1896), concerned about the incessant shouting at the referee, made an appeal through the pages of the newspaper, 'suggesting quieter tactics'. (Intriguingly, officials also discussed ways of stopping 'the Wandering Minstrel' from encroaching on the Reserved side of the ground. Of who he was or how extensive his repertoire, there is no record.) A month later the committee was forced to print 50 notices as a result of spectators shouting at matches, although W.T. Davis obviously had their comfort in mind when he spoke as to the necessity of having a urinal on the Reserved side. They also commissioned a new scoreboard at a cost of 25s and ordered a batch of presentation caps for 6s 3d each.

Of more concern at this time was the sheer logistical difficulty of finding 15 players for an away match – and getting them to their destination in time for kick-off. Contrary to the rose-tinted nostalgia for the Great Western Railway these days, travel was tiring and tiresome. A trip to Old Edwardians in Birmingham on 14 November involved a two-and-a-half hour train journey, followed by 'nigh on an hour of tortuous journey by omnibus, through a seemingly endless succession of side and suburban streets'. Frank Soane routinely made his team change into 'warpaint' and 'football garb' on the train.

During December, the Bath ranks were strengthened by the presence of former Welsh international three-quarter Norman Biggs. One of six brothers born to Mr and Mrs John Biggs, of The Laurels, London Road, Bath, and educated at Mr MacLean's School in Beach Road, Weston-super-Mare, he had been capped eight times as a Cardiff player from 1888 to 1894. His younger sibling, Selwyn, who earned nine caps with Cardiff between 1895 and 1900, also played for Bath but both brothers' appearances were more in the nature of guest appearances than a whole-hearted commitment to the club.

Of the others, the eldest, John, was actually picked for Wales but was deprived of a cap by an intervening injury; Cecil captained Cardiff and guested for Bath but got no further than a Welsh trial; Edgar played for Leeds Parish Church, Cardiff and the Barbarians; and the youngest, Geoffrey, was a wing for United Services and occasionally for Bath, earning selection for Somerset against Devon in 1907. A naval lieutenant, he was a Chevalier of the Legion d'Honneur and was lost at sea in 1916. Norman Biggs, remembered as 'a delightful companion, full of fun and anecdote,' appeared nine times for Bath in 1896/97, scoring six tries and kicking seven goals, but the following season, apart from some junior rugby with Avonvale, was only seen in a Somerset shirt until he suffered a severe injury playing for Richmond against Harlequins in February 1898. There were persistent rumours in July 1899 that Biggs had been offered the Bath captaincy but he never looked likely to accept and within nine years he was dead, felled by a poisoned arrow in Nigeria.

Now he has gone where referees and their peculiarities trouble not.[11]

Unfortunately, the Bath club experienced rather too many reminders of mortality as the Victorian age drew to a close. While Frank D'Aguilar became the first Bath-born rugby player to graduate to an England cap, albeit from the Royal Engineers, his son James was remembered just as fondly by his team-mates. Having been brought into the side against Clifton as a mere sixteen-year-old in October 1892 he became a Somerset player the following season and was a regular fixture in the Bath side for the next four years. Standing 6ft 2in, he was one of the most effective forwards in the club. So his decision to quit medical studies in February 1897 to pursue a career in the tea plantations of Ceylon was keenly felt at the Recreation Ground.

A 10-0 defeat at Neath on 27 February 1897 was an especially sad occasion for Bath players as they bade farewell to their friend, who was being joined in Ceylon by J. McTier and G.O. Hyatt. For D'Aguilar, however, the long voyage to the sub-continent must have been something of a homecoming, having been born at Simla during his father's military service in India.

Good old D'Aggy' had a hearty send-off, and he thoroughly deserved it. If ever there was an instance of the courage of a lion being blended with the gentleness of a woman it is exemplified in the old Hermitage boy. The tea plantation for which he is making tracks is in Dickoya. MacTier, who was to have accompanied him, has left his bed, but is still exceedingly weak.[12]

A year later it was reported that D'Aguilar was doing well on the Ceylon tea plantation and that 'there is footer on the island and recently in a match at Colombo several old Bath faces were seen'. And on 8 November 1900: 'Those old Bathonians D'Aguilar and McTier, I am pleased to hear, are prospering in Ceylon, and still follow the ball there being some very decent "footer" available, in which they play a prominent part.' (*The Bath Chronicle*). Just eight months later, and only five years after his distinguished father, D'Aguilar was dead at the age of twenty-five, having contracted blood poisoning as a result of a rugby injury.

At the time of D'Aguilar's departure in spring 1897, however, Bath and other clubs were becoming increasingly concerned about a Welsh breakaway after International Board disapproval of Newport's decision to reward their talismanic back Arthur Gould, 18 times captain of his country, with a retirement gift of a £700 'furnished villa'. The board resolved that such a gift was an act of professionalism, whether 'on the part of the givers, or Mr Gould.' The likely consequence of this disagreement was to end matches between Welsh clubs and their English counterparts, who placed great value on these fixtures. The RFU secretary, Rowland Hill, eventually stepped in by deciding, pragmatically or rather conveniently, according to your point of view, that Gould's act of professionalism had been committed under Welsh RFU jurisdiction and had not offended RFU rules. In the 'exceptional circumstances then prevailing', he should be allowed to play against English clubs.

Bath's commitment to stronger Anglo-Welsh relations must have been tested after 8 March 1897 when Llwynypia won 37-5 at the Rec. The day started badly for the home side when, after being allowed time off by Stothert & Pitt to play in the afternoon, F.C. Morgan had a finger crushed by a steam hammer at the works and was unable to take his place at full-back. The South Wales team, who came into the game having won 24 and drawn one of their 25 games, with 455 points for and 36 against, were complete masters, as the *Chronicle* observed:

If all South Wales clubs were the same quality as Llwynypia the threatened discontinuance of games with English teams would not cause many tears in Bath. In fact it would be rather a welcome release, for we do not want our incapacity thrown into such strong relief as it was on Monday when the wily Welshmen were making rings round the Bathonians. But as far as our experience goes it points to the conclusion that the Rhondda Valley invincibles are several streets ahead of other combinations in the Principality against whom Bath has been pitted.[13]

Concerns about certain players' commitment to 'out' games surfaced after a 23-5 defeat at Exeter but that was temporarily forgotten when Bath won 3-0 at the County Ground, Bristol, in front of a crowd of 4,000 on 20 March. With Norman Biggs prominent and Joe Long scoring an unconverted try from a combined run and dribble in the second half, Bath claimed their first victory over their near-neighbours in 14 attempts. After home wins over Clifton (13-10) and Bridgwater (6-0) in the space of 48 hours, there was huge anticipation of the return match with Bristol on Wednesday 31 March, a fixture that had been postponed because of flooding on the Rec. *The Chronicle* described the scene vividly:

Crowds of Bristolians arrived by train, and while the spectators were waiting, the Post Office Band played a selection of lively airs. There was a splendid company present, about 5,000 surrounding the arena. The Abbey carillon was still playing the five o'clock tune when the teams lined up.[14]

F.C. Belson, by now perhaps the most effective forward in the Bath team, dribbled across the line for a try, converted by Norman Biggs, who also added a second-half penalty. A defensive mix-up handed Hussey a try for Bristol, converted by Fenner, whose penalty earned an 8-8 draw. Long thought he had won the match for Bath by touching down when Fenner appeared not to have grounded the ball in goal, but the referee sided with the Bristol player and they held out until 'no-side.'

Apart from a creditable 8-3 defeat against the Barbarians, inconsistent performances and reluctance of players to travel blighted Bath's fortunes for the rest of that season and for some time to come. It may or may not have been coincidence that the 'grand old man' Frank Soane was coming to the end of his career. He remained a shining exception to the apparent lack of dedication shown in some quarters.

In February 1898, the management committee decided that the time had come to recognise his unique contribution to the development of the club over sixteen years, both as a captain, a committeeman and a player of huge energy, versatility, skill and commitment.

The arguments over Arthur 'Monkey' Gould were still reverberating around the British Isles, the man himself having guested for Bristol only a month or so earlier. So, mindful of the sensitivities, the Bath club resolved to initiate a testimonial fund to mark Soane's 'proposed retirement and marriage', provided it received the sanction of Somerset RFU. The broad principle to be adhered to was that it should not be a monetary testimonial and that a subscription should not be given out of club funds. A dinner at 3s 6d a head was fixed for 29 March 1898, to be presided over by the Mayor. There was further correspondence with the county body over the form of gift to be presented to Soane. They recommended 'plate' but when the Club Executive proposed a gift of 'a suite of furniture' for 50 guineas, they did not demur.

Soane was to be married in Bristol but that did not make him any more popular with the rival club's supporters when Bath visited the County Ground on 12 March. But for an injury to F.C. Morgan, who suffered a badly twisted knee early in the game, Bath might have fared better than a 3-0 defeat. F. Derrick acquitted himself well despite the fact that a Milsom Street grocer's dog had inflicted a nasty bite on his thigh the previous week, but the *Chronicle* was more concerned about the disrespectful comments directed at Soane:

The animosity displayed by Bristolians of the lower grade to the genial Bath captain is most reprehensible, and I hope that the testimonial to him on the 29th will be of such a generous and general character as to be in striking contrast to the pitiful demonstration of Bristol roughs after Saturday's match.[15]

Those same individuals no doubt cheered Soane when he returned to Bristol on 9 April to play for a West of England XV against the Barbarians, who included his club-mate George Vincent. The West, with players also drawn from Newport, Clifton, Bristol and Gloucester, won 14-0.

After taking a weak team to Exeter where they lost 6-0, there was no 'lemon sucking' and they played half an hour each way so as to catch the 5.37 p.m. train home, Soane led his side out against Percy Park in the final game of the season. Against a team containing five members of the champion county, Northumberland, he played another fine game, although the only try was scored by the excellent Frederick Belson. Soane was 'chaired off' to the pavilion.

There was one more match – and that was a very private affair at St Werburgh's church in Bristol on 21 April 1898 when he married Miss Marion Ellen Macmillan, with his brother, Victor, as best man and only immediate family to share the moment. Who was to step into Soane's boots as captain of the club after eight years? The responsibility fell to F. Derrick but the mantle appeared to weigh heavily early on as the team struggled to find its rhythm and lack of interest affected gates. A.E. Sheppard, skipper of the 'A's, had similarly mixed results.

Soane, now vice president, remained an inspirational figure, travelling to the Forest of Dean to watch a 6-3 win over Cinderford on 1 October 1898. He brought playing kit – just in case – but one item was already on the field, being worn by George Vincent:

It was no wonder Vincent did so well, for he borrowed the ex-captain's [Soane's] 'everlastings', those unmistakable grey worsteds which have been sported on all the principal Rugger enclosures of the country.[16]

For the following match, an ill-tempered affair at Stroud, Soane was back in the team. Although no longer captain, he indulged in some 'deadly tackling' which brought some choice comments from the combative home hooker, Percy Smith, an old adversary from county matches with Gloucestershire. However, the impression that Bath were not quite the force of old was reinforced by heavy home defeats at the hands of Gloucester (18-0) and Bristol (13-0) in which they did not put up much of a fight.

To engender greater enthusiasm for mid-winter training the committee invested in training lights, nine-penny naphtha flares, and a white ball. Results continued to be

Bath 'A' XV 1898/99. From left to right, back row: A. Stiles, W. Puddy, N. Moore, F. Jordan, J.T. Piper (Honorary Secretary), G. Lang, J. Hobbs, H.S. Goldsworthy, W.T. Davis. Front row: L. Heath, A. Osman, W.E. Davies, S. Duck, A.E. Sheppard (captain), A.E. Fry, A.E. Bruton, A.W. Shorland, W. Emery.

patchy but a New Year's Eve trip to Croydon, which necessitated a 7.42 a.m. departure from Bath Spa station (fare 6s return), provides an illuminating snapshot of the social side of the sport at that time:

The visit to the London suburb was marred by the wretched weather that prevailed. Bath players are a happy-go-lucky lot as a rule, and did not grumble at the tediousness of the railway journey. It was undoubtedly economical to take the team to town by excursion, but it was a tiring ride, and the party grew so hungry before they reached Victoria Station where luncheon was served that the robustness of their appetites is said to have given the waiters a fright, and a forward, 'without any rudeness', can be fairly described as 'beefy' when he can accommodate four plates of roast sirloin, and this feat, I am told, was done in excellent time.

The post match hospitality took in various places of amusement in the gay metropolis, and started home at one in the morning. It was half past four on New Year's Day before they landed in Bath, with two bridegrooms among the number.[17]

Exasperation at the team's failure to live up to standards set in previous seasons was voiced with some feeling by the *Chronicle's* correspondent after a succession of unconvincing performances:

That Bath's present three-quarters will ever develop into a smart, capable, scoring line, is almost as hopeless as a quest for blackberries at Midsummer. Their slovenly fumbling on Saturday was about as weak as anything they have done this season, and considering that the same four men have played together practically all the season, such a show of incompetence when half-time has come and gone is disappointing. If it be possible to train three-quarters the process is a confoundedly tedious one; perhaps if we live till the next century, things may be improving. They did give signs of better things at Clifton a week before, and once on Saturday Parker did as smart a thing as could be wished for, but, these flashes are like the proverbial angels' visits.[18]

By February 1899, there was growing concern over falling attendances, as evidenced by disappointing support for an entertaining 9-3 win over Keble College, Oxford, in which the gate takings did not cover expenses. The season had been affected by wretched weather and, with 'fewer clubs of status' on the fixture list, season ticket sales had also fallen off, with the result that the club had begun the season with £90 in the bank as against £120 the previous year.

As if looking for a scapegoat, the committee began to believe that, unless they could negotiate better terms from the Recreation Ground Company, they might have to return to Kensington Meadows. A particular irritant was the capitation charge of a shilling on each annual subscription, which had led to decline in the sale of fixture cards. After spirits were raised briefly by a 5-3 victory over Wellington, Bath players and supporters were brought down to earth by a 14-0 defeat at home to Bristol on 18 February. There was some consolation in a record gate of £104 but a weary Soane, sporting a blackened eye, made it clear that it would be 'absolutely the last derby game' in which he would figure. In fact, it was his final appearance in a Bath shirt, although he would continue to be a towering presence off the field at club and county level.

Meanwhile, *The Chronicle* reported whimsically:

A Bathonian who felt deeply hurt at the result, and may have sought consolation in the flowing bowl, vows that the playing ground was in mourning on Sunday – what he really saw was a whole host of rooks searching among the oat husks scattered o'er swampy patches for grains of corn.[19]

The final away game involved a trip to Exeter amid waning enthusiasm in a mediocre season, with the inevitable cry-offs. *The Chronicle* correspondent was dismissive of the reasons for absence:

The excuses made for absence one heard on the journey were ludicrously childish. Two stalwart forwards were said to have stated that as the saloon would be attached to the rear of an express, they would suffer from 'train sickness' and be no good! True, the train did sway a little, but such pretexts as these are ridiculous.

The timetable on Saturday was a masterpiece in smart management: Leave Bath 1.33: arrive at Exeter – having changed in the saloon – 3.45; drive to field reached at 4: kick-off 4.5: finish 5.15 and drive to St. David's Station; start for home, 5.30: dress and tea in saloon: reach Bath, 7.40.[20]

The 11-0 defeat was notable for brilliant dashes, intercepting and dribbling by J.T. Timmins and, less obviously at the time, for the appearance at nineteen of Frank Cashnella at forward. This remarkable character was to dominate the club in much the same way as Frank Soane, except that Cashnella was to be a regular member of the first team until 1922, and as late as 1927 made an appearance for the 'A' XV at Swindon at the age of forty-seven!

As the season was wrapped up with a 17-0 victory over Taunton, there were rumours that the rugby playing area was to be moved to the river side of Pulteney Meadows. The *Chronicle* was sceptical:

Should the Club Committee agree to this there will be much murmuring in future. The proposed site may look very fair now, but wait till it wears.[21]

The move, eventually completed for the 1900/01 season, entailed a rebuilding of the grandstand in very much the same location as it is sited now, with its back to the River Avon.

There will be advantage and disadvantage attendant upon the change of front of the grand stand on the Recreation Ground. Now it has its back to the west the spectators seated under shelter will not be inconvenienced by the glare of sun in their eyes, and thus a better view of the game is possible in bright weather and the rain which generally beats from the same direction also will not penetrate. But when there is an east wind a blowing it will be nippy in the stand.[22]

Fortunately, the bitter east wind is still a rarer event than the wet westerlies, but the *Chronicle* correspondent remained unconvinced four years later and continued to voice his misgivings:

Before the football arena in the Recreation Grounds was transferred to the river side of the field a slight overflow of the Avon's banks was not to be dreaded so greatly as it is now when the lowest lying portion of the meadow is included within the barrier. Twice last season the enclosure was a swamp, and the Bridgwater Albion match was only brought off by laying out a temporary pitch on the Pulteney Road side of the ground. It would have been far better for the Company, who lost proportionately with the Club, had the football area not been changed.[23]

-6-

The First of the Lions

WINNING AN ENGLAND cap was the pinnacle of representative rugby at the turn of the century but it was an honour that eluded one of Bath's most admired and accomplished forwards. Yet Frederick Belson must be regarded as the first of an elite band of players – those who have represented the British Isles on tour.

There were no official Four Nations tours until 1910 but teams purporting to represent Great Britain or England & Wales had been visiting the southern hemisphere since 1888. Belson's selection for the 1899 tour to Australia – a planned second leg to New Zealand was cancelled – is something of a mystery because there is barely a mention of it in the club archives, although he is incontrovertibly listed as a Bath player in the records compiled by Lions historians.

If further proof were needed, however, the authors of this book have tracked down his ninety-two-year-old son and have seen the cap and badge that the father was awarded as a member of the 1899 Great Britain touring team to Australia, referred to in those days as the 'Anglo-Australian Touring Team'.

Belson's status as a mere county player was no dishonour. Of the twenty-one players who made the long sea journey, just five of the squad had represented their countries, although full caps were to be awarded the following season to J.W. Jarman, of Bristol, and E.T. Nicholson, of Birkenhead Park. The tourists were captained and managed by the legendary Revd M.M. Mullineux, of Blackheath.

Belson was a true 'Lion' in that he played in the first Test in Sydney on 24 June, a match that the 'colonials' won 13-3, although he took no part in the following three Tests which the tourists won by the margins of 11-0, 13-0 and 11-10. Belson is known also to have played against Central Southern Union (won 11-3), New South Wales (won 4-3), and Toowoomba (won 19-4) but whether his lack of involvement in the other Tests was due to indifferent form or injury is not clear.

Intriguingly, in the *Chronicle's* 'Football Talk' on 24 September 1899, it was reported that 'F.C. Belson has obtained an appointment in Sydney and did not finish the tour with the English football team'. According to his son Dorrien, writing to the authors of this history, Frederick Belson had already forsaken his banking career with the National Provincial.

Blazer badge commemorating the Anglo-Australian rugby football tour of 1899. (Courtesy of the RFU Museum)

I do know that my father was working with the National Provincial Bank in 1899 as he told me he had to approach his manager to explain he had been invited to join the tour to Australia, and could he please have six months off! He was told he could go if he wanted to but shouldn't expect his job to be waiting for him on his return.

It must have been a very difficult decision for him as he cannot have been earning very much and could expect very little from his parents and yet would be obliged to pay all his own expenses. I might add here that my father was an Amateur in its strictest sense. I recall his utter amazement and disgust on learning a few years before he died that some sportsmen were actually playing for money! I presume … that my father probably stayed on in Australia for a short while though he must have come home only to be embroiled in the Boer War.

The trail does indeed appear to have gone cold for seven months, until a visit to Bath from United Services Portsmouth, which was to prove fateful for other reasons.

Frederick Belson as a Clifton player.

Portsmouth, where his father had been a sea captain, was Belson's home town and the Services side included his brother, Barclay. The news from the family was that Frank was many thousands of miles away, having enlisted in the South African War as an Imperial Yeoman in Thorneycroft's Mounted Infantry.

The conflict with the Boer also proved irresistible to the Reverend Mullineux. A veteran of the 1896 tour to South Africa, he was an ebullient, outspoken character who used a post-match speech on tour to accuse opponents of ungentlemanly play:

Some of the Australian players were mean enough to call on an opposing player by name to pass the ball. The ethics of the football field have never been on a par with those of cricket, but such downright 'pointing' as above reduces football form to the level of professional pedestrianism.

F.C. Belson in Boer War uniform.

The Australian Press, never ones to duck a fight, countered with:

We've a favour to implore,
Dear Mulli,
Grant it, and we'll ask no more,
Dear Mulli.
Beat us if you can, on the ball;
Beat us badly, one and all;
But, for Heaven's sake, don't bawl
Like Ranji.[1]

The Reverend returned to South Africa, becoming chaplain to General Kelly-Kenny's 6th Division and also private chaplain to Lord Roberts, based at Rondebusch 'where he became very popular' according to a correspondent from *The Times* writing in 1901.

Mullineux's eventful life ended in suicide, suggesting that the extrovert persona concealed a troubled mind.

Tragedy also attended the aforementioned Bath *v.* United Services fixture on Easter Monday, 16 April 1900. *The Chronicle*'s initial report recorded rather matter-of-factly: 'After Merchant had been disabled by a kick on the head and a visitor had also received a nasty smack, the end came with the game in the centre. It was a point-less draw, of which Bath had a full share of the honours.'

Merchant recovered but George Trerise, the US Portsmouth vice captain, had been fatally injured, suffering a skull fracture and bleeding to the brain. The extent of the injury was not at first obvious because the player 'appeared to recover and played out the game', according to a minute of the shocked Bath committee who noted that it had been a match 'conducted in a fair and manly fashion':

Witnesses had observed that Bath forward Merchant had been injured and stayed out of the scrum in a dazed condition. As it happened, the ball came his way – he tried to catch it and failed. After a loose scrum which followed, Trerise lay on the ground and may have collided with Merchant or other Bath men… Afterwards he walked to the Pavilion and on to the Angel Hotel to change, where he collapsed in the yard, and died at the Royal United Hospital. At the City Coroner's Inquest, it was concluded that a skull fracture had caused a brain haemorrhage. A verdict of 'Accidental Death' was recorded.[2]

The club passed a vote of condolence and promptly cancelled the following day's match with Neath as a mark of respect. Although employed as a sailmaker at Portsmouth naval dockyard, Trerise, as his name suggests, was a Cornishman from Falmouth, so subscriptions were raised to a memorial fund for a marble and granite monument which still stands in the churchyard in his birthplace. The stone records the fact that it was erected by the Portsmouth and Bath clubs.

How much appetite the players had for the remaining game of the season, a rearranged fixture at home to Bristol, is not known but there may be some clues in the fact that they lost 9-0 in front of a poor crowd paying just £30, compared with takings of £100 for the corresponding match the previous season.

The whole season had been played out against the backdrop of war in South Africa, which had broken out on 11 October 1899. At the turn of the year *The Chronicle* reported:

Another Bath footballer has been inspired with martial ardour, Bigwood having offered for the Cape with the Volunteer Engineers, in which corps he is rapidly becoming efficient. Soane's appeal to others to join him as a member of the local Volunteer regiment has not as yet met with much response, but there are many who will probably support him in his 'forward' movement.[3]

Unfortunately, that combative spirit was not much in evidence on the rugby field as the Bath team, invariably below strength for away matches, twice capitulated against Gloucester (21-0 and 20-0) and also against Clifton (19-0), Neath (30-0) and Bristol (35-0). Glorious it was not. For the trip to Bridgwater two days before Christmas, they could find only thirteen players and they were not at all pleased to discover that a suspiciously strong 'A' XV had won 51-3 against Eversley on the Rec. Similarly, only thirteen turned up to be trounced at Neath.

Cashnella and his fellow forwards seemed least at fault, the finger too often being pointed at backs shirking tackles. Skipper Jim Long was not exempt from the general criticism, voiced particularly strongly after a 9-0 home defeat by Exeter on 3 March when the backs gave 'a feeble exhibition' and Leonard Edwards was described as being 'more of a Briton than a Boer – in other words, he is better in dashing attacks than in stubborn defence'. That was a little unfair on those doing it for real, especially the 1,200 men under the command of Colonel Robert Baden-Powell, defending the town of Mafeking from 12 October 1899 through to 17 May 1900. When news reached Bath that the siege had been lifted, the *Chronicle* was able to describe celebrations that mirrored those in every other town in the land:

The local demonstrations in connection with the relief of Mafeking reached their culminating point on Saturday night. The streets were gayer with flags and bunting than earlier in the day. The crowds were larger and more boisterous, but always good humoured. The great feature of the evening was the concert at the Sydney Gardens … Decorated cabs, loaded with vociferous loyalists, passed every now and then. Everywhere was life – full of magnetism. Great joyous shouts rent the air again and again. The cheering, shouting, singing crowds, now augmented by hundreds from the Sydney Gardens, went delirious. The most sober man passing through the seething crowds that night could hardly help catching the contagion.[4]

Norman Biggs, like Belson, had joined up as a Trooper in the Imperial Yeomanry and news reached the *Chronicle* that the former Welsh cap had had a narrow escape – 'not from a Boer bullet, but from an infuriated cock ostrich; and I hear his agility developed on the football field stood him in good service when being chased by the dangerous feathered biped'.

The Biggs connection was reinforced during the 1900/01 season by the reappearance of brother Selwyn. Under the captaincy of George Ruddick, Bath won 10 of the 15 games before the New Year. There was no disgrace in losing 9-0 at Bristol or to Gloucester (11-0) and when Penarth won 12-6 at the Rec, Bath finished with 14 men after E.F. Gooding had been sent off. He maintained he only retaliated after being kicked while on the ground.

Aside from that reverse, there were six victories in December including a 36-0 thrashing of Saracens when Biggs made his bow. With Frank Soane stepping in to referee an 11-0 victory over Portsmouth, Bath completed the Christmas programme having scored 63 points in four days with none conceded.

The New Year ushered in cold reality with an unexpected 4-3 defeat at Stroud and then a 33-0 lesson at Kingsholm against a Gloucester side which had already scored 337 points with just 27 against in their 19 games, losing three. Three days after Old Edwardians had been defeated 11-0 on the Rec, rugby and all other entertainment was curtailed by the death of an elderly woman on the Isle of Wight.

Following Queen Victoria's demise on 22 January 1901, after 64 years on the throne, all rugby fixtures were cancelled. Ever practical, Bath's management committee agreed to compensate Taunton for rail fares incurred on 1 December in consideration of Bath's inability to fulfil the 26 January fixture. The old Empress's death seems to have rekindled among some the desire to 'do one's duty' in South Africa, as the *Chronicle* reported:

Several Bath footballers have been seized with a desire for martial glory, and Cliff Lewis is said to have passed all tests for the Imperial Yeomanry. Cashnella got on satisfactorily until it came to managing the gee-gee. H Wyatt who did duty at full-back for the 'A' has gone to Aldershot. Norman Biggs, I hear, is returning to the front with a commission.[5]

The High Command perhaps could have done with a few more like Fred 'Chumpy' Russell, one of the great characters in the history of the Bath club. He had already

Bath 'A' 1900/01. From left to right, back row: T. Davis (touch judge), H.R. Hutton, H.E. Lever, N. Moore, Mr A. Pearce, S.W. Crisp, G.E.G. Phillips, F. Jordan, A.E. Wetten. Middle row: A. Clarke, P. Heath, L.W. Edwards, A.J. Taylor (captain), H. Turtle, C. Spillane, A.J. Rowe. Front row: O.J.R. Edwards (vice captain), F. Russell.

Bath 1901. From left to right, back row: J.T. Piper (Honorary Secretary), F. Cashnella, W. Watts, A. Billett, N. Moore, J. Ruddick, A.J. Taylor, E.W. Clarke, W. Dainton, O. Edwards (touch judge). Middle row: A. Richards, C. Williams, J.T. Timmins (vice captain), G. Ruddick (captain), L.I. Edwards, W.J. Bond, M.S. Bigwood. Front row: L. Edwards, F. Russell.

played a handful of games when drafted in as a late replacement for Selwyn Biggs against Bristol on 16 February – and only because he had brought his kit for the group photograph. But he was the pick of the backs, despite a 6-0 defeat.

Russell graduated through the Parkfield and St George's clubs and took up athletics and boxing to keep in condition for rugby. With his powerful running and stunning hand-off, he was a half-back who demanded, and got, respect. He never lost a boxing match and did not like losing at rugby. That intense competitiveness – and a tendency to rough up opponents – appears to have inhibited his county prospects but he revelled in the 'boos' from a derby crowd. It was said that he once scored five tries and had his jersey torn off his back on each occasion. By all accounts, he was just as competitive as a grower of prize vegetables and as a breeder of both greyhounds and caged birds!

When 'Chumpy' began to lose his pace, he moved into the pack, finally winning a Somerset cap as late as 1920/21. After a spell with Walcot, he retired extremely reluctantly at the age of forty-three. He then refereed for another twenty years, including in the County Championship, and once officiated in a downpour sporting a large umbrella. He also became chairman of the Bath Old Players Association and at the time of his death at the age of eighty-three in 1964, he was a club Patron, outspoken to the last, particularly on the subject of declining standards and players who did not take training or the game seriously. Sadly, he did not live to celebrate the club's centenary. He certainly deserved to.

With Russell in pugnacious mood at the base of the scrum, Cashnella establishing a fine reputation up front and James Timmins an inspirational figure in the back line, Bath began to reassert themselves as a club in 1901. There were defeats but no longer the humiliations of the previous season and the final tally of 17 wins and 15 defeats from 33 matches, with one match drawn, would have been improved but for a bizarre match at Taunton on 20 April.

The scoreline in the archives reads 4-0 to the home team but the result was hotly disputed by Bath who referred the matter to the Somerset RFU and even to the President of the RFU, Hugh Fox. *The Bath Chronicle* correspondent felt so strongly about it that he listed in his weekly *Football Talk* as 'abandoned' a match that involved a disallowed try, three sendings-off and, most controversially, the award of a dropped goal 'that never was'. All but the referee, Mr A.W. Hill, of Bridgwater, seemed agreed on the facts of that 'peculiar incident'. Apparently, Taunton's Darling raced away with the ball and opted to kick over the full-back's head rather than trying to run around him. His punt sailed over the bar and, to everyone's astonishment, Mr Hill awarded a dropped goal, then worth four points.

The sequence of events is not clear from the club records but there was little doubt that the game degenerated into a farce, with Ruddick actually taking his team off the field at one point. S.W. Crisp, of Bath, was dismissed for an unspecified offence although his disciplinary sentence of a week's suspension was subsequently regarded as tantamount to acquittal. The others to be sent from the field were his team-mate, A. Richards, and Paul, of the home team.

As to the fight between Richards and Paul there could be no mistake. The men gave each other some punishing blows before they could be separated, the claret was beginning to flow, and as Richard's jersey had been torn off his back, the affair looked worse than it otherwise might have done. As to who was the aggressor accounts differ, but it is certain that when Richards had gone off the enclosure and was leaving the pavilion Paul attacked him, and there was thus a repetition of the encounter.[6]

Richards claimed that his opponent had been the aggressor but received a three-month ban while Paul, having previously come before the Somerset committee for a similar offence was 'forbidden to play football again under the auspices of the Rugby Football Union'. Still the row over the result rumbled on, with the county feeling unable to deal with Bath's protest and the RFU president writing to say that the governing body could not annul the decision unless the referee admitted he had been in error. 'As Mr. Hill will not do that the matter will have to rest where it is.'

Frank Cashnella played in all but one of Bath's 33 fixtures that season, one more than the skipper, George Ruddick, who was also top try scorer with 10. James Timmins was the most consistent of the backs, with 7 tries from 27 appearances, and was chosen as vice captain under Ruddick for 1901/02.

Unfortunately, pre-season optimism was not matched by results and Bath won only 8 of their 30 matches, losing 17 and drawing 5. An unexpected defeat at Lydney in early November prompted serious discussion on the homeward journey about the need to get down to serious training, 'resolves as to sprint, bathing and rub-downs'.

At a fully attended committee meeting on the Monday night, Mr Joe Webb was appointed as the club's trainer, introduced as 'the well known long distance runner, who has had much experience of getting men fit for athletic contests'. It was decided that 'players selected for the matches and reserves were to train under his superintendence on two evenings in the week – Tuesdays and Thursdays – until their condition warrants a reduction to one evening weekly'.

It was rather late in the season to decide that players had to be fit to play the game, but no time was wasted in completing the arrangements The clubroom of the Mason's Arms in Ferry Lane, just fifty yards from the Recreation Ground, had been chosen as 'a most convenient rendezvous. The first training is fixed for to-night.'

However, injuries and illness severely depleted playing resources during the season and there were heavy losses against Gloucester and at Neath, where Timmins suffered a wrenched knee and Bath had to borrow a player, G. Watts having missed the train. *The Chronicle's* 'Football Talk' pointed out the difficulties of fielding a full-strength XV in West Wales in an era when the working week included Saturday mornings and, for some, the afternoons.

Neath is a far cry, and when Bath has to travel thither in the darkest days of winter it is not the easiest matter to raise a full team, and it speaks well for the keenness of Bath footballers that many of them who had to make pecuniary sacrifices, cheerfully got off to take part in this engagement, while several employers have to be thanked for their kindness in facilitating matters.[7]

Cashnella missed the 32-0 defeat at Bristol on 1 February 1902, having been injured on a snowbound pitch at Clifton the previous weekend, and the club was forced to field a scratch side at Bridgwater, going down 19-3. This time there was less sympathy from the Press:

What happened on Friday and Saturday morning was a painful reminder of what constantly occurred a few seasons ago when there was a desperate effort just before the time to start for an away fixture, to whip up a fifteen.[8]

On 1 March, the fixture at Penarth was scratched because of illness and injuries within the Bath club and the following week they suffered a humiliating home defeat at the hands of a junior Bristol club, Knowle. Further away defeats followed, at Bridgwater and Cheltenham, before the visit of Bristol on 29 March when their rivals ran in seven tries, prompting *The Chronicle* to note that 'our neighbours' enthusiastic supporters include business men of influence, who are always willing to help on the interest of the team in a hundred and one ways which make for success'. Fortunately, morale was restored with a scoreless draw on Bridgend's first visit to the Rec and, more remarkably, a 3-3 draw with the formidable Neath club, who had recently routed Bristol.

Another notable event during the 1901/02 season was the inauguration of the Bath & District Rugby Combination, whose founder members were Walcot, Combe Down, Oldfield Park and Batheaston, soon to be joined by Fairfield Rovers. After a match between Bath and Oldfield Park on 5 April, which raised £16 for district funds, rules were drawn up which were approved by the junior clubs in time for the start of the following season.

The Combination was initially dominated by Oldfield Park, with three league championships in the first four years, Walcot winning in the third year. Clubs joined and dropped out; many struggled financially and the Bath cub, far from prosperous itself, helped out with occasional cash contributions. By 1909 organised Combination competition ground to a standstill and the administration remained dormant until the concept was successfully revived in the 1920s.

Despite the very odd hiccup, and minor 'family' squabbles, countless youngsters were called to senior rugby, and many promising players recommended by the clubs themselves. However, the Bath club's selection of players from the junior ranks did sometimes lead to objections and occasional accusations of poaching. As early as 3 October 1903, a special executive committee meeting was convened to discuss the refusal of the Oldfield Park captain, F. Smith, to play for Bath when selected, as required by Combination rules.

Cashnella's injury on the frosted pitch at Clifton in January 1902 had been serious enough to require an operation and several weeks' recuperation in hospital, which had ruled him out for the rest of the season. Chosen as captain for 1902/03, he was understandably keen to get pre-season training under way and no doubt encouraged to welcome some new faces, including the Oxford University fullback from 1889, W. Grischotti, and a Welshman, J. Biddulph, who had been introduced to the club by fellow three-quarter G.S. Parkinson during their military service together in South Africa.

Despite the inspiring leadership of Cashnella, who finished as top try scorer with 12 from 29 appearances, it was another mediocre campaign, with 16 matches won, 16 lost and 2 drawn. Grischotti's duties as an officer in the South East of Scotland Militia Artillery delayed his debut until the December visit to Bristol, although he dropped a magnificent goal in a 14-6 defeat. Then a fall from a bolting horse left him too 'knocked about' to take the field for a 3-0 win at home to Bridgwater. The pitch had to be re-marked away from flooded areas of the Rec on a day when Wales hosted England at Swansea and the bandsmen providing the pre-match entertainment had to give up because their instruments kept filling up with water!

The annual trip to Exeter proved as testing as ever, the team arriving at St Thomas's Field at 3.50 p.m. for a 3 p.m. kick-off and eventually losing 3-0.

They came uncommonly near victory as it was. It is always playing a team at a disadvantage to rush down the fastest stretch of the Great Western line in a saloon swinging and rocking at the tail of the Cornishman, like a small boat on a rough sea, to change en route, jump into an omnibus, and be whisked on to the ground before they have recovered from the railway oscillation … the Devon officials were not in the most amiable mood, and although they said little perhaps, like the monkey, they thought more.[9]

After an ill-tempered 14-0 defeat at Cheltenham in which home supporters had to be reprimanded for foul language by the referee the conflict spilled over into a neighbouring hostelry where H.R. Tutton was pushed to the ground 'but a sturdy Bath forward had satisfaction for this, as he forthwith toppled over four or five of the rowdies with his fists'.

The Bath team that played Bristol on 21 March 1903. From left to right, back row: C.H. Hacker (touch judge), J.T. Piper (Honorary Secretary), H.R. Tutton, F. Marshman, J.T. Timmins, J.S. Andrews, A. Baverstock, G. Parfitt, G.A. Roberts (Honorary Treasurer). Middle row: P.J. Cooling, W.F. Long, R. Meister, F.J. Cashnella (captain), S.W. Crisp, G. Parsons, J. Godwin. Front row: H.W. West, F. Russell.

A 6-5 defeat at home to Bristol a week later engendered emotions of pride and frustration in equal measure:

There was but one exclamation on the lips of every Bathonian at the conclusion of the game. 'What hard lines!' And this scarcely implies what was in the minds of all. It was the cruellest of cruel luck that the home team had to leave the field a solitary point to the bad. Every man was at his best and the game excelled any predecessor in the intense excitement which it evoked ... It was a grand game and a grand gate for, without the stand, over £60 was taken. The Bath treasurer is smiling.[10]

Raising a team for the trip to Neath the following weekend (28 March) was no easy task. Substitutes were 'picked up on the platform' and local player T. Davis guested for Bath in a Llanelly jersey as the home team completed a 17-3 victory. *The Chronicle*, while acknowledging that they were 'superior in all departments', wondered 'if it is ever dry at Neath?'

They cannot be troubled with water problems over there. Every time the Bathonians visit the place, the Welsh hills that tower behind the town are enveloped in watery clouds, and the ground is running with sticky grimy mire.[11]

Easter 1903 was memorable for a mixture of sunshine and snow showers and only £21 was taken at the gate for the Tuesday afternoon meeting with Pontypridd, which Bath won 9-0.

Matters sartorial dominated discussion at the summer management committee meetings, with resolutions passed both to increase the width of the hoops on the jerseys from four to six inches and to have black sleeves. The final touch was to incorporate the letters 'B.F.C.' within the black band on the chest. Of greater priority to the players was a decision to guarantee hot water on training nights, at a cost of £1.

None of these innovations seemed to have an impact on the field during 1903/04 as Bath won only nine matches under the captaincy of T.B. Timmins, with 19 lost and 3 drawn. The season began with nine defeats in the first 11 games and finished almost as dismally although it did have its lighter moments, as in the opening match against the Rest of Bath, which served as the Club trial. When the combined side's full-back, H. Vanstone, sliced the ball into the river behind the stand, Sam Crisp, the Bath wing, laid on an 'aquatic exhibition which greatly delighted the crowd'.

Crisp, amid the applause of the onlookers, who crowded to the bank, jumped in the Avon after the ball, which he successfully recovered. He was too wet for football now, and Cashnella left the pack to deputise as three-quarter... Crisp, as we all know, has been in strict condition as a swimmer, so fond of the water is he that he may almost be classified as amphibious.[12]

Having been Somerset 100 yards swimming champion in 1901, Samuel William Crisp won the Western Counties freestyle title in 1903 and 1905 as an outstanding member of Bath Dolphins Swimming Club. He also won numerous prizes at running, hurdling and jumping.

Things did not go so swimmingly on the rugby field, although Crisp made more appearances than any other three-quarter, 19, and scored four tries. Cashnella again finished top try scorer with six but there were too many occasions when below-strength sides were sent to 'out' matches. Only ten players turned up at the GWR station in frosty weather for the 12.04 to Exeter on 2 January 1904 and the match had to be cancelled. The Devon club sent a 'moderately worded telegram' asking Bath what they intended to do about the lost gate money, estimated at around £80, but the fixture was rearranged for 30 March when Bath lost 9-5.

Among the few highlights was an 8-7 victory at home to Lydney. According to the *Chronicle* reporter, the cheer that greeted Grischotti's winning conversion 'was so resonant that a friend who lives on the hills a long distance from the ground told me he was quite sure Bath had won before he heard the score. It caused quite a flutter among the Abbey jackdaws and the Guildhall pigeons.'

Not so well appreciated was their reaction to the referee's handling of the home defeat by Bridgwater the following Saturday, 14 November 1903. The official, Mr Satterley, reported Bath to the Somerset RFU, complaining that: 'Never in his refereeing experience had such offensive language been used towards him.' His statement was corroborated by the Bridgwater touch judge and an official warning on behaviour was posted on the Rec.

Although fixtures in Wales were valued highly as a measure of the club's seniority, they appear to have been endured rather than enjoyed, as the *Chronicle* correspondent outlined all too graphically under his by-line 'Play Up Bath' following a 5-0 defeat at Penarth on 12 December. The referee blew 'no-side' fifteen minutes into the second half:

It had just commenced to rain when we left Bath, but in Wales, from the look of things, it seemed to have been raining incessantly for weeks, it was still drenching down, and a keen East wind pierced every marrow of your bone. The changing loft is half a mile from the station, and the ground three-quarters of a mile further on; by the time the players got to the field they were wet through and shivering with cold. Then they had to wait for some belated members of the home team. But the ground! It was unfit for football, indeed, football was impossible and none was seen…

…To add to the misery of the situation there was a lack of hot water and towels when the benumbed and drenched Bathonians reached the changing quarters again. So utterly sick of it all were the players that they vowed they would never visit Penarth again, at least, not on a football bent.[13]

Bath 'A' team, 1903/04. From left to right, back row: J.T. Piper (Honorary Secretary), E. Hodges, F. Marchman, H.W. West, W. Gunning, H. Clow, H.W. Vanstone, C. Clements, W.T. Davis (touch judge). Seated: D.J. Francis, H. Baker, S.S. Bristow (vice captain), J. Hobbs (captain), R. Meister, V. Biss, C. Weston. Front row: H. Meddick, A.E. Cleall.

With just £37 17s 6d being taken at the gate for the game against Bristol on 20 February, compared with £60 18s for the corresponding game the previous season, it was a depressing time on and off the field. In presenting the accounts at the annual meeting at The Foresters' Hall on 28 June, Mr G.A. Roberts said he could remember only four fine days during the season. A Mr Mullins queried 'training expenses' of £12 5s 6d because he did not think that 'training nights were doing any good as the players seemed stiff when it came to Saturday'. Mr Messer retorted that this was because they did not train enough and then made the radical suggestion that the several working men in the team should be paid 2s for tea rather than have it provided. George Roberts, pointing out that this was contrary to RFU laws on amateurism, said that in any case he was not in favour of a separate payment.

He believed it was very enjoyable to have the men together after a match. The system suggested would lead to disruption and not encourage that social feeling which they all liked to see existing in the team. In that respect he considered it would be a mistake. [Applause] [14]

Ironically, after such a poor season, another Bath player was to emulate Belson's example by representing Great Britain on one of the periodic tours to the southern hemisphere. Lieutenant R.J. Rogers, a front row forward who played nine games for the club during 1903/04 scoring one try and also being capped by Somerset, was invited to join D.R. 'Darkie' Bedell-Sivright's party to Australia and New Zealand that summer.

Rogers played in at least one of the Tests on the Australian leg, all won by the tourists, before they set sail across the Tasman Sea. The All Blacks had made their international bow a year earlier with a 22-3 victory against Australia.

Sivright, of Cambridge University, who was to be killed in the Gallipoli landings in April 1915, was injured in the opening match of the New Zealand leg and the honour of leading the first Great Britain side to face the All Blacks therefore fell to a Welshman, left wing Teddy Morgan. Rogers packed down on the right-hand side of the front row alongside the Guy's Hospital hooker, D.H. Traill, and D.D. Dobson, of Newton Abbot. Denys Dobson, a former Oxford Blue who had scored a try on his England debut against Wales the previous year, was sent off in one of the later matches in New Zealand for using obscene language. Bizarrely, he was killed by a rhinoceros in July 1916 while working for the Colonial Service in Nyasaland.

For their first meeting with New Zealand, played out in front of 20,000 people at Athletic Park, Wellington, on 13 August 1904, a fine Saturday afternoon, Great Britain wore red, white and blue hoops with black shorts. After a successful kick by Billy Wallace, Welsh forward Arthur Harding kicked an equalising goal on half-time before the All Blacks pulled clear in the second half to win 9-3 with a brace of tries from the Wellington right wing, Duncan McGregor. Rogers also featured in a scoreless draw with Taranaki in New Plymouth the following Wednesday, and did well enough to be selected for the meeting with Auckland three days later. Sadly his contribution to a match won 13-0 by the home team was limited by injury, as the *New Zealand Herald* reported:

Great Britain touring team 1904. Bath's R.J. Rogers is fifth from left in the back row. (Courtesy of the RFU Museum)

Tight work followed about midfield, and in the melee Rogers had his leg injured to the extent that he had to leave the field, hobbling away in a manner that gave the impression that there was little likelihood of his returning. Only 13 minutes had gone, and the crowd generously urged the local skipper to give Britain another man, but evidently the understanding that no substitutes should be allowed had been arrived at beforehand, and Rogers was not replaced. Some few minutes later the plucky Somerset forward again joined his comrades his leg in bandages, but was not able to render much assistance.[15]

It was the last time for eighty-five years that a Bath player was to represent Great Britain or the British Isles.

-7-

Gone North

OLDFIELD PARK CAPTAIN Tom White was one of the most talented players on the local Bath rugby scene in the early years of the century, blessed with quick feet, a long and accurate pass and a prolific boot.

When he first made an appearance in the blue and black of Bath, guesting at scrum-half in a 20-0 victory over Knowle on a frosty February afternoon in 1902, he attracted attention by converting all four tries. That achievement earned him another game the following week at home to Weston-super-Mare when he landed another 'fine kick' to convert the only try.

The young bricklayer was back on the Recreation Ground a month later, leading Oldfield Park to an 8-0 win over the Rest of Bath, and turned out at fly-half for Bath on 1 April in a battling 3-3 draw with the mighty Neath. When he led his own Park side out against Bath a few days later, they were by no means disgraced, losing 8-0, and finished the season having won 18 of their 24 matches, scoring 248 points with just 52 against.

White also featured in Bath's final game of the season, a 3-3 draw at home to Bridgwater in which he helped set up a try for W.G. Marsh. It was no surprise therefore that he was summoned to a Somerset trial the following September.

Bath, no doubt having redoubled efforts to recruit him to their ranks, must have been frustrated to learn that he had joined neighbours Bristol. That association lasted only until November 1903 when the *Chronicle* carried the following report:

It was reported that Tom White had left the Bristol Club. Along with many other Bath artisans – he had been out of work for a long spell. The ex-Oldfield Captain had evidentially obtained employment in Bath and might be returning to his old club.[1]

White made one appearance at the end of the season, at Exeter, but he was very much first choice at the start of the 1904/05 campaign and had enthusiastically accepted the offer of the vice-captaincy under T.B. Timmins. A popular performer, he had an outstanding game at outside half in the opening game, getting the back line moving to devastating effect in a 25-3 win against Cardiff Romilly.

With White continuing to be an inspiring playmaker and a reliable goalkicker, Bath rattled off 8 wins from their opening 10 games and the *Chronicle*'s report of a 23-10 win at home to Weston-super-Mare left no doubt about the extent of his influence:

Bath's genius, Tom White, was the keystone of success. The baffled visitors tried to mark him, stifle him, and otherwise render him ineffective, but he baffled all these laudable endeavours, and was a veritable thorn in the flesh. He had a hand in so many of the tries that the spectators were delighted to see him get three points of his own.[2]

Next up was the first derby match, played on compacted snow at a fogbound Bristol ground on 26 November. The home pack held the whip hand and ensured a 12-3 victory although the *Chronicle* declared: 'No praise would be too lavish for the game Tom White played. Frank Soane described it as "brilliant" and likened White to Parham at his best.'

Praise indeed from 'the grand old man' who had served for many years as County Secretary and was Somerset RFU President in 1902/03. He must have been just as pleased with White's match-winning performance for the county against Gloucestershire the following week – but the fly-half's ability was now attracting attention from further afield, as the *Chronicle* noted:

After the encounter in which he had been so prominent a figure, some smooth-spoken strangers waylaid the Bath vice captain, and soon made it known that they were empowered by the Oldham Club to make him a tempting offer if he would throw in his lot with that team. As is always the case with these sneaking poachers, they drew a most alluring picture of the monetary advantages that would accrue if the player were willing to relinquish his freedom and independence as a sportsman, and sell himself to them.

They offered White £50 in cash, constant employment at 28s a week, £2 10s a week in addition for his football services, with a bonus of half-a-sovereign for every win. They invited Tom to dine with them at a favourite restaurant in Bristol to talk over the subject, where the principal agent pressed the Somerset half to 'Fly with me now.' But they did not find the Bathonian so willing to yield to their solicitations. To his credit, White refused to be captivated by their bribes and wiles, and at the end of a long parley these emissaries were no nearer securing his entrance into the Northern Union fold than when they accosted him.[3]

While White was masterminding the win over Gloucestershire, his club-mates might have earned a draw at Gloucester but went down 8-5. White was back for a 5-3 win over Neath a week later – their first over the 'Welsh All Blacks' – and for a 3-3 draw against Bristol on 17 December. White was unable to convert Cashnella's try on the final whistle but it was the first time for seven years that Bath had avoided defeat against their neighbours.

Bath continued to win more matches than they lost and on 28 January 1905 topped 300 points for the season with a 40-0 victory over Bristol North, which also marked White's return after a month out injured.

Despite White's rejection of the Oldham overtures the previous autumn, rumours had persisted about a renewed offer. It must still have come as a shock to supporters when the *Chronicle* revealed on Friday 24 February that Tom White had 'Gone North'.

This afternoon Tom White, the Bath and Somerset footballer, about whose intentions various rumours have been in circulation, left Bath to join the Oldham Northern Union Club, who approached him last December, and whose attentions have been renewed... White, who is a Twerton man, was a bricklayer in the employment of Mr Loxley, builder. He stated that he was receiving £110 down from the Oldham Club, £2 10s a week, with bonuses for every training and every win. White left by the 1.20 Midland train, and was seen off by some Bath football friends. T West will play half in his place against Taunton tomorrow.[4]

His team-mates had known something was up when White appeared at the pavilion on the Recreation Ground the previous night only to pick up his kitbag. It was common knowledge that the player had been in dispute with county officials following a midweek match with Devon at Plymouth on 8 February. *The Chronicle* laid out in its 'Football Notes' what it claimed were the true facts relating to 'The Breach with Somerset':

As various reports more or less inaccurate have been circulated as to why White did not appear against Yorkshire at Weston last Saturday, it maybe well to recite the correct version. The game at Plymouth against Devon on February 8th necessitated White losing a day and a half's work. Every expense of the journey was met by county officials, but White asked for two day's pay. On being told that he could not be paid it as it was against the rules of the E.R.U., White said he should not play for Somerset again unless he received it. The Somerset Committee duly picked White against Yorkshire, and he sent back his post-card to the secretary just as he received it. No effort was made to induce White to change his mind, and he did not play. And it cannot be said his absence was much felt, for the Somerset backs could not have played better. After White's action the Somerset Committee did not again chose him for the Cornish engagement. Altogether White appeared in six Somerset matches, two last season and four this.[5]

The very Press who had been hailing him as 'a genius' now suggested that his form had fallen off, that 'probably Oldham will conclude that they have been too generous' and that 'probably Tom will have a touch of home sickness when it is too late'. Bath had no option to soldier on without their fly-half, eventually registering a record-equalling 21 victories and amassing an unprecedented 401 points. The skipper, Timmins, appeared in every one of the 39 fixtures.

At the start of the following season, the *Chronicle*, noting the importance of having a recognised 'convertor', acknowledged that 'Tom White was a rare man in this respect' and that the Bath club had had 'remarkably few conversions since he went to the North. I trust the captain will give an eye to this, and see that one or two of the likely kickers indulge in the required practice.'

It was a remarkably prescient observation. Bath did not manage a successful kick at goal until J. Prosser landed a straightforward conversion of Tom West's try against Mountain Ash on Boxing Day! Throughout the whole of 1905/06 there were only eight conversions and no penalty goals, dropped goals or goals from marks. The season's record was dismal – 7 games won, 2 drawn and 24 lost. From early November through to March, the team managed just one victory in 15 matches, a 3-0 win at Clifton which remained their only success away from the Rec.

Looking for solace in the midst of their misfortune, rugby people in Bath had begun to take a greater interest in schoolboy rugby, desperately hoping to spot another Parham or White. They were not to be disappointed.

Bath had been among the clubs represented when the English Schools Rugby Football Union was formed in Leicester on 26 March 1904 and had played a match with Bristol in aid of the new body on 6 April 1905, eventually contributing £11 10s 1d. The first annual meeting of the Bath Rugby Schools Union was held on 2 August, presided over by Mr R.R. Stephenson, Headmaster of East Twerton School. He announced that the founder members, Oldfield Council, East Twerton, Widcombe and St Paul's, would be joined by Weymouth House, Bathforum, St Stephen's, and Batheaston & District.

On 18 November, Bath Elementary Schools met their Bristol counterparts at Lambridge where 'without doubt the hero of the match was little Vowles. It did one good to see the sturdy little chap tackling the-to him-giants of the other backs. His try was a beauty too.' Harry Vowles was to be an outstanding scrum-half in the inter-war years.

Vowles was unlucky to miss out on an England Schools cap later in the season after excelling in the trial at Gloucester on 10 March 1906, at which he was joined by two other Bath boys, Parsons and Hingston, both forwards. All three had splendid games according to a *Chronicle* report the following week but it was Parsons who had the honour of becoming Bath's first schoolboy international, lining up against Wales on 7 April. Vowles – 'this diminutive boy … in the thick of every rush' – was nominated as reserve but was capped the following season, impressing against the Welsh at Leicester.

After such a disappointing season in 1905/06, the Bath committee had to do something to restore the club's reputation. What could they do? The answer seems to have been to ditch the traditional blue and black strip for white jerseys, adorned with the City Arms. The new jerseys were to cost 54s a dozen and three dozen were ordered along with the same number of badges at 36s a dozen. Boots were to be ordered from Messrs Cash & Co at no more than 8s 11d a pair.

Season ticket prices were held at 6s and Richard 'Dick' Meister took over as captain, managing to get the players training two nights a week from mid-August. With a sensible eye on the future, the management committee at its meeting on 24 September decided to set up a Junior Section for boys aged fourteen to seventeen, with an annual subscription of 2s 6d. The club accepted an offer from St John Ambulance to send two men to attend at home matches.

The hazards of playing the game were underlined in November when a Widcombe player was paralysed in a match against Combe Down. All the local clubs rallied round:

I am asked to say that a definite endeavour to raise funds for the poor fellow Hawkins, who is a cripple, probably for life, as a result of the accident on October 27, is being undertaken by Mr. A J Stride, of the Widcombe Club. Every club will be asked to help, and subscription lists will be out shortly. The accident is undoubtedly the worst that has occurred at the game for many years in Bath. [6]

Frank Cashnella renewed the appeal for assistance for Hawkins as late as 1920, prompting Bath to organise a fund-raising match.

Meanwhile, Meister turned out on the wing for Somerset in their match against the touring Springboks at Taunton on 20 October and also scored the only try when Bath achieved a rare 5-3 victory over Neath a fortnight later. A heavy defeat at Penarth was followed by narrow reverses against Pontypool, Bristol and in the return match at home to Penarth.

This was also the first season of the Somerset county knock-out cup and Bath negotiated the first round with a 19-0 victory over Wellington before coming away from Bridgwater with a 5-3 win to secure their place in the final. The opposition were Bridgwater Albion and, much to Bath's displeasure, Taunton was chosen as the neutral venue which meant that, even with a special excursion fare of 3s, the 386 Bath supporters were outnumbered nearly four to one by the 'bricktowners'.

On the field, things began badly for Bath when Alby Hatherill was sent off in circumstances so mysterious that he was allowed back on the field for extra time after the sides completed 80 minutes without scoring. As darkness fell, Pippin scrambled over for the winning try in the first period of ten minutes, also adding the conversion as Bath complained in vain to the touch judge, Mr Donne, president of the Somerset RFU. It was eventually acknowledged that the referee had acted in error in sending off Hatherill and no penalty was applied but Bath's letter of protest over the handling of the match was brushed aside by both the county and the RFU. Their only recourse was to refuse to play Bridgwater Albion the following season 'on grounds of ill feeling and danger of trouble'. The first Somerset cup competition had ended on an acrimonious note.

Weakened by the late defection of Tom West to Gloucester after the right wing had been named in the Bath line-up, they lost 14-0 at home to Bristol on a sweltering afternoon on 30 March 1907. The first win at Taunton for some years (8-0), followed by a scoreless draw with Cheltenham, left Bath with 12 victories and 14 defeats from 28 games, with two matches drawn. In an odd postscript to the season, Bath officials were summoned to a Commission of the RFU in Bristol on 3 May to have their books inspected and to answer charges of 'infringing the professional rules of the Union.' Management Committee minutes of 6 May record only the fact that the books had been inspected, suggesting that the charges were not pursued.

Tom West's exile at Gloucester was short-lived and easily forgiven by those who chose him as captain for 1907/08. He must have been having second thoughts though after overseeing seven successive losses from the start of the season. They included a 49-8 defeat against London Harlequins on Wandsworth Common, the first meeting between the clubs.

Harlequins experimented with seven forwards and two stand-off halves, the brothers Adrian Dura and Frederick MacFarlane Stoop operating in tandem with deadly effect. Bath actually led early on with an opportunist try by West but the home team eventually totalled eight goals and three tries, although West added another for Bath near the end.

Both Stoop brothers were wounded in Mesopotamia during the First World War, Adrian also being awarded the Military Cross. Immortalised in the Stoop Memorial Ground at Twickenham, he was Harlequins' guiding light for many years, acting as secretary from 1920 to 1938, the year he made his last appearance for the club aged fifty-five, and as president from 1920 to 1949. A barrister, he was also an England selector and president of the RFU.

Bath's losing run finally ended on 1 November when the Recreation Ground played host to Racing Club de France, the match ending 6-6. Cashnella crashed over in the corner with two Frenchmen on his back and C. Brown kicked a goal from a mark while the visitors, dismissed as 'heavy, fast and dashing but clumsy when handling', scrambled a late try. The game also marked the first team debut of an Oxford scholar, Alfred Kitching, on the left wing.

Kitching, educated at Keble College, was to become Senior Master at Monkton Combe School on the south side of Bath from 1936 to 1947, gaining a reputation as a talented and well-liked teacher who combined academic excellence with an unflagging interest in school sporting activities. But first, as a rugby player, he was to prove an important figure in a Bath revival in the years leading up to the First World War.

There was little sign of that revival when he first came into the side. The first win, against Wellington (10-3), did not come until 16 November and although Bath managed a scoreless draw against Bristol, it was only because their neighbours had to fulfil a fixture with Cardiff on the same day. For the visit of Clifton on 7 December, Bath officials found the pitch partly covered at one end by the River Avon so they shortened the playing area into four '21's rather than four '25's and the crowd were treated to a spectacular touchdown by Kitching, 'sending the spray everywhere', as they splashed to a 21-0 victory.

After further encouragement with wins over Taunton, Old Edwardians and Stroud there were then six defeats on the trot going into the New Year. The Penarth fixture, always an unwelcome trek, began badly with just twelve players gathered at Bath Spa, although they joined up with C. Wyer at Cardiff. Unfortunately, the team then boarded the wrong connection at Cardiff, found themselves at Barry and by the time the thirteen players alighted at Penarth, the kick-off had to be delayed until 4.15. Losing 3-0 was no disgrace in the circumstances.

Disgrace, even dishonour, tainted the following Saturday's Somerset Cup tie at home to Weston-super-Mare, however. On a wet and windy day, Bath never really came to terms with the visitors' big, bustling forwards and, although Meister dodged through for a try in the left corner, his side lost 6-3. Three players were sent off – W. Watts, of Bath, and Perkins and Fear, from Weston – but the worst aspect of the tie was the reaction of certain Bath supporters who mobbed the referee, Mr H. Smith, of Bridgwater, when he refused to award a dropped goal to J.C. Robinson. Not surprisingly, Somerset RFU took a very dim view of this behaviour and ordered use of the Recreation Ground to be suspended for a fortnight.

When they returned to their own patch, Bath edged a 9-8 victory over London Harlequins and collected three more wins before the end of the season, finishing with 10 victories from 32 games played, with 20 lost and 3 drawn. Still they could not beat Bristol, however, losing 13-3 after their finishing let them down.

Not accredited as an official fixture, but great fun nonetheless, was a Bath *v.* Old Crocks match on 24 April which featured Capt. G. Perreau, of the Ghurkha Regiment, who had played seven years previously, as well as Dr Jim Long and his brother W.F. Long, now a Bath city councillor. Cashnella's try was the only score.

Resentment over their exit from the county cup was still simmering five months later when club members gathered for the annual general meeting. It was chaired by Mr A.F. Florian who, deploring the result of the cup-tie, maintained that the previous season's poor results were 'more a result of ill fortune, than bad play.'

In seconding T.B. Timmins' proposal that Tom West be elected captain, Cashnella hoped the team would have a good season, making the point that last year 'hearts were broken by heavy defeats in away matches at the start of the season'. For a team that had won only 11 matches away from home in seven seasons, a 0-0 draw at Cheltenham in the opening fixture of the 1908/09 campaign was therefore seen by the *Chronicle* to be 'exceptional in every way'. Away victories followed against Wellington and in Birmingham against Old Edwardians to help quell the 'travel sickness', if only temporarily.

Bath fancied their chances against Bristol on a fog-bound Rec on 19 December but had to settle for a scoreless draw, while one of the biggest Boxing Day crowds seen on the ground saw them avenge the previous month's loss at Mountain Ash by winning 17-3. Arthur Ford, chosen to captain the side in the absence of West, had to pull out because of pressure of work at the Post Office and was replaced by an Ogmore Vale forward, Jack Chilcott, who was staying at Bath.

Jack later turned professional and toured with the Great Britain Rugby League side. Of more significance to this history is the fact that he was great-uncle to Gareth

Chilcott, cornerstone of the great Bath pack of the 1980s. Jack's brother Jim, who sired ten children, was father to Dai Chilcott, Gareth's father, and also to Iris, whose grandson is Nathan Thomas, of Bath, Wales and now Cardiff.

The return match at Bristol was played in freezing weather and, after a try apiece in the second half, it took a late penalty goal from a Bathonian, Norman Moore, to earn a 6-3 win for the home team. Some 200 Bath supporters wondered if their team would ever beat their rivals!

Progress in the Somerset Cup began with a 38-0 romp over Combe Down before Weston-super-Mare were overcome 9-6 on the Rec in front of 1,700 people paying £49.

The enthusiasm was simply too intense for words, and what with the rival exhortations of the contending partisans, the keenness of the players, and the tough struggle for supremacy, the excitement was at boiling point throughout. As a spectacle the match was of the usual Cup-tie order, plenty of vim, tons of energy, heaps of pluck, and desperate endeavours, but mighty little science.[7]

The competitive atmosphere surrounding cup-ties seemed to bring out the worst in the clubs, with objections to the eligibility of three Bath players and the winning team threatening to call off all fixtures. After the dust settled, Bath disposed of Stothert & Pitt 28-0 to earn the right to play Bridgwater in the final at Weston-super-Mare. Some 900 Bath supporters, wearing lily-white hats with Bath Buns attached, paid the 2s excursion concession from Bath Spa, only to see their favourites well beaten by 9-0.

A sequence of four victories over Penarth, Leytonstone, Cheltenham and away to Taunton lifted spirits before the curtain came down on an improved season with a 13-0 defeat at Pontypool. Ford's captaincy, after taking over from West in mid-season, had yielded a respectable record of 18 wins from 35 games, with 15 lost and 2 drawn, and on 28 May grateful players and officials gathered at the club's headquarters, The Crown Hotel, New Orchard Street, to present him with a wedding gift.

A number of personalities spoke in his praise and he was presented with a handsome oak framed photograph of himself in his County jersey. All present sang 'For he's a jolly good fellow', and the company drank his health with enthusiasm.

The proceedings were of a most convivial and enjoyable character. Songs were given during the evening by Messrs: A.H.W. Taylor, W.L. Angell, E. Cambridge, C. McCoombe, W. Fear, G. Taylor, Higgs, Simpkins and J. Smith. Mr J. Broom very kindly contributed a flute-solo in a most excellent manner, while Mr. Porch's remarkable whistling solos were also greatly appreciated. Mr W.E. Angell made an efficient accompanist.[8]

Although not one of the older members of the team at twenty-five, Ford had proved a popular figure blessed with the rare gift of being able to enthuse those around him. According to the *Chronicle*: 'He was full of go, and for grim determination could not be excelled, being of the "never say die" order; a genuine scrummager and a resolute tackler, and a speedy man at following up.'

Not surprisingly, he retained the captaincy. The committee also decided it was time to ditch the experiment with white shirts in favour of a return to blue and black, with the addition of white hoops. It is worth pointing out, however, that in the modern era, Bath famously won their first Twickenham final in a change strip of white shirts!

Club officials were not concerned entirely with parochial matters and could occasionally be far-sighted. On May 20, the Rugby Football Union voted by 44 to 27 to accept a Bath proposal, presented by club treasurer George Roberts, that the value of the drop goal be reduced to three points. It was then carried forward to the International Board but there was some delay before it was incorporated into the Laws of the Game – forty years, to be exact.

While rugby balls were a far cry from the pigs' bladders in use forty-five years previously, their propensity to absorb water made handling and kicking something of a trial in wet weather. The 'Orb' football being marketed by Messrs A.G. Spalding and Bros, 'well known athletic providers of London, Edinburgh and Birmingham', was greeted with acclaim by players at Bath and other clubs, at the start of the 1909/10 season. The innovation does not seem to have been fully developed or marketed, however, and the slippery leather ball was in use well into the 1970s, until plastic coatings were applied.

The faith placed in Ford's captaincy for a second season proved well placed as the team lost only two games before December. Bristol snatched a try two minutes from time to win 13-11 at Ashley Hill in a match described by the *Bristol Echo* as 'quite the most exciting game ever seen between these teams, and to do Bath justice they deserved to leave the field victorious instead of a defeated team.' Kitching and Hurst scored Bath's tries with Hatherill converting one and adding a penalty. They also lost 8-6 to Plymouth on a day when both sides were weakened by county calls.

The conduct of spectators at home matches continued to concern the committee and the Secretary was instructed to write to King Edward School 'to stop boys from blowing whistles on Saturdays, other than that used by the Referee, as the annoyance interfered with the Bath Club games'. It was also reported: 'One too ardent supporter has been forbidden the field, and the officials are determined to keep in check any indications of rowdyism.' The players themselves appear to have been men of some restraint and the *Chronicle* of 25 October, noting that the Temperance movement was much in evidence, pointed out that 'those who are interested in it may be pleased to know that most of the Bath team are teetotallers.'

For some it was still a gentlemen's sport. In a 13-10 home win over Clifton, the Bath full-back E.C. Hartell suffered a blow to the head and took some time to recover.

The Cliftonians once more proved themselves splendid footballers and capital sportsmen. When Hartell was knocked out, and the ball lay at the Cliftonian's mercy, they pulled up and made no attempt to profit from the occurrence, thus exemplifying the real spirit of 'rugger'.[9]

Conversely, the county cup had already demonstrated a propensity to bring out the worst in sides, but there was no denying the intensity of competition. The 1909/10 season was to feature a remarkable contest between Bath and Weston-super-Mare which saw three games drawn before the Seasiders finally prevailed.

A howling gale, which blew down the canvas screens designed to deter non-paying spectators gathering on the North Parade bridge, was blamed for the first scoreless match on 19 February. The following Thursday, storm clouds cleared over Weston's ground to leave it in its worst state for forty years, according to locals who were still clearing pools of water with buckets and pails right up to kick-off. No score again.

Some 3,000 people packed into the Rec for the second replay on 10 March but there were wrangles even before kick off as Bath objected to the inclusion of W. Hawkins, who had not appeared for Weston that season, and the visitors said they would not play extra time to achieve a result. Hawkins' penalty was matched by one from Alby Hatherill before the break and Cashnella might have won the tie for Bath had he not ignored an overlap and been tackled just short of the line.

The marathon tie was finally decided 48 hours later back at Weston as the home side won 17-3 against a Bath team weakened by the absence of Cashnella (knee injury), F.S. Cambridge (leg strain) and W.H. Thomas (dislocated thumb), among others. Cup rugby had its attractions but you could sometimes have too much of a good thing, it seemed.

There was a feeling of thankfulness among the Bath players – those that were left sound and fit – that there has come an end to cup ties.[10]

The Somerset officials could not have been happier, however, after banking their share of the total gate takings of £134. For Bath, the need to pay the Recreation Ground Company their cut made away ties more profitable.

Bath's home record stood until 26 February 1910, when they lost 5-0 to Plymouth but there was further recognition of their improved standing when W.H. Thomas was put forward as a candidate for Great Britain's summer tour to South Africa. An invitation does appear to have been forthcoming but the player's business commitments denied Bath the honour of providing a third tourist in the space of 11 years. Having made his debut in a 5-3 win over Abertillery in November, the former Penarth player had been identified by the *Chronicle* as 'a tall, strong, vigorous forward, just the stamp we want'.

An unwelcome distraction at the annual general meeting of the Recreation Ground Company that season was a proposal to consider the introduction of Association Football, alternating each Saturday with rugby. Shareholders pressing for such an arrangement thought it would be worth an extra £50-60 a year in revenue but Thomas

Gandy, founder member of the old Bath Zouaves, said he could not see how this would be possible and this view was supported by Mr Lewis, on behalf of the directors.

Having originally set up home at the Belvoir Ground at East Twerton, 'the Association men' failed again in June 1913 in an effort to persuade the rugby club to share the Rec. While the soccer players moved first to the Horse Show Grounds at Lambridge and then in 1933 to Twerton Park, the Recreation Ground became synonymous with rugby.

-8-

Fields of Glory

TINTED – OR TAINTED – by nostalgia, according to your point of view, the years immediately preceding the First World War came to be regarded by chroniclers as a 'golden age'. It was certainly a glorious episode in the history of Bath Football Club, all the more welcome after those fallow years in which results had been mixed at best and no player had merited selection for the England team since Frank Soane in 1894.

No one could have burst more spectacularly onto the scene than Vincent Middleton Hope Coates. Called into Monkton Combe School first XV while still a junior and awarded his School Cap in 1904 when only fifteen, he maintained his startling progress at Hailebury Imperial Service College. After being capped in his first year and elevated to captain of the Haileybury XV the following season, he impressed the Somerset selectors to such a degree that they picked the strapping young wing for the senior county side at the age of seventeen.

Going up to Caius College, Cambridge, to study medicine he won a Blue as a Fresher in 1907 when still only eighteen and, after a spell with Bridgwater, joined Bath with his brother Norman when their father, Dr Charles Coates, moved into Hopecote, Combe Down. The medical profession was something of a family vocation, their grandfather, Dr Charles Coates MD FRCP, having been 'one of Bath's most esteemed citizens and trusted physicians of his day'.

Norman made his debut on Christmas Eve 1910 in the customary defeat by Bristol, who had strained relations between the clubs earlier in the season by luring St Clair Johnstone, 'the Silver Fox', from the Bath ranks. The brothers finally lined up together against London Welsh three days later and Norman scored one of the tries in an 8-3 victory.

If their appearances were restricted by university commitments in that first season, one in particular was unforgettable and it established Vincent's reputation forever among Bath followers. When Bristol arrived at the Rec for a Thursday evening fixture on 6 April 1911, every rugby follower in Bath was painfully aware that they had not beaten their neighbours since 20 March 1897 when a crowd of 4,000 saw Soane's side win 3-0 at the County Ground. This time, in addition to club members, just 800 people paid £18 at the gate, braving a biting wind and flurries of snow, but Bath set a hot pace.

ketch decorated the front of the menu card at the congratulatory dinner given to incent Coates, by the Bath Football Club, on his being capped for England in Lord Alec Thynne—so soon afterwards to be killed in action in the Great War— at the banquet, which was attended by many famous figures in West Country rugby.

Coates capped.

Cashnella made a grand burst into the Bristol quarter. Here the ball was thrown out from touch to N Coates, who handed smartly to his brother, Vincent. The left wing made a splendid run; he shook off several men who attempted to tackle him, and scored. It was a fine try, and Brooks converted with a grand kick.[1]

The brothers combined impressively again before half-time to create a try for W.H. Thomas for Bath to lead 8-0 at the break.

Then V Coates made a brilliant run on the left, dodging and sprinting grandly. He tried to drop a goal when a few yards away, but the ball did not rise. He seemed to have a try at his mercy had he gone on. Bath were doing all the attacking, and one of the forwards seemed to be over, but the whistle had gone. Then the ball was passed to the left near the Bristol line, but went into touch before V Coates could gather it. But just after, Vincent Coates was over with another try, amid deafening cheers and Brooks goaled.[2]

The closing stages were contested in semi-darkness to the extent that the referee felt unable to award E.J. Hodges a try in the corner. No one was complaining however when he blew for no-side with the score 13-0 in Bath's favour, and the *Chronicle* singled out the right wing for special praise.

Vincent Coates was the hero of the match, and whatever else the Cantab. may do for Bath, and I trust his achievements may be many and brilliant, he will never do anything more popular with Bathonians than putting the winning spirit into the side as he did on Thursday.[3]

Bath had lost 10 of their 16 matches up to Christmas; they lost just six of the 19 games afterwards, Alby Hatherill being a cheerful and enthusiastic captain. He even turned out against Abertillery on his wedding day, 11 February, entering the dressing room to cheers from the team. His brother, Alfred 'Loo' Hatherill, also captained the 'A' XV in 1910/11, making five appearances for the first team and scoring the only try in a 3-3 draw at home to Cheltenham, 'a disagreeable game' in which Cashnella was sent off with an opponent. 'Cash' was in rare form at this time, scoring two tries the following week, 4 March, in an 11-11 draw with Pontypool on the Rec. Not the sort of individual to allow opponents to take liberties, Cashnella was sent off almost exactly a year later

Vincent Coates (left) with brother Norman.

The Bath team that faced Bridgwater on 15 October 1910. From left to right, back row: W.T. Davis (touch judge), J. Dainton, J. Heitzmann, J. Carpenter, F.J. Cashnella, E.S. Cambridge, B. Hurst, W.H. Thomas, A. Ford, J.T. Piper (Honorary Secretary). Middle row: G.A. Roberts (Honorary Treasurer), R. Ascott, G.W. Powell, A. Hatherill (captain), S.E. Brooks, A.F. Kitching, F. Soane (vice president). Front row: W. Fear, E.C. Hartell.

at Neath, although his part in the fracas was later judged by the Somerset disciplinary committee not to merit a suspension, suggesting that he was becoming a 'marked man' with certain referees.

Norman Coates had taken over the captaincy for 1911/12, a campaign which began at the annual meeting with a warm tribute to the Honorary Treasurer, George Roberts, by the club chairman, T.B. Timmins.

He could remember him when he (Mr. Timmins) first started to play football, and no man in Bath, or even in Somerset, gave such time and so much ability to the game of rugby football as did Mr. Roberts. If every cause was supported by the hard and splendid work such as Mr. Roberts put in on behalf of football they would have a good deal more success, and a good deal less failure than occurred in affairs generally. Mr. Roberts spared himself in no way whatever. He worked hard, he went away with the team every week, and when the finances of the Club required looking after he was ready with his advice.[4]

A handsome new grandstand had been erected on the riverside during the previous season and it was decided that season tickets be issued for the stand at 3s 6d for the season, with the price of admission to the stand being 6d for First XV games and 3d for 'A' fixtures. With the brothers Coates in fluent form and well supported in the back line by Kitching and Clifford Walwin, a centre from Gloucester Old Boys who had come to Bath to complete pharmacy studies, twice as many games were won as lost before Christmas.

Unfortunately, Welsh opponents invariably proved the stronger, although Abertillery had been defeated 13-9 at the Rec on 30 September. The goalkicking of 'nippy' Dickie Ascott proved decisive and there was some satisfaction that he was intending to move to Bath from Radstock.

Not so popular was Mr Wyer, a supporter who was censured by the Management Committee for 'his noisy behaviour at matches'. Other matters dealt with at their meeting on 3 October concerned the provision of 'tea at Training Evenings until further notice' and the need for the railway company to be notified at least two weeks in advance of bookings of saloons.

Later that month, it was reported that W.H. Thomas, who had continued to play for Bath after his job had taken him to Swindon, was soon to be posted to Cardiff by his company. Thomas, who had been prevented by business commitments from accepting an invitation to tour South Africa in 1910, was destined to serve the Cardiff club with distinction.

After a crowd of 3,500 packed into the Rec on 18 November to see Somerset play Gloucestershire, the club staged its annual 'smoking concert' at the Crown Hotel and players and officials regaled a large audience with a varied repertoire:

A very enjoyable programme was gone through during the evening, the following being the names of the contributors and their contributions: Messrs. Syd Rouse, 'The Village Pump'; Arthur Taylor, 'The Lighthouse Keeper'; A F Kitching, 'A suicide' (humorous recital); W Fear, 'No, no, no'; E Cambridge, 'Haste to the fair'; E Simpkins, 'Veteran's song'; R Hulbert, 'Roll on the dark and deep blue ocean'; F W Porch (siffleur) 'The last stand'; Finch, 'Put on your coat and come home'; John Smith, 'Adieu, Marie'; G A Roberts, 'Cockles and Mussels, alive, alive O'; Fred Russell, 'Don't go down in the mine, dad'; Poole; and Stevens.[5]

Singing, whether organised or impromptu, was very much part of the after-match routine, and many of these ditties had been rehearsed on homeward journeys, to the metronomic accompaniment of the Great Western Railway.

Henry and Cecil Biggs impressed against Bath two days before Christmas in a strong Bristol team that scored five tries to three in a 24-9 victory and, although a draw with Mountain Ash was followed by wins over Ferndale and Penylan, the rest of the holiday programme was spoilt by wretched weather. The *Chronicle* contended: 'Everyone will agree that Bath have seen about enough of Welsh teams for a while. The clamorous, contentious, and critical shouts of their obtrusive supporters got on the nerves of a good many during the Christmas games.'

The view from the Principality was more generous, as expressed by the *Llanelly Mercury* of 11 January 1912, which declared that the local team would have 'the finest fixture list on record next season. The new teams likely to appear at Stradey include Coventry, Bath, Cheltenham and London Welsh'.

The spectre of the Northern Union re-emerged in January as Dicky Ascott and Riley West signed for Hull Kingston Rovers, Ascott making his debut against no less than the touring Australians. According to the *Sportsman* newspaper: 'Of Ascott splendid impressions were formed; he shirked nothing and bore out his reputation for pluck.'

Meanwhile, the grind of weekly fixtures was enlivened for the Bath players on 24 February by lunch at the House of Commons, at the invitation of their President, Lord Alexander Thynne MP. Responding to words of gratitude from Mr G.A. Roberts, Lord Alexander Thynne said that among the many visitors he received at the House no visit had given him greater pleasure than that of the Bath team, adding:

The strength of the British people was founded on sport. As long as British people continued to be sportsmen, so long should we flourish as a people. Of all the forms of sport there was none that developed the best spirit of Englishmen better than football, and especially Rugger [cheers]. It was quite true that English Rugger had made great strides in the last few years and if the All Blacks came here again they would experience a very different reception. He hoped if the Colonial team came here they would be seen at Bath and they would be there shown the quality of West Country Rugger at the present time [cheers].[6]

The players then set off for Wandsworth Common to face London Welsh, only to discover that the game had been called off. The sense of anti-climax was only partly relieved by a dinner hosted at the Holborn Restaurant by Sir Charles Bart MP.

As the 1911/12 season progressed, Bath struggled for consistency, crashing 43-4 at Pontypool in one of their heaviest defeats, such a humiliating experience that players were reportedly reluctant to venture from their homes the following day. The concluding game brought success, however, an especially sweet finale because Bristol were beaten 21-4 at the Recreation Ground, leaving Norman Coates with a playing record in his first season as captain of 20 victories, 11 defeats and 1 draw.

Apart from the permanent stand erected in 1910, spectator accommodation was spartan until agreement was reached with the Recreation Ground Company for a temporary stand to be installed on the opposite touchline. A tiered affair which had previously been used for county cricket, it replaced rough boards. It remained in situ for ninety years in different forms of construction, open to the elements and passing into Bath folklore as 'the Flowerpots'.

On 17 August 1912, an explosive letter was received from the Honorary Secretary of Plymouth Grounds and Stands Company, E.H. Searle, inviting Bath to join six other clubs in forming 'a Western League to play under Northern Rugby Union rules in this approaching season'. When Bath's Management Committee discussed the matter, it was at first proposed that the letter be left to lie on the table but G.A. Roberts moved a resolution, seconded by Norman Coates, that Mr Searle be informed 'that the Bath Club had no idea of forsaking its loyal allegiance to the Rugby Union and could not for one moment countenance the proposal contained in his letter.'

It was a wise move. Not surprisingly, the guardians of the amateur game took a dim view of any attempt by the Northern Union to establish a foothold in the South West and the *Chronicle* reported on 21 September that the Devon RFU had suspended seven past and present officials for their perceived treachery. Two months later an RFU Committee decided to 'expel, remove or suspend' certain officials and players of the Newton Abbot, Torquay, Plymouth and Devon Albion clubs and to close the grounds of all those concerned. The treasurer of Devon RFU was suspended.

In this sort of fevered atmosphere, it was no surprise that the merest suspicion invited immediate and draconian sanction, as the Bath forward, Arthur West, discovered. Selected by Somerset along with Vincent and Norman Coates, Fred Hill and W.F. Wardle to face the South Africans at the Recreation Ground on 3 October, he was temporarily suspended on the eve of the match by an emergency disciplinary committee of the county union. Rumours persisted of a clandestine visit to Rochdale.

West denied the charge of consorting with Northern Union representatives but when his case was finally heard in London at the end of the month he felt the full force of the RFU's disciplinary machine. West was formally suspended from all Rugby Football Union clubs, a decision which, if he had not made up his mind already, confirmed him in his decision to 'go North.' It is rather reassuring to learn from *The Bath Chronicle* that when he boarded the train at Bath on 10 January 1913 several of his old chums gathered to give him a send-off and wish him every success.

After the excitement of the South Africans' visit – Somerset were defeated 24-3 in the first game of their tour – Bath continued to prosper under Norman Coates's captaincy, losing just 5 of their first 20 matches.

What fresh can I say about the Brothers Coates? They have exhausted all my stock phrases, for they utilise the whole gamut of Rugby proficiency. Norman, both in running, kicking and tactics generally is quite on a par now with Vincent, and if there is a better all round pair in the South I don't know them.[7]

The highlights of the pre-Christmas programme were home and away wins over Bristol by 8-0 and 12-0 respectively; a further home derby was scoreless and Bristol finally won a fourth match at Nevil Road 8-0. The only home reverse during the season was a 3-0 defeat by Pontypool on 14 December when Bath were weakened by county calls.

All this was achieved by a side who, with the exception of Alfred Kitching, resident at Monkton Combe School, all lived within the city boundary. The undoubted star was Vincent Coates and it was with great acclaim, if no great surprise, that the twenty-three year old was selected to play for England against South Africa at Twickenham on Saturday

4 January 1913. The tourists triumphed 9-3 by a try and two penalties to a try but, by all accounts, regarded Coates as the best wing three-quarter they had faced on tour.

It was eighteen years since Frank Soane had won his first England cap and 'Buster' contributed in his usual jovial manner when a large number of 'Rugbyites' dined at the Assembly Rooms to celebrate Coates's achievement. As ever, it was the sheer physicality of the young medic's approach to the game that appealed to Soane, according to reports of his tribute: 'It was worth going a long way to see Vincent Coates play. There were generally six laid out and the ambulance was very busy and, as for the full back, he was generally in a blue funk for, if he did not get out of the way, he got a push in the jaw.'

Apart from reminiscences of Frank Soane's playing days and of Tommy Parham who, despite his lack of caps, was thought to have 'had no equal in England as an outside half-back', there was a cameo appearance from a 63-year-old Bath supporter, Harold Freeman. The old Marlborough Nomads player recalled his debut against Scotland in 1872 as the only three-quarter in the England team. They played 20-a-side, with three full backs, three halves, one three-quarter, and 13 in the scrum!

Four days after that dinner, Coates scored one of two England tries in a 12-0 victory at Cardiff. He followed that up a week later with a hat-trick in a 20-0 win over France at Twickenham and crossed twice more against Ireland on 8 February in Dublin (15-4). Although he was not on the scoresheet in the 3-0 win over Scotland, which secured the Triple Crown and the Grand Slam, he was properly feted as top try scorer in the Championship with six tries.

That tally, a championship record, was surpassed a year later by Cyril Lowe with eight and Coates never played for his country again, but his impact on the game was not forgotten. O.L. Owen, in his 1955 book, *The History of the Rugby Football Union*, wrote: 'Coates made his great name as a powerful runner carrying a hand-off comparable with Maclear's in the course of five matches in one season. A more formidable meteor never shot through the Rugby sky into that strange never-never land known as memory.' (Basil Maclear was an equally formidable Irish wing of the 1900s.)

Back on the club scene, Bath's resurgence was heartening news for the Recreation Ground Company. At its annual meeting on 8 November 1912 reference was made to the growing popularity of rugby in the city: '... the Bath Football Club was looking up in such an excellent way, showing the best of play and winning matches.' However, the condition of the ground was causing concern, as the soil had become greatly impoverished, 'due to the tremendously hot summer of 1911, which actually burnt up the turf, followed by the excessively wet summer of 1912 which helped to make matters worse'. The Company also received that season a letter from the Club Secretary drawing their attention to 'the nuisance caused on the playing patch by sheep.'

At the start of the season, the Honorary Secretary's position had passed to E.F. (Eddie) Simpkins from the long-serving John Townend Piper, who had been a member of the Club since 1887 and Club Secretary since 15 May 1890. Piper continued to share

Vincent Coates, capped by England in 1913.

secretarial duties with the younger man for another thirty years, being rewarded for his devotion to the club with the first Life Membership in 1922, and was still in harness at the time of his death in 1942. But that commitment was more than matched by Eddie Simpkins and his son, Jack, who eventually took over from his father and was still in the post when Bath were conquering all at Twickenham in the 1980s.

To return to the first 'golden age', the 12-0 win over Bristol on 21 December 1912 – Bath's first away win in derby matches for more than fifteen years – sparked a remarkably successful run of 13 matches in which the only defeat was at Coventry (23-0) on 8 February. The spell was broken in mid-March but Coventry were beaten 15-0 in the return and Norman Coates's second season as captain was more than respectable – 21 victories, 12 losses and 1 drawn game.

One fixture quietly dropped for the following season was the double header with Mountain Ash. As if a four-hour railway journey to the Valleys was not ordeal enough, the return trip lasted more than nine hours, with some of the party only having time to go home, change their clothes and then be at work at 6 a.m.!

Having regained their status as a premier club in the eyes of English and Welsh opponents, it was clear to many that a steady stream of talent would be needed to sustain

J. Townend Piper.

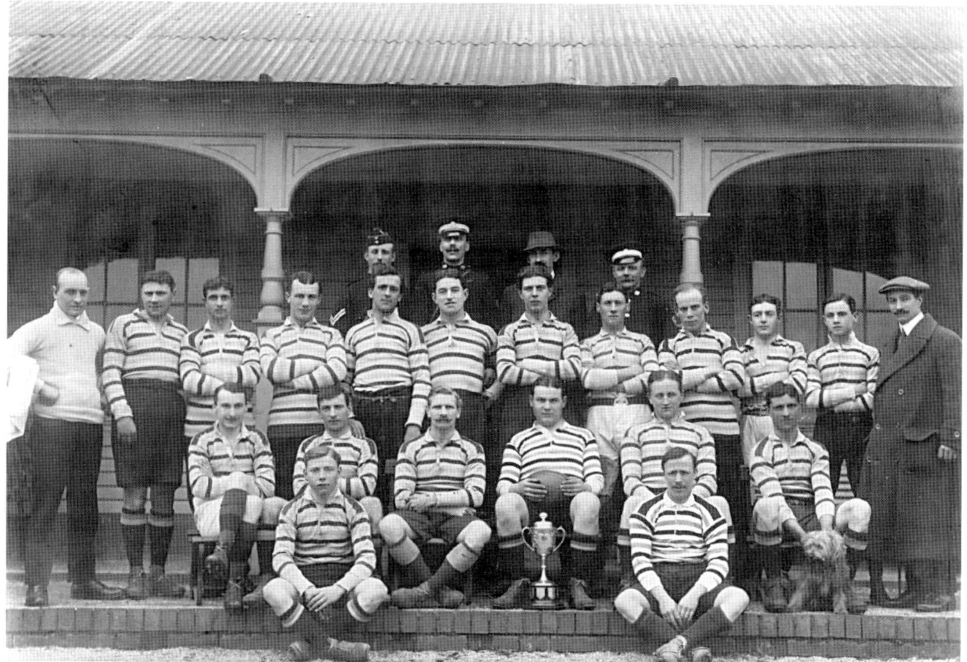

'A' XV. Winners of the Bath Knock-out Cup, 1912/13. From left to right, back row: Sully, J. Abrahams, A.B. Moore, C. Curtis. Second row: N. Bristow (trainer), S. Holman, F. Dixon, C. Gibbs, H. Burt, B. Hurst, T. Pyatt, W. Locke, B. Isaacs, E. Horsell, R. West, W. Cleall. Third row: P. Hawkins, W. Stevens, A.E. Cleall, G. Chivers (captain), W. Lewis, L. Hatherill. Fourth row: H. Vowles, A. Russell (vice captain).

it. The Bath club therefore took it upon itself to reorganise schools rugby in the city, each school to send a representative to work with a sub-committee of the club, meeting every Tuesday evening. The Management Committee also instructed on 18 February 1913 that Middle Common (Victoria Park) be secured as a ground for the Schools Union and that funds be raised at a summer carnival and, more immediately, through an 'Old Crocks' match; Alf Cleall, Club vice president and captain of the 'A' XV, offered to raise a team.

Middle Common on Victoria Park was duly secured at a cost of £7 for the season from 1 October and further playing space was reserved for the Schools Union at the Horseshow Ground and on part of the Rec. The sports day took place at Kensington Meadows on 7 July, officiated by John Piper, Frank Cashnella, Eddie Simpkins, C.C. Wills and George Roberts.

At the beginning of the 1913/14 season, it was thought that the following schools would be operating rugby teams: Bathforum, Oldfield, East Twerton, Bathwick St Saviours, St Stephen's, Widcombe and probably St Luke's and Batheaston. Finding somewhere for all the schools to play was still something of a headache, although a good pitch was found at Claverton and also a rough patch on North Parade, only suitable for practice. Another ground was sought in the Grosvenor or Walcot district.

Old Crocks *v.* Bath 'A', 1913. From left to right, back row: J. Abrahams, C. Curtis, C. Wills, H. Parsons, E.W. Austin, G.T. Dando, P. Cox, W. Watts, J. Darke, J. March. Second row: Sully, W. Dolman, G. Parsons, T. Hanney, W. Gunning, R. Hulbert, A. Taylor, F. Russell, A. Marshman, J. Rowe, H. Vanstone (referee, Somerset RFU), W. Cleall. Third row: W.F. Long, J.W. Gibbs, Dr J.E. Long, A.E. Cleall (captain), E.F. Gooding, G. Parfitt. Fourth row: W. Curtis, W. Holmes. (Old Crocks 16 Bath 'A' 3)

If there were any doubts about the benefit of an effective grooming policy through the schools, it was very evident in the progress of the up-and-coming Harry Vowles. He made a good showing for the Possibles in the club trial but his opposite number, Husbands, was regarded as the 'find' of the day in the Probables' 27-0 win. Not all the entertainment was on the field of play, however, as the *Chronicle* observed:

So engrossed was a baker's boy in watching the trial that his basket was dispossessed of two loaves by a couple of pigs before he was aware of it.[8]

One of rugby's most enduring rivalries began on 13 September 1913 when Bath opened hostilities with Leicester in front of a crowd of 7,000 at Welford Road. Bath found themselves eight points down at half-time and eventually lost 17-5, scoring a last minute try through G.G. Powell, converted by Norman Coates. Three-quarters of a century later, the opening game of Bath's season was still away to Leicester.

Despite the absence of Mountain Ash, there was no shortage of Welsh opposition to spice up the fixture list in those days, with Llanelly the biggest draw of them all, supplemented by teams such as Penylan, Crumlin, Machen, Pontypool, Abertillery and

Penarth. Rapid expansion of the South Wales coalfield had led to new rugby-playing communities springing up all over the valleys – but at a cost.

On 14 October the colliery at Senghenydd in the Rhymney Valley was shattered by an explosion which claimed the lives of 439 men and boys, including eight 14-year-olds, making it the worst disaster in British mining history. One street lost 18 men. The Bath Management Committee, meeting that night, voted to arrange a benefit match against Bath Old Boys and a collection from the 4,000 spectators attending the derby match at Bristol four days later yielded £12 0s 6d.

Bath lost that one 5-0 and also went down at Llanelly 15-8 on 8 November as results followed the pattern of 'home win, away defeat' until a run of nine successive victories stretching into February. Pontypool, arriving as Welsh champions, then claimed Bath's home record but notable scalps were taken in the second half of the season, including Bristol (9-0), Llanelly (5-0, beaten by a try from the skipper Philip Hope), Coventry (41-10) and Leicester (14-3) on their first visit to the Rec.

A 16-0 reverse at Penarth, only the 12th defeat in 33 games, rounded off an otherwise 'happy and successful season' in the words of the Report and Accounts submitted to the annual general meeting at the Red House Restaurant on 30 June. The one note of

Bath 1913/14. From left to right, back row: W. Rosenburg (touch judge), S. West (trainer), F. Froude (forward), R.R. Stephenson (committee), A. Ford (forward), R. Husbands (half), A.H.W. Taylor (chairman), B. Hurst (forward), D. Fisher (forward), G.G. Powell (forward), W.H. Royal (forward), E.F. Simpkins (Honorary Secretary). Second row: E. Warde (forward), E. Russell (forward), S. Head, (forward), P.P. Hope (three-quarter, captain), V.M.H. Coates (three-quarter), N. Coates (three-quarter), H.E. Shewring (three-quarter). Third row: F.J. Cashnella (forward), A. Hatherill (half), H. Vowles (half), S. Pratt (three-quarter), G.A. Roberts (Honorary Treasurer).

disharmony surrounded the Somerset RFU's allegedly 'shabby' treatment of the club treasurer, George Roberts, after he had raised £215 for county funds through his assiduous work in organising the South Africans' fixture.

It is with the utmost indignation we record the ingratitude displayed towards our esteemed Hon. Treasurer – who took the lead in organising the reception of the South Africans, and managed all the details of the fixture – at the recent meeting of the Somerset Union, for we know the keen interest he has ever taken in Somerset Rugby Football during the thirteen years he sat on the County Committee.[9]

There was talk of breaking with Somerset over this slight but those present contented themselves with re-electing the Honorary Treasurer unopposed and looked forward with justifiable optimism to another good season, one in which the club would celebrate its golden jubilee. Just two days previously, Archduke Franz Ferdinand, heir to the Austro-Hungarian Empire, had been assassinated in Sarajevo. What no one could have known was that this outrage was rapidly to set in train a series of events that would make Vincent Coates a war hero – and also claim the lives of committeemen in that very room. There would be no jubilee celebrations until 1925, the sixtieth anniversary. Otto von Bismarck had, of course, predicted that a European War would result from 'some damn foolish thing in the Balkans'. By midnight on 4 August, Britain was at war with Germany, but as late as 22 August the *Chronicle* was reflecting opinion within the club that 'football might be a welcome diversion in the war trouble.'

A letter from Leicester intimated that Bath were expected there on 5 September and a trial match was fixed for 29 August on the Recreation Ground, kick off 3.30 p.m. On Tuesday 25 August the Management Committee, giving 'officials power to act in any Emergency which might arise owing to the present crisis', decided to take soundings from local clubs and quickly discovered that St Stephen's had abandoned all matches. By 1 September it was learned that the Frome club had disbanded and that evening's issue of *The Bath Chronicle* carried a plea from the Mayor of Bath urging the rugby club not to permit games during the crisis.

No man, he said, would care to play or look on at football while his fellows were sacrificing their life and time on the Continent.[10]

That effectively ended any debate on the matter and an Emergency Committee of the club immediately met to cancel the visit to Leicester, upon which George Roberts moved the following resolution, seconded by the chairman Arthur Taylor and carried unanimously, without discussion:

That having regard to the grave crisis through which our country is passing and the urgent call to every eligible man to take up arms for Britain's honour and security, this Committee decide that no matches be played before Christmas and that in December the situation be further considered. The Committee feel sure that the many members of the club will appreciate the patriotic motive inspiring this resolution and will rally to their support when under happier auspices it will be possible to resume club games.[11]

With commendable tidiness they also resolved that arrangements be made with the Recreation Ground Company for the ground to be kept for the Schools Rugby Union and that all club property be collected and stored at the Red House. All club accounts were to be paid and the balance banked on deposit. Far from curtailing boys' rugby, the suspension of the senior game was seen to be an opportunity to expand the sport for those aged fourteen to seventeen and a junior section was quickly formed so that 'by playing rugby football, the lads would be keeping in training in preparation for the time when they were old enough to enlist, and they would be ready to play football when the war was over'.

Before the end of September, Norman Coates and his other brother, Adrian, were off to the front, along with Philip Hope, to serve as motorcycle dispatch riders attached to the Royal Engineers. Among the first to be sent to France was Billy Fear, who had made his debut for the club way back in 1898/99 before enlisting in the 2nd Battalion Prince Albert's Somerset Light Infantry and then seeing service in the Boer War and in India. On returning to Bath in 1908 he established a strong half-back partnership with Alby Hatherill for nearly five years. Called up as a Reservist on 5 August, he was soon in the thick of the fighting, serving in the same Company of the Somersets with the Bath fly-half, Lieutenant J.C.W. MacBryan. Both were wounded at Ligny in the first few weeks of the war and remained prisoners of the Germans until the Armistice more than four years later.

Meanwhile, a Bath XV took the field against Kingswood School on 14 November in aid of the Belgian Relief Fund and to defray ground expenses. The Recreation Ground Company had also made the area available to Territorial forces, the Royal Engineers, The Yeomanry and the 4th Somersets, until they could find grounds to drill on. There was a further Bath XV fixture on 16 January with a Canadian Highland Regiment, billeted on Salisbury Plain. With members of the 10th Devons (Kitchener's Army), supplementing home favourites such as 'Podge' Blanchard, Alby Hatherill, Harry Vowles and Frank Cashnella, Bath managed a 6-6 draw but there was a sad sequel as news came through in April that one of the Canadian forwards, C.B.C. Cream, had been killed, shot through the head. A more cheerful, if rather gung-ho, message was received by George Roberts from another Bath player, Sergeant Ben Hurst, of the Royal Wessex Engineers:

I hope you managed to beat the Canadians. I tried the 'loose head' on the Germans last night, and was not penalised. Neither did the whistle go for 'offside.' Quite fit. Kindest regards to all.' [12]

But the First World War was continuing to take its toll. Philip Hope had a narrow escape in January 1915 when a shell crashed through the bonnet of his motor car, injuring his driver and companion. The Bath skipper of the previous season was taken unconscious to the cellar of a house which remained under bombardment for several hours. A request for his leave to be extended was refused and he was returned to the Front, still seemingly shell-shocked.

Norman Coates was granted leave to attend Vincent's wedding in July but according to the *Chronicle*, 'owing to the war, the ceremony was of a very quiet nature indeed; only immediate friends of the families were present'. Within four months Vincent was in uniform himself, speedily commissioned by the Royal Army Medical Corps after qualifying as a surgeon. He was soon transferred to the Royal Fusiliers as regimental medical officer while his bride devoted herself to nursing wounded soldiers in Bath.

There was more action on the Rec in September as Bath City were allowed to stage a soccer match against the 1st Footballers' Battalion of the Middlesex Regiment as part of a Recruiting Rally, with a strong appeal for unmarried men to come forward.

A week later, a telegram was delivered to 17 Stuart Place, Twerton, home of Mr and Mrs Walter West, informing them that their thirty-three-year-old son, Rifleman Tom West, of 'A' Company, 10th Battalion, King's Royal Rifle Corps had been killed in action on the morning of Wednesday 29 September. Tom West, a winger and Bath captain in 1907/08 before going north to join Rochdale Hornets, thus became the first player from the club to join the roll of the 'fallen'.

Even more shocking was final confirmation that none other than the club's vice-chairman, Alf Cleall, a tireless committee-man and former skipper of the 'A' team, was dead. As a Sergeant with the North Somerset Yeomanry, he had been shot in the throat on or around 17 November 1914 while holding off a massive German attack. First listed as 'missing', he was posthumously mentioned in despatches on 15 February 1917 but his death was not officially communicated to the family by the War Office until the following December.

Alf, a forty-year-old veteran of the Indian Frontier and South African campaigns, had been landlord, along with his mother and brother, Wilfred, of the Rising Sun in Grove Street and later the Full Moon in Upper Borough Walls. It was several months before the Management Committee of the club could pay their tribute, in the form of a resolution proposed by George Roberts:

At this their first meeting since it was officially announced that Sergt Alfred E. Cleall N.S.Y. was killed in action at Vlamertinghe, Flanders on November 17th 1914, the members of the Bath Football Club Committee desire to place on record their sincere sorrow at the loss of an esteemed colleague, who was at the time of his gallant death their Vice Chairman. As Captain of the 'A' team and as an ever willing player in the

Recreation Ground marked out for soccer, 1915.

1st XV, Sergt. Cleall rendered valuable services to the Club and was always held in high regard for his sporting and genial qualities. As a British soldier his bravery was attested by his mention in despatches and the noble nature of his death. (Resolution carried with members standing).[13]

Private Eddie Clarke, a half-back with the Oldfield Park Club and Bath 'A', and occasionally the First XV before emigrating to Canada, was reported killed in action on 8 July while serving with the Canadian contingent, presumably on the Somme where their divisions were massed. Eddie's 'Maple Leaf' was delivered to his mother at 13 Brunswick Street, Bath.

Meanwhile the Recreation Ground hosted an Army Service Corps Sports Day incorporating the following activities: '100 yards flat race, throwing the cricket ball, three-legged race, wheelbarrow race, boxing exhibition, quarter-mile flat race, sack race, officers' race, blindfold boxing and kicking the football.'

Still the Somme claimed its victims. Lord Alexander Thynne, who as MP for Bath and vice president of the club had entertained the players to lunch at the House of Commons four years previously, was wounded in action on 30 July while leading a battalion of the Glosters.

The Chronicle did its best to keep readers in touch with their old sporting favourites and this article on 30 September 1916 would have been widely read:

IN THE BIG PUSH
BATH FOOTBALLER'S IMPRESSIONS
Tribute to British Artillery
A most interesting letter has just been received by Mr Arthur Taylor, Chairman of the Bath Football Club, from Private Loo Hatherill of the Gloucesters, eldest brother of Alby Hatherill, himself an old Bath forward and a member of the club committee. Private Hatherill was on the staff of Messrs. Horton Brothers, Northgate Street, when he enlisted. It will be noticed that he has seen Mr P.P. Hope, the captain of the Bath Club, who is still a dispatch rider at the front. Private Hatherill says:

We have been in the big push, and succeeded in taking two lines of German trenches and a good number of prisoners. We were told afterwards by the General how pleased he was with the way we went over like one man. It was not a very pleasant feeling waiting for the order to charge, but once you were over the top you forgot everything except that the German trenches are in front. The noise is terrific, what with the artillery and machine guns...

IN TOUCH WITH FOOTBALL FRIENDS
One of our fellows from Bath met Dr Vincent Coates, and he asked him if there were any of the football club in the Gloucesters, if so to remember him kindly to them. He told me he could not think of my name till after Dr Coates was gone. So I went back the next day to try and see him, but had no luck. But I saw Philip Hope on his motor bike. I think he recognized me as he went past, but he seemed in a hurry. He looked pretty fit and well. We have moved now, so I do not expect to see him again for a bit. We have a couple of officers in our regiment from the Clifton Club, Captain A.J. Gardner and Captain Sellman. It makes one think of the good old tussles on Westbury Down and on the Rec. I wonder how many of the old brigade will be left when Bath and Clifton meet again!

The big news, however, was that Vincent Coates, already a hero on the football field, had been awarded the Military Cross 'for conspicuous gallantry and devotion to duty in action. During an attack he tended the wounded under very difficult circumstances, working without assistance after his orderly was hit. He was under heavy shell fire.'

The former England wing was decorated in the field near the scene of his bravery, Delville Wood, the notorious killing ground on the Somme. The Management Committee meeting of 23 October duly sent its congratulations to Lieutenant Coates who later went to Salonika as bacteriologist and completed his war service as Medical Officer 2nd Infantry Brigade, 49th Division.

In December 1916 Mr and Mrs John Biggs of the Laurels, London Road, Bath, were informed that their second son, Lieutenant Commander Geoffrey Nepean Biggs, brother of Norman, Selwyn and Cecil, had been lost at sea, aged 31. He had played one game for Bath in 1904/05.

Kitching, Cashnella, Blanchard, Fred Russell and others provided welcome opposition to army units on the rugby field during 1916/17, including the Army Cyclists Corps (3-3), London Rifle Brigade (9-0), Royal Naval Division, Blandford (no score recorded) and Downside College (5-3). However, Bath could not raise a team to play the New Zealanders on 11 January 1917.

Rugby provided no real respite from the losses across the Channel. Poor Arthur West, summarily suspended from the Somerset side to face the South Africans four years earlier and then banished from Rugby Union to pursue an ultimately unsuccessful career with Oldham, met his fate serving as a Sergeant with the Manchester Regiment. Posted 'missing believed killed' on the evidence of a comrade, he joined his cousin Tom West on the roll of the fallen.

It could be weeks or months before the battlefield surrendered remains or evidence of identity. Eleven months after the Ascott family had been told their rugby-playing son, Wallace, was missing it was finally confirmed on 3 February 1917 that Dickie, Stan and Bob had lost their brother. Further afield, Lieutenant Colonel Gustavus Arthur Perreau, of the Indian Infantry, was reported killed in Mesopotamia, aged 43. A clever rugby player, he was a regular for the Hermitage School and played for Bath on a number of occasions, particularly when on leave during the 1900/01 season.

As a despatch rider, Sergeant Philip Hope endured as hazardous an existence as any. By October 1917 he was back in Britain with broken ribs and other injuries although, as he explained to Arthur Taylor and George Roberts when they visited him in Beaufort Military Hospital in Bristol, it was as a result of colliding with a water cart in the dark. Although unconscious for some time, he had remounted his machine and completed his mission. According to the *Chronicle*, he had 'rendered useless' a dozen machines or more during his three years' active service.

1918 brought no relief for family and friends back in Bath. On 12 January came the shocking news that Alfred 'Loo' Hatherill, one of the great characters of the club and brother of Alby, had been posted 'missing' by his unit, a TA battalion of the Gloucestershire Regiment. Previously injured by an exploding shell, he had spent months in hospital in Newport before returning to France. The death was confirmed later.

It also became known that Sub-Lieutenant Fred Hill, the Bath fly-half who was picked by Somerset against the South Africans in October 1912, had been killed in France on Christmas Day at the age of 26. Having emigrated to Canada later that season, he had returned with the Canadian forces and then obtained a commission in the Royal Naval Division.

Walter Fletcher, a Bath forward and contemporary of Dr J.E. Long, died in London Military Camp aged 41 after being invalided home with shell shock. Dave Fisher, a regular in the Bath pack in the immediate pre-war seasons, came home wounded from France and died on the Isle of Wight, where he was working on munitions.

The war appeared to be drifting to its close but carried a sting in its tail, claiming a distinguished member of the club on 15 September, none other than Lord Alexander Thynne. After being wounded in the chest during the Battle of the Somme, he returned to Parliamentary duties while recuperating but was back in France in February 1917 in command of a Wiltshire battalion, only to be wounded again, this time in the forearm. Third time around, he was even unluckier. Although titled, twice mentioned in despatches and Gazetted as a Companion of the Distinguished Service Order, Lord Alexander proved as mortal as humble Loo Hatherill.

Ceasefire was sounded in Bath at 11 a.m. on 11 November by bugler Sydney Golledge, of the Somerset Light Infantry, and by Christmas there were joyful and emotional reunions with Billy Fear, J.C.W. MacBryan and others returned from captivity. Life – and rugby – could begin again.

-9-

They Played the Game – They Crossed the Line

ONE OF THE first tasks of the Management Committee in resurrecting the Bath club was a poignant one, to elect a replacement for Alf Cleall. Fittingly, Wilfred Cleall was invited to occupy the seat left vacant by his brother's death on the fields of Flanders more than four years previously. Some 100 rugby players were reckoned to have been among the 10,000 men of Somerset who had lost their lives in the First World War. One of the Bath junior sides, Widcombe, sacrificed a dozen of their team.

It is impossible to imagine the mix of emotions that attended the resumption of fixtures at Bath on 22 February 1919, when wounded soldiers gained free admission to the Recreation Ground for the visit of Bristol United. Of the Bath XV that won 8-3, only Harry Vowles and W.H. 'Billy' Royal remained from the team that had lost to Penarth on 25 April 1914.

Other familiar names such as Philip Hope, Alby Hatherill, Alfred Kitching, Fred Russell, Norman Coates, Cliff Walwin and the ageless Frank Cashnella returned to action over succeeding weeks against a variety of opposition, including the New Zealand Command Depot, the Auckland Battalion, Avonmouth Old Boys, Bristol University, the Australian Army Service Corps (the 'Kangaroos') and the Canadians as well as renewing Welsh acquaintances.

A return match against the New Zealand Command Depot featured a Bath debut for 17-year-old Eton schoolboy Isaac James (Jim) Pitman, also the Public Schools middleweight boxing champion. As talented a scholar as he was an athlete, Pitman, from Newbridge Hill, Weston, near Bath, was a descendant of shorthand system inventor Sir Isaac Pitman, to whom he was said to bear a remarkable resemblance. An Oxford Blue and an England cap beckoned.

An even more precocious talent appeared in the following game, a 42-0 rout against Burnham on 17 April. Stanley George Ulick Considine, born in India on 11 August 1901 – three days before Pitman – remains one of the most gifted individuals ever to have worn a Bath shirt. Considine, home from Blundell's school, Tiverton, also helped Bath beat Pontypool 8-3 on Easter Monday, meriting a brief but prescient end-of-season commendation:

Bath 1919/20. From left to right, back row: E.S. Cambridge, E.J. Hodges, L.J. Richardson, R.S. Chaddock, C.E. Carruthers, W.H. Sheppard, A.H.W. Taylor (chairman), H. Gregory, G. Wilkins, F.J. Cashnella, C. Whittaker, T. Hanney (trainer). Second row: H. Richardson, L.F. Burt, F. Russell, P.P. Hope (captain), W.H. Royal, A. Woodward, C. Lock. Front row: E.F. Simpkins (Honorary Secretary), L.V. Burt, H. Vowles, H.G. Walker, S.G.U. Considine, G.A. Roberts (Honorary Treasurer).

The Blundell School boy played two excellent games during Easter, and is no doubt a player of whom a lot will be heard.[1]

With Cliff Walwin making 'a most efficient referee', Considine made another promising showing for the Probables in the August trials on the Bristol Boys Home field, Lower Bristol Road, in preparation for a 1919/20 programme of 42 fixtures under the captaincy of Philip Hope. Among the absentees was one of the severe war-wounded, Ted Russell, brother of Fred, Bill, Tom and Jim.

Although Norman Coates was to throw in his lot with Leicester, the brief and glittering rugby career of his brother Vincent was one of many that had been ended by the war. He settled into the practice set up by his grandfather at Combe Down and was also Senior Physician to the Royal Mineral Water Hospital in Bath until his untimely death in a railway accident in 1934.

A fresh ten-year lease on the Recreation Ground was secured from 1919 but the price of a season ticket had gone up from 6s to 12s, with a consequent doubling of the capitation charge payable to the Recreation Ground Company. With 1s 6d also going to the Government in Entertainment Tax, the net increase in revenue to the club was only 3s 6d. With reluctance, the cost of a lady's season ticket also rose to 5s.

A PRELIMINARY LOOK ROUND
By 'AN OLD PLAYER.'
Since I penned my last 'Causerie' in the spring of 1914 the world has been devastated by the greatest war on record and many stalwarts of the Rugby world have laid down their lives for the sake of liberty. The same excellent characteristics which go to make the perfect footballer have proved also to make the perfect soldier. 'Playing the Game' has been our proud boast in the war, and thank Heaven, our victorious record was won by clean methods, well worthy of an Empire of true sportsmen.[2]

A huge crowd of between 8,000 and 9,000 crammed into Leicester's Welford Road ground on 6 September 1919 to see Bath win 16-3 with two tries from the skipper Hope and others from Fry and Cashnella, the latter ten days short of his fortieth birthday.

Another significant meeting was the resumption of fixtures with Bristol. Three sets of brothers – Richardson, Considine and Coles – lined up for Bath at Radnor Road, Horfield, on 4 October but Reg Pickles and Len Corbett were outstanding in a 9-0 home win. They also won the return match 16-3 on 29 November, although there were strongly-worded allegations of foul play against the home team in the *Bristol Times & Mirror* after Corbett suffered a badly twisted right knee in a tackle. The referee, Tommy Vile, of Newport, later came to Bath's defence

The Somerset Rugby Football Union had had to be reconstituted at the start of the season and Clarence Whittaker, Philip Hope, Harry Vowles, W.H. Royal, S.G.U. Considine and the ex-miner from Abertillery, J.D. Pope, did well enough in the county trial to be picked for the opening championship match against Cornwall.

Tragedy on the Recreation Ground, 27 December 1919.

After the anguish of the war years, people in Bath were able to enjoy their sport again. They were therefore totally unprepared for the saddest day in the club's history, the second fatality on the Recreation Ground following the death of Portsmouth's George Trerise in April 1900.

This time it was one of their own. Cliff Walwin, pharmacist in the local branch of Boots, was one of the most popular personalities in the club although no longer a first-team regular at full-back. He was not even originally selected for the home game against Cross Keys on Saturday, 27 December but, offered the chance of a game, made the fateful decision to stay in Bath rather than spend Christmas with relatives in Gloucester.

By all accounts it was a fair tackle, although a severe collision, and both Walwin and his opponent, George Greenslade, were clearly badly hurt; the Bath man had taken a blow in the kidneys and the Welsh miner was also laid out. Walwin was carried to the pavilion in great pain and from there to his home at Grosvenor where he was examined by Dr Lindsay, of No. 1, The Circus. *The Chronicle* takes up the story:

With fear of internal bleeding, he was taken to the Church Street Nursing Home where Mr. Forbes Fraser was called into consultation and an operation performed. Unfortunately after a brief revival, at 11pm his pulse weakened and he tragically died from the injury at 12.05 on Sunday 28th December 1919. Coroner Frederick Shum certified – 'Accidental death from shock + Collapse through internal injury whilst playing Football.'[3]

The New Year's Day fixture with Clifton was cancelled, as was the Exmouth match on the following Saturday along with the entire programme of rugby in the city. The funeral of this 'clean and manly sportsman' at Walcot Wesleyan church on the last day of the year drew a huge gathering of mourners from the family, Boots, Bath Pharmaceutical Association, Somerset Red Cross and other local organisations as well as reading like a 'who's who' of the region's rugby fraternity. At the graveside at Lansdown to hear the Last Post, were the following representatives of the Bath club: 'Capt. Vincent H. Coates MC, Messrs. A.H.W. Taylor, G.A. Roberts, C.C. Wills, J.T. Piper, E.F. Simpkins, F.J. Cashnella, W.T. Davis, A. Hatherill, A.J. Bennett, A. Ford, W. Cleall, G. Gray, H.W. Considine, S.G.U. Considine, C. Lock and E.S. Cambridge. Additionally, Bath Players – Messrs. E.J. Hodges, C.E. Carruthers, T. Fry, J. Fry, C. Tucker, S. Horwood, F.D. Stickler, J. Richardson, R. Richardson, F. Russell, L.V. Burt, W. Wilkins, H. Vowles, S. Vowles, F. Smith and T. Hanney (Trainer).'

Tributes were not confined to his friends, colleagues and team-mates in Bath, and they were all the warmer it seemed because he genuinely epitomised all that was admirable in the honest, committed amateur rugby player. Dai Gent wrote in *The Sunday Times*:

A more genuine sportsman never played for Bath or any other club. He was not quite a first class player but he was a first class sportsman, a man the club could always rely upon to turn out, even at the last minute, and every minute of the game he was heart and soul for his side. What admirable fellows these are; always at their club's disposal, consistently good in their play, and ever clean in their tactics. They are to be found in every club – its backbone, really. They do not get the plaudits of the crowd or Press, like the 'stars', but their worth is appreciated by the players, officials and all who understand the stuff of which the torch-bearers of the traditions of Rugby are made. Of such was Walwin.[4]

In addition to a contribution to the 'Clifford Walwin Fund' from the club of £150, a memorial match between a West of England XV and South Wales at the Rec on 18 March 1920 raised a further £200 9s 6d. Whittaker, Hope, Considine and L.J. Richardson were selected from Bath as the West won 13-8.

Bath won 21 of their 40 matches, losing 15 and drawing 4. The double was achieved over Leicester, one of whose tries was scored by ex-Bath skipper Norman Coates. The final game ended bizarrely when the London Welsh captain, Michael, led his team off the field having had a man sent off following warnings about foul play. Bath were leading 18-0.

If there was anything to celebrate after Walwin's death, however, it was the consistently outstanding form at fly-half of the teenager Considine. There was also some satisfaction that club accounts showed cash in hand, at the bank and invested, of £535 18s 11½d, providing the wherewithal to make improvements to spectator accommodation for the following season. The Management Committee eventually authorised £110 to be spent on stand construction, the repair of terracing and the purchase of 100 forms (seats) at 2s 6d each.

Bath 1920/21. From left to right, back row: R.S. Chaddick, Dr F.A. Meine, C.J. Whitaker, L.J. Richardson. Second row: Dyte, C.C. Wills (vice chairman), J.T. Piper (Honorary Secretary), H. Loader, W.H. Sheppard, A.H.W. Taylor (chairman), E.F. Simpkins (Honorary Secretary), C. Mannings, N.J. Blake, Geo Romans (Gloucestershire RFU). Third row: C. Curtis, H. Richardson, F.J. Russell, Dr W.H. Royal (vice captain), P.P. Hope (captain), H. Vowles, A. Woodward, I.F. Burt. Front row: F.J. Cashnella, L.V. Burt, J. Pope, A. Hatherill, A.E. Morgan, S.G.U. Considine, G.A. Roberts (Honorary Treasurer).

Some 2,000 who descended on the Rec on 28 August 1920 to watch the final trial were delighted to see Considine arrive ten minutes after the start, straight from a cricket match. He had made his first-class debut for Somerset in 1919 and was already making his mark as a batsman and a supremely athletic cover point.

At Leicester in the opening match of the season 'he jumped clean over the outstretched arms of Wilkinson' to score a try but missed most of the second half with concussion after a clash of heads with his team-mate, Royal. The East Midland side won 37-6, watched by a crowd of 8,000.

New 'Flowerpot' stands were in use for the first time for the visit of London Welsh, beaten 26-3. The following Saturday, 2 October, Bath made a splendid first impression at Swansea, losing 6-5 to the All Whites in front of 5,000 at St Helens. Considine was considered the best back on show and Vowles had his best game for some time, although Bath's second-half try went to Philip Hope, converted by Whittaker, after 'some delightful open football'. Cashnella, now 41, made a rare appearance and the travellers were so pleased with their collective showing that they sang all the way home.

Next up was United Services Portsmouth and the ultimate challenge for the fast-developing partnership of Vowles and Considine, a confrontation with the England half-backs, C.A. (Cecil) Kershaw and the legendary W.J.A. ('Dave') Davies. Davies had made his debut against South Africa before the war, his only experience of defeat in an England jersey, and was first paired with the submariner scrum-half in March 1919, for the Fleet against the Rest of the Navy. They began their England partnership in 1920 and retired together from representative rugby after the 1923 Grand Slam season. Kershaw was on the winning side 13 times in his 14 internationals, having to be content with a draw against the French in 1922.

With Vowles keeping a close watch on Kershaw, Bath won 9-0 thanks to two tries from Philip Hope.

The visit to Cross Keys on 13 November must have been a sombre one but there was heartening news of George Greenslade, who had turned out for the Second XV the previous weekend in his first match since the tragic tackle on Walwin. The miner's own injuries had necessitated months of convalescence. Unbeaten all season, Cross Keys saw off a gallant Bath challenge by 11-0.

A week later it was announced that Considine had been named as a reserve by England, but his County Clare surname had also alerted Ireland to his talents. As the son of Irish parents he was selected for the Possibles in the final Irish trial at Lansdowne Road on 29 January and scored a try after being moved to the Probables at half-time. But it was England that eventually won his allegiance, although recognition was some time in coming.

Poor Coventry copped it 33-0 on the Rec on 27 December as a powerful Bath line-up accommodated Norman Coates, home for Christmas, and ran in nine tries. Even more satisfying was their achievement just 24 hours later in taking Cross Keys' unbeaten record with tries by Fred Russell, Harry Vowles and L.V. (Victor) Burt. All were converted by Clarence Whittaker in a 15-4 win which also maintained Bath's unbeaten home record.

The pre-war custom of a visit to the pantomime was revived that winter and nearly 100 players, committee and ladies, not to mention opponents from Bridgwater, adjourned to the theatre for a lively performance of Aladdin in which Widow Twanky added the following verse to 'her' song:

It fills my heart with joy to see you Rugger boys tonight;
Good sportsmen all, who in each match do play the game a-right.
There's Considine and Captain Hope and 'Chumpy' to the fore;
And Dilly never dallies, but does his best to score.
So here's good luck to all the team in the new year begun,
And may they never lack success in Nineteen-Twenty-One.

This tradition echoed down the decades more than 70 years later when England and Lions prop Gareth Chilcott entranced his team-mates in the role of the villainous Broker's Man in *Cinderella* at the Theatre Royal over Christmas 1992.

There was more serious ceremonial for Philip Hope's team on 29 January when, before facing London Welsh, they gathered at the new Cenotaph in Whitehall to pay tribute to their team-mates who fell in the First World War. A 'handsome laurel chaplet' tied with the blue, white and black colours of the club was laid by Alby Hatherill, who had lost his brother Loo at Cambrai. The party dismounted from their charabanc, heads bared, and remained standing for a few minutes after the chaplet was laid, oblivious to the large number of people who had stopped to witness the little ceremony. Had they looked closely, they would have seen that on the chaplet was a card carrying a simple inscription:

In proud memory of those members of the Bath Rugby Football Club who laid down their lives in the Great War. They played the game – they crossed the line.

Other teams had also suffered and Bristol were especially thankful that the redoubtable Sam Tucker had recovered from wounds received on the Somme while serving with the Royal Engineers. Bath found the 24-year-old hooker a particular handful when they lost 10-4 at Bristol on 19 February although a semblance of honour was restored in a 3-3 home draw a month later.

A weakened Bath team lost 16-0 at Llanelly on 12 March, but the match launched one of the most enduring traditions in British club rugby. For the return match at the Rec three weeks later, the Scarlets brought a rag doll dressed in their colours and pinned it to the crossbar at the Johnston Street end of the ground. Things began none too promisingly for the home team when Whittaker gave away a converted try with a mis-kicked clearance but Bath responded with a spectacular three-quarter move to send Pitman over in the corner. Harry Richardson added another unconverted try before Vowles landed a beautiful drop goal to establish a 10-5 interval lead.

Harry Vowles' daughter, Mollie Hall, recalls that on this particular day her father was feeling considerably under the weather following the previous night's excesses – the current phrase would have been 'Harry's got the brewer!' At half-time his team-mates decided to shove him under a cold shower – and it had the desired effect.

Another four-pointer from the hung-over Vowles got Bath's tails up and Pitman shook off the Llanelly try-scorer Thomas to cross again. Then Considine broke through in the centre and, when faced by the full-back, punted ahead and picked the ball up on the bounce to score. After Vowles landed his third dropped goal to complete a 24-6 victory, he was carried off the field shoulder-high. Harry enjoyed another night of celebrations as the Rag Doll changed its livery!

Relations with the Somerset RFU, occasionally fractious, hit another low that April when Considine and H. (Bert) Loader opted to play for Bath against Weston-super-Mare rather than for the county XV against Middlesex. Eddie Simpkins, informed by the Somerset County Secretary that if they refused to play for the county, they must not play for Bath, fired off a telegram to Twickenham requesting clarification of the players status as 'free agents' in such circumstances. The correspondence went as follows:

Has county union power to suspend players who play for the club after declining place in county side? Reply urgently needed.

To this came the reply from the Honorary Secretary of the RFU, C.J.R. Marriott:

Cannot prevent such player playing for his club. Marriott.

Somerset officials were not going to take that lying down, however, and at their meeting at Taunton on 21 April passed a resolution charging the Bath club with a 'flagrant breach of their rules' in fielding Considine against Weston-super-Mare two weeks previously. On 31 May the matter came before the RFU Committee and, amid furious backtracking, they delivered a severe censure to the Bath club for both fielding a player contrary to Somerset's instructions and for sending a telegram to Twickenham without details of the circumstances and without advising the county union. Bath, having declined to affiliate with the county union for 1920/21 over the 'free agent' rule, now withdrew completely.

On a more constructive note, the Bath Supporters Club was inaugurated and it was decided also to re-establish the Combination structure, under the title of the Bath and District Rugby Combination, 'to promote and foster the game, having particular regard to the welfare of junior clubs'. In the same spirit, Walcot Rugby Football Club changed its name in the summer of 1921 to 'Walcot Old Boys RFC' to strengthen ties with Walcot Council School and, in the words of its chairman W.J. Sheppard, might consider 'going in for drawing, singing or literature, as well as games'.

At senior level, the annual meeting of the Bath club noted 'a marked improvement in play' from a season which saw 48 players utilised in 39 matches, of which 22 were won, 14 lost and three drawn. Philip Hope led by example as top scorer with 24 tries, followed by Considine with 18.

Further ground improvements were authorised and a tender of £457 16s 6d was accepted from Messrs E. Chancellor and Sons, of Lower Bristol Road, to extend the grandstand at both ends and to erect corrugated iron shelters on a series of 15 cantilevers in front of the current structure. The Recreation Ground Company made a contribution to the cost.

The atmosphere of expectation was more than matched by a 12,000 crowd at Welford Road for the now-traditional opener against Leicester, who won 16-3. After a 20-0 loosener at Teignmouth the following week Bath journeyed to Kingsholm where they had always come off second best. This time they earned a 9-9 draw, with Harry Vowles playing the game of his life and Considine scoring two tries, as the whole team produced a magnificent performance. It augured well for the 1921/22 season and, sure enough, they were unbeaten until a 16-5 defeat at Llanelly in mid-November.

Nearly 500 members of the new Bath and District Rugby Supporters Club made the trip to Newport on 3 December for the first meeting between the clubs, an indication of Bath's rising stature. The visitors lost 8-5 to a controversial penalty but the post-match convivialities organised by the Newport Supporters Club at the Westgate Hotel, with entertainment from the Alexandra Dock Male Voice Choir meant the upset of defeat was soon forgotten.

Considine was summoned to Bristol two weeks later as first reserve for England while I.J. Pitman was selected to represent the South of England. Pitman was awarded his Varsity Blue and it was as a member of the Oxford University club that he achieved his one and only England cap against Scotland later that season.

There was no denying the virtuoso talents of Considine, although international recognition would not come his way for another three years, but Philip Hope was one of the most influential figures in the club, both as a prolific try-scorer and as a captain. It was a sad day therefore when he followed his brother Archie's example by emigrating to North America. Hope, who had survived a hazardous existence as despatch rider in France, was presented with a Mauser sporting rifle, a silver salver and a framed picture of the 1921/22 team at a gathering at the Red House, the scene

Bath 1921/22. P.P. Hope was the captain.

of so many memorable rugby dinners. Happily, he returned three years later for a guest appearance.

Harry Vowles took over the captaincy for the last six weeks of the season and, after a successful tour to South Devon, the Easter programme was enlivened by the visit of Stade Bordelais. After Bath pledged a guarantee of £170, the match attracted 6,000 to the Rec to see Bath win 11-3 before Leicester were overcome 8-0 some 24 hours later and Bristol (6-3) succumbed on the Saturday following. The season's record was even more impressive – 25 victories, 6 draws and 9 defeats – and Considine finished top scorer with 66 points, including 20 tries.

The wrangle with Somerset rumbled on into the 1922/23 season, Bath still refusing to affiliate, yet the club supplied players for the county XV. Ironically, they carried all before them in winning the County Championship for the first time and there were seven players from Bath in the team that conquered Leicestershire on 14 April.

Somerset: W.F. Gaisford (St Bartholomew's Hospital); F.A. Meine (Bath), J. Jarvis (Bridgwater) (Captain), E.G. Hammett (Blackheath), and A.E. Thomson (United Services); S.G.U. Considine (Bath) and H. Vowles (Bath), A.L. Spriggs (Bridgwater), F. Spriggs (Bridgwater), P. Lewis (Bridgwater), J. Reed (Bridgwater), L.J. Richardson (Bath), C.N. Mannings (Bath), W.H. Sheppard (Bath), and L.W. Bisgrove (Bath).

Bath's first full season under Harry Vowles saw 45 fixtures fulfilled, with 25 games won, 16 lost and 3 drawn. An early highlight was an 18-0 win over Aberavon on 8

October in which Pitman sprinted away for two magnificent long-range tries but, on returning to Oxford later in the month, the new England cap suffered a compound fracture of the leg against Leicester.

His Bath team-mates captured Cross Keys' unbeaten record by 4-3 in December and achieved a first-ever victory over Gloucester. That 9-6 win on 27 December not only preserved Bath's unbeaten home record but also earned them the distinction of being the first English side to beat the Cherry and Whites that season. The most formidable team in the land were Newport, who remained unbeaten all season, with 35 wins and 4 draws. Bath held them to a single dropped goal at the Recreation Ground on 10 February.

Spectators had not only benefited from an extension to the 'Flowerpots' and other ground improvements but, from the United Services match on 23 September 1922, an official match day programme (price 2d) had been produced and circulated at each home game by the supporters club. For 1923/24, responsibility for the match programme was assumed by the committee of the Club.

The season had hardly begun when the Club was cast into mourning by the death of long-serving Honorary Treasurer George A. Roberts. As a mark of respect, the players wore black armbands for the visit of Aberavon on 8 September.

Bath 1922/23. From left to right, back row: W.T. Davis (touch judge), F.J. Cashnella (committee), L.J. Richardson, L.W. Bisgrove, W.H. Sheppard, J. Dobson, C.C. Wills (vice chairman), R.S. Chaddock, J.T. Piper (Honorary Secretary), C.E. Carruthers, C. Mannings, E.F. Simpkins (Honorary Secretary), A. Hatherill (trainer). Middle row: H.J. Comm, H. Richardson, G. Woodward, H. Vowles (captain), Dr F.A. Meine, W.J. Gibbs, G.A. Roberts (Honorary Treasurer). Front row: L.V. Burt, S.G.U. Considine.

With Vowles retaining the captaincy, Bath experienced mixed fortunes before stringing together an impressive run of ten victories, culminating in a 12-5 victory over Gloucester on 27 December. But the rest of the campaign brought only five more wins, leaving the team with a record of 18 matches won, 18 lost and four drawn.

Considine finished with just eight tries, including a remarkable effort against United Services when he 'jumped' the full-back, allegedly crossing the line five feet off the ground. His involvement had been restricted by law exams and illness, however, while the skipper had also missed the early weeks of the season after a collision in training resulted in the loss of several teeth.

The spat with Somerset appeared to have been resolved by an extraordinary general meeting of the club at the Red House on 16 November 1923 when a resolution to affiliate to the county union was passed by 129 votes to 73 in a card ballot. By the New Year, it was reported in the *Chronicle* that Somerset had voted to readmit the Bath club.

Meanwhile Club officials approved plans for what was called the New Pavilion on the northern end of the pitch, with provision for the stand to accommodate almost 1,000 spectators above the changing room area.

We the sub-committee have decided unanimously to continue negotiations with the Rec. Gd. Co. with a view to the early erection of the suggested pavilion, providing bathing accommodation and stand on the North bank and the sub committee suggest that an amount of £1000 be provided by the Club to facilitate the erection of the structure and that in return, a lease of at least 21 years at the expiration of the present lease be granted the Bath F.C.[5]

Working just as hard to keep pace with the modern world, The Recreation Ground Company had already made arrangements for an officer of the Royal Automobile Club 'to be present at all home matches to organise the parking of motor cars'. Both parties' efforts to bring facilities up to the highest standards were recognised later that year by the RFU's decision to hold an England *v.* The Rest trial at the Rec.

In a bizarre footnote to the season, the Management Committee discussed on 13 May a suggestion that they hold a 'Smoking Concert' in aid of the Mayor's Fresh Air Fund!

Bert Comm, who had made his Bath debut back in March 1921 as a product of the St Stephen's junior club, had been virtually ever-present at full-back since the retirement of Clarence Whittaker. In the final game of the 1923/24 season he kicked five conversions in a 28-3 thrashing of Leicester, so it was a considerable blow to preparations for the following season when he announced he was turning professional with Oldham Northern Union Club. There was no hint of recrimination, however, in the comments of 'Mascot' in the *Chronicle*:

Bath team that faced Bristol on 20 January 1923. From left to right, back row: Tommy Davis (touch judge), Reg Richardson, R.S. (Dick) Chaddock, Charles Carruthers, Charlie Mannings, Charlie Curtis (St John's Ambulance), Joe Blake, W.H. (Bill) Sheppard, Len Bisgrove. Middle row: Harry Richardson, George Woodward, Harry Vowles, A.E. Morgan, Jim Russell. Front row: Bert Comm, S.G. Ulick Considine, Len Burt.

Before facing Aberavon on 8 September 1923, players can be seen wearing black armbands after the death of long-serving treasurer, George A. Roberts. Note: the team changed in the cricket pavilion.

THE BATH HERALD, MONDAY, JANUARY 7, 1924.

MOTOR PARK FOR RUGBY MATCHES — GUARDIANS' FIRST CHURCH PARADE — THE MAYOR AT OLDFIELD PARK BAPTIST CHURCH.

Car parking.

Had he been able to secure a better situation in Bath, there is little doubt he would have remained in the city, and no one can blame him for seizing the opportunity of improving his position in life when it came his way.[6]

With Ulick Considine taking over as captain and choosing to play mainly in the three-quarter line, Bath made a slightly hesitant start – two defeats and a draw – before defeating Gloucester 16-7, with the skipper and the young Harry Slade in outstanding form. Perhaps they had been inspired by the visit only a few days previously of Cliff Porter's All Blacks, entertained to lunch by the Bath Committee in the presence of the Mayor and Mayoress? Destined to enter legend as 'The Invincibles', although they did not play Scotland, they became the first New Zealand team to tour the British Isles without losing or drawing a game. Somerset's XV to face the tourists included Considine, Dick Chaddock H.B.L. Wake, Len Bisgrove, Bill Gibbs and Tom Rose. A depleted Bath side went down 3-32 to a strong United Services outfit the same afternoon.

As the All Blacks continued on their all-conquering tour, Bath slipped up 11-0 at Plymouth, hampered by the loss of Considine with a muscle strain and Chaddock, who stayed on the field but was a virtual passenger because of a shoulder injury. They had already 'lost' another member of the party during the outward journey when Alby Hatherill, now the team's trainer, was left behind at Exeter.

He emerged from the restaurant room with a cup of tea in his hand; he made a dash for the open carriage door, but a rather officious porter slammed it closed – just as poor Alby was about to launch himself into the air.[7]

As Bath played Old Edwardians to embark on a run of seven successive wins, the spectators included several students from the new Prior Park College 'who intend to take up Rugger seriously in the near future'. It was another thirty years before the school produced its first international in an Irishman, J. Murphy-O'Connor, brother of the current Catholic Cardinal. The most famous international 'old boys', both capped from the Bath club, were to be John Palmer (England 1984) and Damian Cronin (Scotland 1988).

After a handsome 20-6 win at home to Pontypool, some 1,000 Bath supporters travelled to Bristol on 6 December with high hopes of an away victory in a derby match for the first time since before the war, partly because the home side were without four players on duty at the international trial. Bath did not disappoint, winning 11-7 with tries from Considine and Vowles, dribbling half the length of the pitch. The performance of a young lad from Larkhall, Ralph Banks, partnering Harry Richardson in the centre, held out particular promise while Considine was again magnificent, as predicted by the Bristol match programme:

Young Considine takes the Bath Bun. He starts like a shot from a gun.
His manner elusive
Is very conducive
To scoring. Just watch how it's done!

Considine was named as reserve for the final trial on 20 December and therefore missed the fixture against Mr Freethy's XV on the Rec, although the match did mark the return of Jim Pitman for his first game since breaking a leg two years previously. Albert Freethy, a Neath schoolteacher and a distinguished referee, made rugby history two weeks later by ordering the All Black lock Cyril Brownlie off the field in a stormy opening to the international at Twickenham. It was the first dismissal of a player in a Test match.

Christmas Eve 1924 marked Bath's first visit to Cardiff. The scoreline read 22-6 to the home side but for all who were there it imprinted itself in the memory as a virtuoso display from Considine on the left wing. The Cardiff press abandoned any parochial sentiments to declare:

By far the most outstanding man of the day was S.G.U. Considine, whose dashes on the left wing were things of joy. He was a constant thorn in the Cardiff side, and his try was one of the best seen on the Cardiff Arms Park for many a day.[8]

Which one, exactly? His first-half effort involved beating half a dozen opponents and being pulled down three times before he eventually reached the line; after the break, he intercepted a pass near his own line, dodged the Cardiff full-back Collins and raced to the other end of the field to touch down, applauded loudly and generously by the home crowd.

How long could this talent by ignored by the England selectors? In fact, they resisted his claims until the very last match of the 1925 championship season in Paris on Easter Monday 13 April, when he was picked on the left wing. At 23 years old, he was at the height of his powers, which made the outcome all the more tragic for Considine and the Bath club.

England were leading 13-0 when the Bath man suffered the kind of knee injury that these days could no doubt be successfully treated by reconstructive surgery, intensive rehabilitation and expert physiotherapy. For Considine, who recklessly returned to the field of play rather than go to hospital, it brought a savagely sudden end to a glittering career. At first, as he indicated to the *Bath Herald*, it appeared that it would be a temporary, if lengthy, absence.

His injury occurred in the second half. He cut inwards and then dodged back to avoid opponents, when his knee suddenly gave way, and he fell helpless. After he returned to the field, although he could hardly limp about, he was rather lucky to stop what might have been a score for France. The two centres had the ball at their toes when he fell forward, and his head striking the ball, averted the danger.[9]

S.G.U. Considine, capped by England in 1925.

When 6,000 crammed into the Rec on the following Saturday afternoon for the Bristol derby, Considine appeared on crutches and was given a huge ovation. Without their talisman, Bath lost 5-3 and were also trounced 40-5 in the final game at Aberavon, leaving him with a playing record as captain of 22 wins from 37 matches, 13 of which were lost and two drawn.

It fell to Arnold Ridley, sometime Bath team secretary and later president of the club but also an accomplished playwright who later became even more famous as Private Godfrey in the *Dad's Army* series, to pen Considine's obituary after his death in Bath on 31 August 1950. The tribute is worth printing in full because it tells us as much, if not more, about Considine than mere match statistics:

To many of us, especially those connected with rugby football and cricket between the wars, the idea of Ulick Considine being dead seems unbelievable and absurd. So often did we share or witness his triumphs that it did not appear possible that he must fall to the inevitable and final tackle. Perhaps this idea has persisted in our minds even during these past months when we have been only too aware of his failing health. But the final whistle has blown; the umpires have pulled up the stumps.

The late Hugh Walpole once wrote that genius could be applied to the playing of games every bit as much as to the writing of books, the painting of pictures or composition of music. He could have had no better illustration of this than in Considine. He was a genius indeed. There are many (not only in Bath and England) who share my view that he was one of the greatest individual players of rugby football of all time. As a team player maybe, he was not quite so outstanding.

Genius is built upon individuality and Ulick Considine was an individual. This does not mean that he was a selfish player or did not fit into club life. Nothing could possibly be further from the truth. It means that the audacity of his play, the instantaneous nature of his reactions, made him a 'match winner' all on his own.

There were those who said it was nearly as difficult to play with him as against him. There were times when unconsciously he could fool his own side just as successfully as he fooled the opposition.

This probably was a reason why his selection for England was delayed until he changed his position from half-back (the connecting link between the forwards and backs) to that of wing-three quarter. Another reason lay in the fact that at the time of his greatness, England's outside half position was so firmly held by W.A.J. Davies. Davies was a far more conventional player: more than that, the ideal captain and a difficult man to displace. But it was 'Consi's' boast, the only one I ever heard him make, that when playing against Davies, either in a club game, county match or international trial, he was never on the losing side!.

Naturally he was a great favourite with the spectators. Who present at that memorable Christmas Eve match between Cardiff and Bath can forget those two second half tries which bought the Welsh crowd cheering to their feet?

Ulick Considines's cricket, good as it was, was somewhat effaced by his rugger. But he was a fluent and forcing bat – who will forget that 'wristy' shot that sent the ball flashing past backward point to the boundary? And a steady County one. At cover point he had few equals. Jack Hobbs describes his as one of the greatest. His seeming nonchalance was a trap to many a batsman who dared push the ball away to the off for an easy single.

The disaster that befell him in his first international was a tragedy not only for himself, but for Bath, Somerset and England. His courage proved his undoing. After a severe knee injury, he remained on the touchline instead of going to hospital and when England's 13-point lead had been reduced to 2, he returned to help his side.

According to Wakefield, it was 'Consi' who saved the game for England in the closing seconds by falling on the ball to stem a French rush. Even then, he made light of his injury and several days elapsed before he saw a specialist. By then the damage was done, his rugger career was ended and although he appeared for Bath and Somerset at cricket for some seasons afterwards, the 'quickness of foot' which was the inspiration of his play, was missing.

Off the field Ulick Considine was sometimes considered a 'queer bird'. Even his friends did not find him easy to approach. He was inclined to be taciturn and sometimes a little intolerant. His brusqueness of manner sometimes caused him to be misunderstood and he lacked tact in his outspoken comments.

But against these small defects can be placed two of the greatest attributes of human character. He was a man of the highest possible integrity, incapable of a mean thought or action, and his loyalty towards his friends was unshakeable. Woe betide the person who was guilty of malicious gossip in his presence. The flashing eye, the angry twirl of the moustache and the gruff 'I wouldn't say that!' was only a mild indication of what was to come!

As a sportsman (in the true meaning of the word), citizen and friend, Ulick Considine had few equals.

Arnold Ridley

While his rugby career was over, Considine continued with Somerset County Cricket Club until 1935, by which time he had amassed 3,000 runs at an average of 21.33. His only century had been an unbeaten 130 against Worcestershire at Taunton in 1921. Articled as a solicitor to former Bath player W.F. Long, Considine rose to the rank of Squadron Leader in the RAF during the Second World War but was afflicted by ill health in the years afterwards.

Selection committee, 1925. From left to right, back row: A.I. Ford, F.J. Cashnella, G. Parfitt. Front row: E.H. Davies, E.F. Simpkins, C.C. Wills, W.T. Davis.

-10-

Diamond Jubilee

WHEN PLAYERS PAST and present, dignitaries and guests gathered at the Red House, New Bond Street, for a gala dinner to celebrate sixty years of the Bath club on Thursday, 15 October 1925, there was one conspicuous absentee.

Walter Sants, a founder member of the club and later Honorary Secretary (1868-82) and Treasurer (1899-1901), would have occupied pride of place as one of those pioneering spirits, resplendent in their dark blue jerseys and red caps, who had embraced the new game of rugby football in 1865.

His death just 19 days previously, on the morning of a home match against Devonport Services, robbed this grand occasion of a living link to the men who had been responsible for the birth of a great club. Sants himself was still playing in the three-quarters until 1883.

A few remained from that era, notably Herbert Perry, whose playing career also had begun in the 1860s and 'still hale and hearty', occupied his favoured seat in the front row of the stand at every home match.

The dinner had been preceded that afternoon by a Diamond Jubilee match against South Western Counties. Declared an 'All Pay' fixture, 'with reserved seats to be had at 3/-'. The new North Stand was not quite ready but still able to accommodate some of the 5,000 spectators who packed into the Recreation Ground.

With luminaries such as Reg Pickles and Sam Tucker, from Bristol, and Tom Voyce, from Gloucester, turning out in opposition, the Invitation XV was always going to be too strong for the home side. It was a brave rearguard effort nonetheless as Bath went down 3-19, the South Western Counties scoring two goals and three tries. Len Corbett, from Bristol, and the unfortunate Ulick Considine were the respective touch-judges while the teams lined up as follows:

Bath: H.G. Slade, W.J. Gibbs, R. Banks, S. Watts, J. Armour, F. Rhymes, J.W. Colquhoun, H.B.L. Wake, L.J. Richardson, R.S. Chaddock, C.E. Carruthers, C.N. Mannings, J. Dobson, G. Woodward, A. Morley.

South Western Counties: W.F. Gaisford (Bart's Hospital and Somerset), H. Smith (Barnstaple and Devon), J. Hanley (Plymouth and Devon), Reg Pickles (Bristol and

Gloucestershire), S. Jago (Plymouth and Cornwall), C. Carter (Bristol and Gloucestershire), Dr Taylor (Gloucester and North), T. Voyce (Gloucestershire and England) (Captain), J.S. Tucker (Bristol, Gloucestershire and England), M. Shaw (Bristol and Gloucestershire), A. Spriggs (Bridgwater and Somerset), C. Gummer (Plymouth and Devon), W. Roscolla (Cornwall), E. Stanbury (Plymouth and Devon), and H. Rew (Exeter and Devon).

Referee T.H. Vile (Wales).

Expressing himself in language and sentiment so alien to the modern day, W.S. Donne, past president of the RFU and current president of Somerset, proposed a toast to 'The Bath Football Club', commiserating with them on their poor record to date (seven straight defeats):

It was true that they had yet to win a match this season, but what did it matter? [applause]. They did not play rugby football to get a great record – they played Rugby for the great game that it was [applause] and if they were having a bad innings just at present moment, they had got to remember there was a future, and he was quite certain that their record in the immediate future would equal those of some of their best records in the past [applause]. Many old players would agree with him, Mr Donne continued, that some of their very best and most enjoyable games had been those that they had lost, and so long as they kept that spirit in the game, so long would Rugby be the game it was – the greatest of all British games [applause]. He would yield to no one when he said that rugby football was the best and brightest that a Britisher could play; it was the one game in which a man played for his side and not for himself [applause]. Whether they won or lost, so long as they played the game, so long would rugby football be prominent in the minds of British sportsmen [applause].

On his left was Frank Soane, who was received with cheers and regaled the gathering with memories of his first game for Bath all of 45 years earlier. On a more serious note, the old international urged the club to rely more upon their own young players, and not go 'skying' round the country for others. That was an opinion shared by Len Corbett, of Bristol, who said they should look to Bath for their players and, even if there was a lean season or two, they could soon get a team second to none in the country. Tom Voyce, the rugged Gloucester forward who was to win the last of 26 caps for England later that season, averred that he 'had played rugby ever since he could walk and hoped to play it until he was unable to walk! [Applause] Rugby was the most wonderful game in the world. The spectators might say it was rough, but the players enjoyed it.'

Two days later, Bath won their first game of the season, 6-0 against St Thomas Hospital, but it was a poor display – described by one follower of 30 years as the worst exhibition he had ever seen the club give. Considine's enforced retirement to sit on the selection committee had undoubtedly cast a pall over the squad and county forward Len Bisgrove had also left to join Weston-super-Mare, having secured a teaching post in the town.

An improvement in form came too late to bolster Bath's meagre representation in the Somerset XV to face Cornwall, Bill Gibbs being joined by H.V. Wake, Tom Rose and Harry Richardson. A trip to Pontypool ended in a 9-8 defeat but it was considered a fine effort and that was despite the fact that Milsom, from Radstock, had left his kit in the charabanc, forcing him to play in uncomfortable borrowed boots. Harry Vowles and Ralph Banks had particularly good games against strong opposition and Harry Slade performed well at full-back. *The Chronicle*, however, observed gravely:

It will probably be Bath's last visit to Pontypool for some seasons. After all there is practically little pleasure in visiting such a place, and especially now when Pontypool are not playing the kind of football which will attract good opponents.[1]

This was a touch ungracious considering that Pontypool had lent a player, Daniel, to the Bath side after L. Seal had failed to turn up!

The new North Stand, completed in time for the England trial on 19 December, was 86ft long by 24ft deep and provided cover for 800 spectators. Underneath were dressing

Bath 1926/27. From left to right, back row: R.F. Farnham (committee), J.T. Piper (Honorary Secretary), F.J. Cashnella (committee), W.S. Bascombe (committee), G. Gray (committee), H. Bowen (vice chairman). Third row: C. Curtis, A.I. Ford (committee), A.N. Goold, L.M. Basden, S. Weekes, P.R. Skinner, N. Matthews, E. Dunscombe, H. Burgess, A. Milsom, W. Usher, W.T. Davis (committee), G. Burden (committee). Second row, sitting: H.W. Vanston (Honorary Treasurer), J.B. Hannah, A.E. Anderson, H.B.L. Wake, W.J. Gibbs (captain), I.J. Pitman, K. Holmes, R.I. Collett, E.F. Simpkins (Honorary Secretary), C.C. Wills (chairman). Front row: W. Hancock, A.J. Tomlinson, R. Banks, D. James.

rooms for teams and referee, six baths, four hot and cold sprays and lavatories as well as a secretary's office and a committee room. Installed the following spring on the front of the stand was a clock, commissioned from Messrs Mallory to commemorate the unique contribution of George Roberts as Honorary Treasurer from the turn of the century until his death in August 1923.

The Pavilion Clock and this Photograph perpetuate the memory of the late Mr G.A. Roberts, for upwards of 20 years the indefatigable Hon. Treas. of the Bath Football Club. Erected by Members of the Club as a token of the esteem and gratitude for ungrudging services – 1926

With forecasts for a sharp frost on day of the trial the Bath club hurriedly arranged for 20 tons of straw to be supplied and laid the day before by Messrs Tucker and Sons, of Broad Quay, Bristol. They began removing it again as early as 5 a.m. and the ground was cleared, rolled and ready well in time for the match.

Bath players acted as stewards, facilities were provided for 40 members of the Press and special arrangements were made for parking in Henrietta Street, Bathwick Street and Pulteney Road. With seated stands erected on the Popular side, the Recreation Ground was thought to be able to accommodate up to 10,000 and 'by one o'clock, as the Abbey chimes were playing "Tom Bowling", perhaps the greater part of a thousand spectators had gained their points of advantage'. It was estimated that 7,500 watched the Possibles beat the Probables 22-14, giving the selectors pause for thought during their deliberations at the Pulteney Hotel that evening.

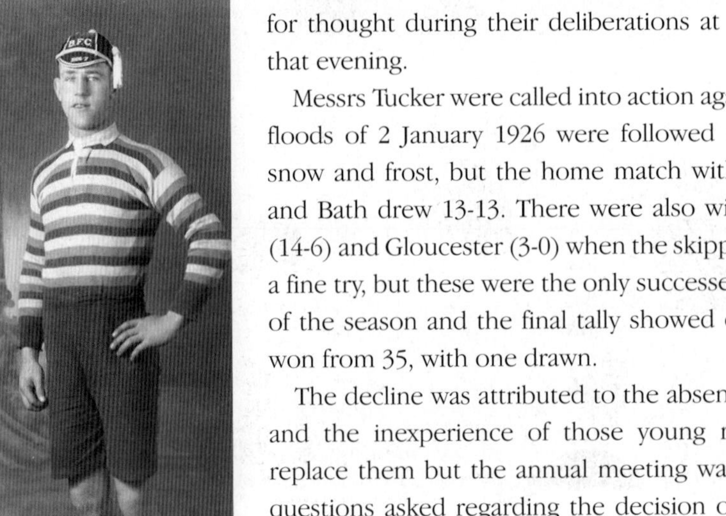

A.S. 'Shammer' Weeks during the 1926/27 season.

Messrs Tucker were called into action again when the severe floods of 2 January 1926 were followed two weeks later by snow and frost, but the home match with Cardiff was saved and Bath drew 13-13. There were also wins over Cross Keys (14-6) and Gloucester (3-0) when the skipper Bill Gibbs scored a fine try, but these were the only successes in the second half of the season and the final tally showed only seven matches won from 35, with one drawn.

The decline was attributed to the absence of senior players and the inexperience of those young men brought in to replace them but the annual meeting was a lively affair with questions asked regarding the decision of the committee to commit £1,000 of club funds to building of the North Stand without consulting the membership.

Bill Gibbs, entrusted with the captaincy for a second season, was relying on experienced performers like George Nudds.

The Bystander, February 15, 1928

Leading Rugger Clubs

BY MAC

No. 15.—BATH

Bath Rugby Football Club always produce a strong side, and they prove very pleasant opponents. Pitman, the captain of the "Red Sox Brigade," is the well-known Oxford and England threequarter

Pitman's Press.

However, the 1926/27 campaign began badly for Nudds when he suffered a facial injury working at Stothert & Pitt during August and was then incapacitated by a kick in the opening game, a 14-0 defeat at Leicester. He was eventually rewarded for a succession of fine performances with a call up for Somerset.

With Nudds and three others on duty for Somerset, a long injury list and Harry Slade on a boat to Bermuda, finding a XV to travel to Plymouth on 16 October was more than usually difficult. Eventually, at 10 p.m. on the Friday night the call went out to a 17-year-old wing, Bill Hancock, who had represented Weymouth House School at rugby, soccer, running and swimming. He had to go to his employer next morning and ask permission to travel with the team but made an instant impression by running half the length of the field for a debut try and then laying on another for his captain in an 11-9 victory.

There was a more notable triumph a fortnight later when Newport were defeated 8-6 at the Rec. With I.J. Pitman providing a cutting edge in the centre, Nudds touched down under the posts to open the scoring while the second half opened with a forward rush carried on by one of the most improved players, Norman Matthews, and finished off by W. Usher for A.S. Weeks to convert.

At the Remembrance ceremony at the gates of Bristol's Memorial Ground on 13 November 1926 Bill Gibbs laid a tribute reading: 'In grateful remembrance of those gallant members of the Bristol Rugby FC from their friends, the Bath Football Club.' On a sombre, wet day Bristol won 8-0.

Llanelly, the only Welsh side to beat the touring Maoris, captured Bath's unbeaten ground record the following week by winning 6-0, and a 6-3 half-time lead was surrendered against Gloucester who won 13-6 at the Rec on 28 December. A scheduled visit to Cross Keys on 18 March was cancelled by the Bath committee at 48 hours notice, in view of 'the prevalence of smallpox in that district'.

With easier opposition from the New Year and notwithstanding another defeat by Bristol (15-3), performances picked up and by the end of the campaign Gibbs was able to show a much-improved record of 21 victories from 35 matches with one draw. Among the successes was forward Arthur 'Shammer' Weeks, who played in 14 matches, converting six tries, but when the Bristol Harmonic Male Voice Choir was hired for three guineas to perform at the derby match on 26 March, they seemed to inspire Bristol, who won 15-3.

Again, the perennially edgy relationship with Somerset erupted over the infamous Rule 18, preventing players turning out for the club if they declined to appear for the county, reviving memories of the 'Considine affair'. This time it was employed against another ex-England cap, Pitman, prompting the Bath club to resign again from Somerset RFU.

Amid general condemnation of the county's stance, *The Times* of London thundered to Pitman's defence (4 December 1926) and Oxford University, supported by their

Cambridge counterparts, were reported to be preparing a motion to the RFU outlawing any rule by a county preventing a player operating as a free agent. Bath described it as 'a blot on the amateur game' and the question of re-affiliating was not raised for another 12 months.

Meanwhile, 47-year-old Frank Cashnella turned out for the 'A' XV against Swindon in April, giving a creditable performance and maintaining his record of managing at least one game a season since 1898. 'Cash is a wonder, and no mistake about it.' Five months later he was mourning the death of George Ruddick, his captain from 1900-02.

Pitman took over as skipper for 1927/28, maintaining a respectable record of 22 victories and three draws from 35 fixtures despite heavy defeats at Leicester (33-0), Llanelly (37-8) and at home to Bristol (32-0). Hancock, the new star, scored two tries on his debut for Somerset in March and joined Pitman on the scoresheet as the club rounded off the season with a long-awaited win over Gloucester (10-8).

A departure from normal routine involved participation in the Bristol Sevens early in the season, with instruction kindly provided at the YMCA Hall beforehand by the innovative W.W. Wakefield, of Harlequins, the most mobile forward of his day. Bath lost 8-3 to Bristol, leading 'Mascot' of the *Chronicle* to comment:

I don't think these tournaments will catch on to a great extent, although I see no reason why we should not have one here among the Junior clubs at the end of the season. It's a good game, but the element of luck is too strong, there being no time to retrieve a bad start. Make one bloomer, as it were, and it's all over.[2]

A return match was arranged for 17 April, however, and Bath claimed the Arnold Ridley Cup by winning 9-8. Ridley, who had been severely wounded in the fighting on the Somme, was one of many young men from Bath who had been invalided out of the Army during the First World War. (Interestingly, as devotees of *Dad's Army* will recall, one episode of the timeless BBC comedy series had the gentle, bumbling Private Godfrey revealed as a hero of the Great War.) After embarking on an acting career in 1918 his war injuries forced Ridley to return to work at his father's boot shop in Bath. He then turned his hand to writing plays and, inspired by several hours' wait at a lonely West Country station, he wrote his highly successful mystery thriller, *The Ghost Train*, in 1923.

A devoted follower of the club, he had entertained a 25-strong Bath party at the New Theatre, where his new play, *The Wrecker*, was touring. It told the tale of a train wrecker who waged a deadly duel with an England rugby captain; Cashnella, ever the entertainer, amused them all backstage by playing with the props, in particular the signal levers.

Ridley had been voted on to the committee by 27 July 1928 when Cashnella was elected as chairman. They also had to consider a number of edicts from the RFU, including a reminder to clubs not to permit dog racing around their pitches. More seriously:

Bath, 1929/30. From left to right, back row: W.H. Sheppard, E.F. Simpkins (Honorary Secretary), G. Gray. Middle row: C. Curtis, P. Moon, H. Burgess, R.G. Sampson, E.G. Haydon, S. Weeks, M.V. Shaw, P.R. Skinner, J. Cutting. Front row: L.D. Wardle, L. St V. Powell, N.W. Matthews (vice captain), I.F.M. Spence (captain), L.T. Seal, J.B. Hannah, W.E. Hancock. Front row: R. Banks, F. Rhymes.

A fatal accident having occurred through players of two teams forming down some distance apart, and then rushing forward to form a scrummage, the attention of referees has been drawn to the definition of a scrummage, and they have been requested to stop the dangerous practice referred to.[3]

A more pressing matter for the Bath committee, it seems, was the need to prevent people watching games from the North Parade Bridge – dubbed 'The Scotsmen's Gallery'. The solution, as proposed to the Town Clerk by Cashnella, was to be a canvas screen.

The Corporation was not always so obliging to the rugby club and at the end of October refused the supporters' club use of the Guildhall for Saturday dances amid concern over their tendency to celebrate in a 'robust' fashion.

There was not so much to celebrate during 1928/29 under the captaincy of W.H. (Bill) Sheppard. Bath lost 22 of their 41 games in 1928/29 although, with Considine as Honorary Coach, they did famously achieve their potential against Cardiff on 17 November with a 10-3 victory, scoring tries through A. Milson and Hancock.

Bristol again achieved the double over their neighbours, attracting a crowd of 11,000 to the Memorial Ground for the first encounter. Hooker Norman Matthews was absent, the former Avonvale player having been called up for his first England trial, just reward for a series of quality displays for his club and county.

The final 15-a-side match on the Rec that season saw the 'A' team draw 3-3 against an Old Crocks XV led by S.G.U. Considine, who 'had a bit of a game with the opposition, handing off and eluding in something like his old style'.

In his 50th year, Cashnella was perhaps too much of an antique to be risked in that game and at the annual general meeting in July he was made a Life Member of the club 'for his services to rugby football in this city and to this club in particular,' in the words of Arnold Ridley's proposal. Apart from being a first-team regular for 24 years to 1922 and not missing a game, home or away, for six of those seasons, he had attended some 800 committee meetings and had been co-founder of the Bath Schools Union in 1905.

Within three months he had resigned from the club he loved so much, the split being sparked by a half-time spat with the new captain, I.F.M. (Ian) Spence, during a home match against Cardiff when Cashnella insisted, as a member of the selection committee, that he get Lester and Banks to switch positions. While unanimously upholding the skipper's authority the committee asked Cashnella to withdraw his letter in which he adhered to his decision to resign 'unless some arrangements are made whereby the Selection Committee shall be in a position to proffer advice to the captain, when it is obvious, as in the Cardiff match, that the team is not doing well'.

Seven days later, the committee met again and there was no evidence of Cashnella relenting:

Mr. Considine read a letter from Mr. Cashnella, and proposed: 'That as he has not withdrawn his resignation we must accept it.' This was carried. Committee then

The Press Box, 1930.

agreed to write to Mr Cashnella, thanking him for his great services and expressing regret that he had taken the step he had. The Committee was more than sorry that they had no other course but to accept his decision. Consideration of a replacement was held over until the following week.[4]

Intriguingly, it was a dispute at Bristol which was to have rather more impact on Bath's fortunes. The back row forward Mervyn Shaw had been re-elected captain by the players for the 1929/30 season, only for their wishes to be overridden by the members, who chose Sam Tucker. Shaw resigned and applied to join Bath, followed by his vice captain E.L. 'Barty' Stinchcombe.

The first derby match on 23 November was therefore as eagerly awaited as any and some 1,200 Bath supporters travelled by rail excursion alone. A number of the Bristol players went up to Mervyn Shaw before kick-off to shake his hand and, reassuringly, he enjoyed just as sporting a reception from the crowd of 8,000. After the war he was to return to Bristol as committeeman and selector.

Bristol's heavier forwards ensured plenty of possession but they were outshone behind the scrum and Bath's right wing J.B. Hannah eventually scored from a kick-ahead after a smart interception by centre Louis St Vincent Powell. It was not until two minutes from time that Lillicrap touched down to bring the sides level but, with the last move of the game, Powell fed Hancock who 'raced away, jumped clean over Watts, the full-back, and scored amid tumultuous cheering' to secure a 6-3 win.

Back home on the Rec, flooding was a perennial problem, and 48 hours before the home fixture against Richmond on 14 December the ground at the Pulteney Street end was under three feet of water. Even on the morning of the match water was still edging up to the 25-yard line but by kick-off it had subsided, leaving the pitch in remarkably good condition after being flooded for three weeks! Bath won 19-0.

After draws home and away with Gloucester, a courageous 9-8 defeat at Swansea and the first win over Llanelly in 15 attempts, there was huge anticipation of the return match with Bristol on 22 March 1930 and the prospect of the first 'double' over their neighbours since 1888.

Reports varied on the size of the crowd – between 8,000 and 10,000 – although it was judged to be the biggest ever seen on the Rec, with a 200-yard queue at the Riverside entrance and motor cars lined two deep along the length of Pulteney Street. In addition to the contribution from season ticket holders, £300 was taken at the gate from a crowd which included 'a fair sprinkling of the fairer sex'.

Bath were 6-0 ahead within 25 minutes thanks to a charge-down try from Hannah and another from E.G. (George) Haydon. Sherman crossed for Bristol after the restart but the home side finished the stronger to win 9-3, ensuring that they remained unbeaten against Somerset or Gloucestershire opposition for the first time on record. All three teams – First, 'A' and 'Extra' XVs – won more matches than they lost, with the First XV record standing at 19 wins, 15 defeats and three draws. Nine players were selected for Somerset.

Perhaps the most extraordinary story from the season, however, arose from the Wales *v.* England match at Cardiff on 18 January 1930. Norman Matthews had travelled to Penarth the day before as a nominated reserve and when the Exeter prop, Harry Rew, stubbed a toe in training, the selectors switched Joe Kendrew from hooker to prop. But instead of promoting Matthews they put in a hopeful call to Sam Tucker, of Bristol, who had been capped 22 times. It was already 12.25 pm.

Tucker, with extraordinary initiative, arranged a lift from the pilot of a two-seater biplane from Filton Aerodrome and arrived in the England dressing room barely 15 minutes before kick-off, having had some difficulty in persuading the gatemen who he was! Matthews, who had even donned his kit for the official team photograph, dressed and took his place in the stand. And that was as close as he ever got to an England cap.

Ian Spence's second season as captain was even more successful, with 22 victories from 37 matches, 12 defeats and 3 draws. It began with a highly encouraging 3-3 draw at Leicester, although the crowd appeared to have been affected by a visit to the city by that famous aviatrix, Amy Johnson.

For the visit to Plymouth on 11 October, Bath were forced to include an 18-year-old at centre. R.A. (Ronald) Gerrard, born in Hong Kong where his father had been Assistant Commissioner of Police, had moved back to England with his recently-widowed mother three years earlier to be educated at Taunton School. That was the first occasion he had touched a rugby ball but he excelled at all sports, winning the Public Schools 'pulling the weight' championship in 1929 and 1930 and also being lawn tennis, table tennis and fives champion of his school. He headed the school batting averages for three years, was a first-class rifle shot and a member of the school water polo team.

At six feet plus and weighing almost 14 stone, Gerrard was already such an impressive physical specimen and blessed with such pace and resourcefulness that he had 'international' stamped all over him. He was still a teenager when he lined up against South Africa at Twickenham the following season to earn the first of 14 England caps – a club record that stood for exactly half a century, until surpassed by John Hall against Scotland in 1986.

Gerrard was outstanding in a 13-6 win at Weston-super-Mare on 15 November 1930 and scored his first try for Bath in the return, a 9-3 victory on 6 December. Gerrard could not prevent Bristol winning 6-0 at the Memorial Ground a week later but that proved to be the only defeat in 12 matches – including a 9-3 win over Gloucester – until a visit to Llanelly on 14 February (0-8). They were back in the groove against Leicester the following Saturday, however, winning 19-9.

Among other newcomers was Donald Crichton-Miller, who made his Bath debut on 3 January 1931, but who was still technically a Gloucester club player when he won the first of 3 caps for Scotland against Wales three weeks later. The pack was strengthened

Cue the chorus girls... Bath 14 Plymouth Albion 3.

BATH CLUB'S LAST MATCH OF THE SEASON
APRIL, 1931
TAKING THE MATERIAL THINGS FIRST IN THIS WELTER OF WELSH WEIGHT AND BATH BEEF, I MUST REMARK ON THE PECULIAR ABSENCE OF THE BALL, WHICH, IF FOUND LOITERING IN ANY OPEN SPACE,
OH LOOK!
DEM '31
WAS AT ONCE BURIED SO WELL, THAT THE WINNER OF IT MUST HAVE HAD GRAVE DOUBTS ABOUT EVER EXHUMING IT.
PASSING ON TO THE HUMAN INTEREST SIDE OF THE MATCH WE WILL FIRST CONSIDER THE FASTEST MAN ON THE FIELD
MR. BUDD, THE REFEREE, WHOSE SPEED WAS DISTINCTLY GREAT WESTERNISH, AND I WAS SURPRISED
THAT WHEN DAI JOHN DROPPED A GOAL, MR. BUDD WASN'T ALREADY THERE TO SIGNAL IT OVER
MR. BUDD, ALTHOUGH A VERY BUSY MAN, FOUND A FEW SPARE MOMENTS TO ATTEND TO
UP'S A DAISY
SARTORIAL MATTERS.
AND NOW TO FINISH THE CARTOON AND THE SEASON WE SHALL DRAW
MR. CUTTING, FOR RUNNING IN FRONT OF THE BAND WITH THE LEMONS,
MR. GOUGH, FOR NEARLY SCORING A TRY WITH SOMEONES HEADGEAR,
MR. SIMPKINS TO THANK HIM FOR ASSISTANCE RENDERED,
AND MR ARNOLD RIDLEY WELL, JUST BECAUSE HE IS MR. RIDLEY.

'Up's a Daisy!'

further at this time by the arrival of Reading University student Gordon Gregory but again, when the 23-year-old hooker was capped against Ireland on 14 February, it was as a member of the Bristol club.

On 21 March, as Bath were beating Plymouth Albion 14-3 on the Rec, Gregory and Crichton-Miller confronted each other in the Calcutta Cup at Murrayfield and while the former went on to win 14 caps while with Bristol, the Scotsman wrote to the Bath management committee in April regretting the fact that he had made only a few appearances, but he hoped 'to become more regular next season'.

Another occasional player in the early 1930s was a player better known for his exploits on the cricket field. H.F.T. (Bertie) Buse, who scored 10,623 runs and took 657 wickets for Somerset between 1929 and 1953, was also a capable full-back or wing. In describing Buse the cricketer, the incomparable John Arlott likened him to 'a butler bringing in the tea', a description which could not be bettered for accuracy or economy of prose. Naturally, he was to choose the Recreation Ground as the venue for his much-deserved cricket benefit against Lancashire in 1953. In those days, the Bath festival wicket was notoriously dodgy and, sensationally, the match was all over in a day – a financial disaster for a man much loved by Somerset supporters. In his later years he worked as a 'messenger boy' on *The Bath Chronicle*.

Bath's final game of the 1930/31 season was against Llanelly, Wales's champion club, who won 7-3. Referee Budd did his best to keep up with play – until his shorts fell around his

'You know what sisters are!'

R.A. Gerrard gained 14 England caps between 1932 and 1936.

ankles! Such entertainment ensured that sport provided a welcome respite from the dire economic conditions, but it could not isolate itself from the troubles of the ordinary working man and his family. A committee meeting on 25 August resolved that 'in view of present circumstances of industrial depression, the 15s 6d membership tickets be made available on an instalment system'.

Mervyn Shaw's qualities of leadership made him a natural choice as skipper for 1931/32, a decision vindicated by his record of 25 wins, 12 defeats and a draw from the 38 fixtures. A first-ever meeting with Bridgend on 10 October 1931 produced 'some hot exchanges between the forwards' but Bath edged home 16-15, good preparation for the visit to Bristol the following week.

Although Crichton-Miller was absent, playing for London Counties against the Springboks, and second row George Haydon – top try scorer the previous season with 28 – had been permanently lured to the capital by work commitments, Bath did Shaw proud by winning 13-11. Gerrard and A.E. Merritt scored fine tries but the hero of the hour was second-team wing E.J. Eastcott who deputised at wing forward and scored the try that allowed Ralph Banks to add the winning conversion.

Gerrard's thrilling displays in his first season of senior rugby had earned him selection, together with Norman Matthews, for a combined Somerset-Gloucestershire XV against the Springboks on 3 October. The teenager looked so much at home in that

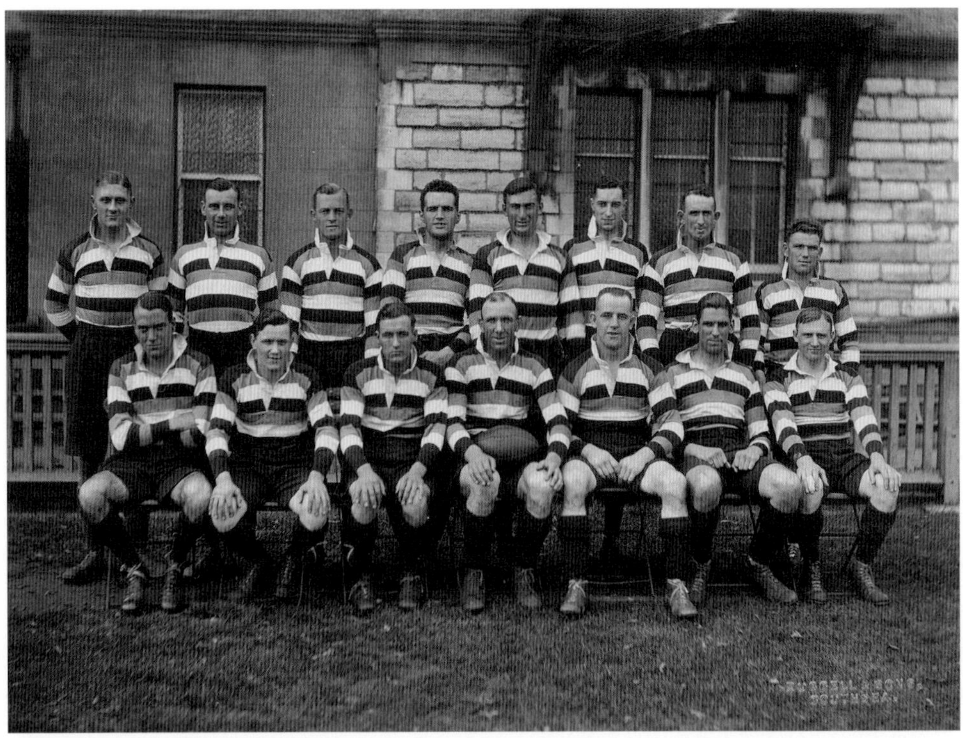

Bath *v.* United Services, 19 September 1931. From left to right, back row: D. Wilson, L. St V. Powell, R.A. Gerrard, N.W. Matthews, D. Crichton-Miller, C.E. Gough, D. Thomas, S. Williams. Front row: E.G. Haydon, R. Banks, A. Merrett, M.V. Shaw (captain), S. Weeks, J. Jones, W.E. Hancock.

exalted company and in the England trials that he was selected for his first cap against South Africa at Twickenham on 2 January 1932, just 24 days short of his 20th birthday.

The Springboks, led by that brilliant midfield tactician Bennie Osler and with the innovative Danie Craven at scrum-half, had already beaten Wales and Ireland. If there is any such thing as a gentle introduction to Test rugby this was certainly not it, yet Ronald Anderson Gerrard earned praise from all quarters for his all-round contribution and particularly for two breaks that might have yielded tries, as the *Bath and Wilts Chronicle & Herald* proudly reported.

FIND OF THE SEASON
SUCCESS IN FIRST RUGBY INTERNATIONAL
DEADLY TACKLING
... The first time he had no one up to support him. On the second occasion Spong had drawn Osler and Waring before sending the Bath man away. Gerrard ran strongly to Brand, with Aarvold in attendance, instead of passing he cut inwards, and was sandwiched between the South African full back and Gray. Still, the Bath centre with his determined running created a very favourable impression.[5]

The *Sunday Despatch* wrote: 'Gerrard put in a couple of splendid dashes that even if they failed in their objective stamped him as a centre who should be of service to England for some years to come. His tackling also was deadly accurate.' The *Morning Post* judged him to be 'the best of the line'.

The tourists won 7-0 and went on to complete the Grand Slam against Scotland (6-3) a fortnight later. England's hopes of a successful home campaign were dashed the same day in Swansea when Wales triumphed 12-5, but Gerrard had kept his place at centre and confirmed his obvious potential in victories over Ireland in Dublin (11-8) and at home to Scotland (16-3). His tenure coincided with the breaking-off of relations with France by the four Home Unions over allegations of professionalism in their club championship. In normal circumstances, Gerrard would have added five more caps to the 14 he won between 1932 and 1936.

Meanwhile, the unfortunate Norman Matthews, captain of Somerset and elevated to the England XV in the trial when Joe Kendrew withdrew, never came any closer to an international cap. Also given an England trial was another Bath forward, Derrick Wilson, while 11 players from the club represented Somerset. Crichton Miller (London and Hampshire) also turned out for a Territorial Army XV while S. Williams was selected for the RAF against The Army.

The 'Match of the Season' at the Rec was the 11-6 win on 5 March which completed the double over Bristol, thanks to tries from L.W. Moore and the unstoppable Gerrard. Among the 8,000 spectators was C.J.B. Moneypenny, who had played in the

A rare double.

very first derby fixture on 27 October 1888 under the captaincy of the redoubtable Frank Soane.

On 2 April, spectators arriving at the Rec for the game with United Services Portsmouth found the club flag flying at half-mast in tribute to Soane, who had died the previous day at the age of 66. It had been half a century since his debut for Bath and no individual had stamped his personality with more effect on the club, not merely as the first home-grown England cap from the club but also as a driving force for progress in the committee room.

The momentum he had created, maintained behind the scenes by dedicated personalities such as George Roberts, John Piper, W.T. (Tommy) Davis, Eddie Simpkins and others, continued to be felt. As they prepared to bury Soane, the committee decided to build a new West Stand for 1,150 seated spectators and to sign a 50-year lease with the Recreation Ground Company. Tommy Davis retired from the committee that summer after 36 years' service, while Simpkins embarked on his 22nd year as joint Honorary Secretary.

With Gerrard's emergence as a world-class talent, the 1931/32 season had been hugely successful. It ended on a suitably triumphant note, with an 8-3 win over Gloucester.

Six wins off the reel set a confident tone for the start of the 1932/33 campaign. The early matches included a tour to Cornwall, with training on Penzance sands and wins over Redruth (10-8) and Penzance (24-9). The *Football Chronicle* was on sale the following morning at 7 a.m. and, as one player was heard to remark, 'Penzance people wondered how it was we could have our own paper following us about'.

Although Bristol took revenge with the 'double' and Llanelly also beat Bath twice, Gloucester lost at the Rec and Mervyn Shaw's second season as captain finished with 24

The West Stand takes shape, July 1932.

victories, 13 defeats and a drawn game (at home to Harlequins). Gate receipts were up £79 at £1,962 and the new grandstand had attracted many new patrons.

Gerrard maintained his international reputation as an ever-present with England but the championship season got off to a poor start with defeat by Wales at Twickenham (3-7) and although Ireland were beaten there 17-6, Scotland won 3-0 at Murrayfield when the Bath man received a leg injury. As ever, he was solid in defence but now not the quickest pair of feet in the three-quarter line.

He returned to club duty for the last month of the season and on 13 May made his debut for Bath Cricket Club against Cardiff, scoring 64 in a total of 203-4 declared, with one S.G.U. Considine contributing an unbeaten 37. Gerrard was also given three games for Somerset in 1935, but without showing any form.

For all Gerrard's exploits with England, almost as much publicity was given to honours awarded in July 1933 to two other Bath players, Bill Hancock and Dan Thomas, a Bath police constable. Their commendations from the Royal Humane Society for bravery resulted from an incident in which a Bathwick woman tried to drown herself and her mentally disabled daughter of 28 in a canal lock at Widcombe. After the woman tried to resist attempts to rescue the daughter with a grappling iron, PC Thomas leapt into the water to effect a rescue, closely followed by Hancock. Court officials recorded that the conduct of the rescuers was 'deserving of the highest praise'.

Meanwhile, Gerrard was awarded the captaincy of Somerset at the tender age of 21 and rugby fans in Bath were beginning to wonder if the club could possibly keep him. First he turned down a Rugby League offer from Leeds in October 1933, amounting to a signing-on fee of £1,000 in cash, a job in Leeds and £4 per game.

At around the same time, he was offered a job opportunity with British Reinforced Concrete Company in Stafford but, to everyone's relief and much rejoicing in the Bath club, he decided to stay with the City Engineer's department in Bath. It was all terrific copy for the local sports pages in the run-up to the 14 October visit to the Memorial Ground, the scene of as extraordinary a denouement as witnessed in any match between the old rivals.

Bath were leading 3-0 in the closing seconds when the Bristol centre, Rugg, ended a spell of intense pressure by crossing the visitors' line. But, in trying to make the conversion easier, he ran on towards the posts only to be gathered up by Norman Matthews and Peter Moon and 'pitchforked' over the dead-ball line.

After the coldest December snap for 40 years – the Avon was frozen over from Pulteney Weir to North Parade Bridge – Gerrard needed more matches to overcome a leg injury that had taken the edge off his pace, according to the England selectors. They therefore asked him to turn out for Leicester against the Barbarians on Boxing Day and he played only one more game for Bath before winning his eighth cap against Wales on 20 January 1934.

Bath were playing Leicester at the Rec that day, the home team without 'Gerry' and the visitors missing Bernard Gadney, the England scrum-half and captain. Leicester won

BATH v. LLANELLY

AS A SPECTATOR AT THIS MATCH I WAS THRILLED BY THE FACT THAT THERE WERE 7 INTERNATIONALS IN THE WELSH TEAM.

AS A BATH SUPPORTER I WAS DELIGHTED WHEN MINTO MADE BATH'S SCORE 8 POINTS! (LLANELLY GOT A POINT FOR EVERY INTERNATIONAL THEY POSSESSED)

AS AN ARTIST I APPRECIATED THE BEAUTY OF FORM AS EVINCED IN THE DIMPLED CHIN OF H. DAVIES (I GOT THIS CLOSE-UP IN THE DRESSING ROOM)

THE RHYTHM OF GERRARD'S MOVEMENTS WHEN HE HELD THE BALL

AS A CARTOONIST I WAS FASCINATED BY A HAT. THIS HAT WAS THE FEATURE OF THE GAME; THE FEATURE, IN FACT, OF EVERY GAME WHICH MR SIMPKINS ATTENDS. MR SIMPKINS (KNOWN TO THE FRATERNITY AS EDDIE) IS THE HON SECRETARY AND HAS GIVEN MANY YEARS SERVICE TO THE BATH CLUB – AND SO I SHOULD THINK HAS HIS HAT!

I HAD THE PRIVILEGE OF BEING HIS GUEST ON SATURDAY AND WAS ABLE TO STUDY IT. WHEN PLAY WAS HELD UP WHILE THE BALL DID A STEP-DANCE ON THE ROOF OF THE STAND I FULLY EXPECTED HIM TO FLING THE HAT INTO PLAY

AND THE OBVIOUS STRENGTH OF MR JONES'S ANATOMICAL STRUCTURE (HIS BONES WITHSTOOD THE WEIGHT OF THOSE SEVEN INTERNATIONALS)

UNFORTUNATELY HE DIDN'T – BUT THE MORE I STUDIED IT THE MORE I FELT THAT MANY A TRY HAD BEEN SCORED WITH IT.

P.J. JAN. 27 193–

The rag doll retrieved.

Gerrard heralds changes in 1934.

12-8 but there was so much interest in the international that score updates from Cardiff were thoughtfully displayed on a blackboard paraded around the touchline.

Three unconverted tries saw England home 9-0 and they then travelled to Dublin, where they defeated the Irish 13-3. When the Scots were beaten 6-3 at Twickenham, Gerrard became the first Bath player to celebrate a Triple Crown since Vincent Coates 21 years earlier.

Under the leadership of B.C. Barber, Bath had wrested the 'rag doll' from Llanelly with an 8-7 victory on the Rec on 27 January 1934, the winning conversion being retaken by Jock Minto after the opposition charged early. Home advantage also accounted for Gloucester (13-8) and Leicester (8-0) but Bristol took revenge and Bath finished their programme of 36 matches with 20 wins and 16 defeats.

Gerrard took over the captaincy for 1934/35 with a clear idea of what was required:

...a little more keenness and of the wish to train and a little more football sense on the playing field. During the coming season my chief aim will be to create a more intensive team spirit.

The skipper was magnificent in the opening game at Llanelly, doing 'a couple of men's work' and collecting a black eye, but was unable to prevent Haydn Tanner inspiring a 13-4 home win. Four days later, the teams met again and this time Bath scored five tries in winning 21-3, capped by a spectacular dropped goal from Buse. When the teams met again at Stradey at the end of the season, however, Bath were trounced 42-0.

In the end, Gerrard's record was no better than that of Barber, with 20 wins from the 40 fixtures, 19 defeats and a draw, although fresh talent was emerging in the shape of players like Les Matthews, the brother of Norman. Barber deputised on the occasions when Gerrard was required for representative duty but the younger man's fortunes with England were equally mixed – a draw with Wales, victory over Ireland and defeat by Scotland.

The saddest event of the winter, however, was the shocking death of Vincent Coates in a fall from a GWR express at Maidenhead on 14 November 1934. The former international and war hero, now a world authority on rheumatic diseases, apparently stepped out of the carriage thinking he was alighting at Bath Spa. A former patient penned the following tribute:

Brilliant upon the football field,
Brave on the field of war,
Beloved and honoured in his work,
Why had death closed the door?

Bath, 1934. From left to right, back row: G.V. Wynne-Jones, J. Minto, H.T.F. Buse, A. Weeks, J. Wilkins, J. Davies, C.E. Gough, H. Oak, B.C. Barber (touch judge). Seated: J.S. Bartlett, P. Moon, J. McKay, R.A. Gerrard (captain), D. Wilson, N.W. Matthews, L.D. Wardle.

So strong of frame, so frank of face,
So generously gay,
Quick, resolute, yet truly kind,
He went his healing way.

At first that steadfast, searching gaze
Through to the soul he'd send,
Questioning, noting all, and then
He'd smile and be your friend.

A faithful friend, a sturdy friend,
And bracing too at need,
In pain or grief a gentle friend
And comforting indeed.

His kindly clasp, his cheerful words,
His look, and merry smile –
Oh! It is only fit and right
To mourn him for a while!

Yet – 'Keep a stout heart' – at the door
He'd sometimes pause to say;
And 'Keep a stout heart' echoes still –
Tho' he is gone away.

The 1935/36 season began badly with five successive defeats, including a 34-0 thrashing at home by Llanelly, so it was a surprise to many that Bath, without the injured Gerrard, rediscovered their pride to show remarkable battling qualities in a scoreless draw at Bristol. It was a 'grim struggle' and the referee afterwards entered the Bath dressing room, carrying a blood-stained handkerchief, asking: 'Who gave me this tooth on the field?'

For all the club's travails, Gerrard was selected by England to face Jack Manchester's All Blacks on 4 January 1936 – 'Obolensky's match'. As everyone knows, the Russian prince scored two tries, one of which has passed into Twickenham legend, and England won 13-0, not least because Gerrard and his fellow back line were unyielding in defence. He was singled out for special praise.

Three weeks later, Bath's game with Moseley and all other fixtures were cancelled as a mark of respect following the death of King George V. When rugby resumed on 1 February, Bath lined up against Swansea wearing white, with black armlets. The following week there was news of a former Bath player, Tommy Rose, and his attempt to beat Amy Mollison's record for a non-stop flight from London to Capetown. Although forced down at Haifa, he had made a 25-minute stop-over at Khartoum before continuing on the next stage to Kismu. His aircraft, a Miles Falcon, had won the King's Cup the previous year and was capable of flying for 1,000 miles at 160 mph.

'Ash, Wood and Oak!' From left to right, back row: A. Ash, R. Banks, G. Gray. Front row: J.S. Wood, W.E. Hancock, H. Oak.

Bath's own high-flyer, Gerrard, won his 11th cap in a scoreless draw at Swansea, which was followed by a 6-3 defeat in Dublin and, fortunately for England, a face-saving 9-8 victory over Scotland at Twickenham. Gerrard, increasingly troubled by injury, never played for England again. For a man who harboured ambitions of captaining his country, it must have been a huge disappointment for his international career to end at the age of 25; he was, however, to prove an outstanding leader of men in another conflict about to engulf the world.

In the meantime, Gerrard turned up 'fighting fit' for the 1936/37 season under the captaincy of Norman Matthews, who had come out of retirement in the previous mid-season. It was an honour long overdue for another inspiring leader. In one of those delightful quirks of happenstance, the front row in the mid-1930s regularly included Harry Oak at hooker, propped by A. Ash, with John Wood at lock behind them, but the player who caught the eye in September 1936 was T.R. (Roy) Harris, a young fly-half and product of King Edward's School who had played the occasional game the previous season.

Bath on their 1936 Cornish tour. From left to right, back row: Dick Chaddock (forward), unidentified supporter, Bill Barber (forward), Arnold Ridley, Charlie Gough (wing), lady companion, Peter Moon (forward), Dickie James (centre), Bertie Buse (full-back), Cyril Bailey (utility back), Ron Gerrard (centre), unidentified supporter, Arthur Francis (forward). Front row: Harry Davies (scrum-half), Albie Hatherall (baggage man), Freddie Wills (committee), Norman Matthews (forward), Leslie Mathews (wing), local boatman, Arthur 'Shammer' Weeks (forward), Bill 'Kipper' Hancock (wing), Lance Wardle (fly-half), Captain Leslie Amor (club president), Harry Oak (forward), Norman Willis (supporter), president of Penzance RFC.

Roy Harris makes a break against Leicester on 30 March 1937; Leicester's Prince Obelensky is on the extreme left.

He was outstanding in the early weeks of the season, especially on the tour of Cornwall, but was uncharacteristically nervous in the 101st meeting at Bristol on 10 October 1936 – the 21st derby for Norman Matthews and Hancock's 19th. Gerrard landed a magnificent 45-yard penalty against the wind to open the scoring but went off injured in the second half and Bristol completed a 6-3 victory with tries by Woodward and Baynam.

Rugby supporters in Bristol owe much to Bath. From 1865 to 1888 numbers of enthusiasts used to travel here to see Bath – not the simple journey it is today – and one Saturday evening in Sept 1888, a few of them, while on the way home, decided to start a club of their own.[6]

There was better luck when Bath returned to Bristol a fortnight later to face Clifton, where Flying Officer Basil Robinson (RAF and Durham) was paired at half-back with Lance Wardle. A 35-yard run-in by skipper Matthews was the highlight of an 18-5 victory and there were further tries from Robinson and forwards Leslie Phillips and Peter Moon.

The other West Country derby against Gloucester was kicked off by the Mayor of Bath, W.F. 'Joe' Long, who 42 years earlier had scored the first try on the Recreation Ground as a teenage wing. Having performed his civic duty, he apparently took some persuading to leave the field of play, but Bath still won 11-5. Meanwhile, a new generation was coming through and Norman Halse was promoted from the Colts XV for his debut at scrum-half on Boxing Day in a 35-0 win over Old Blues. Halse, known to all as 'Curly', was destined to become a Club stalwart, long-serving committeeman and Club President.

Frost and floods caused several cancellations but Bath put together a run of five wins through March, culminating in a 17-13 win over Leicester, for whom Obolensky scored a spectacular try. Defeats by London Scottish, Neath and Bridgend brought the tally of losses for the season to 13 against 18 victories and 3 draws. There was still one more reverse, on 27 June at the annual meeting of the RFU when Bath's attempt in concert with Bristol to get broadcasting of internationals discontinued was ruled out of order. Both clubs were concerned about the effect on gate takings.

Gerrard, troubled by a persistent thigh strain, lost his international place to Peter Candler, of Bart's Hospital, as England carried off the Triple Crown, but the Bath man was restored to his club captaincy for the 1937/38 season. It began spectacularly with a 19-17 home win over Llanelly, in which Basil Robinson scored four tries, ably fed by his skipper and the darting Roy Harris. Gerrard's only visit to Twickenham that season must have been a depressing affair as Bath lost 3-14 to Harlequins in the echoing vastness of a stadium whose advantage to Quins as a home venue must have been marginal.

A match might just as well be behind closed doors for all the vocal support they receive in such a vast stadium. A dozen Pressmen have a whole stand to themselves, and find Twickenham as great a solitude as the Mendips.[7]

A far more agreeable occasion was Gerrard's wedding to Miss Molly Taylor at St Mary's church, Bathwick, on 19 November 1937. England captain H.G. 'Tuppy' Owen-Smith was best man as 400 guests celebrated the union and marvelled at the wedding cake, designed by the bride to reflect her family's architectural prowess.

The tiers were not circular, but rectangular, and the top was modelled to convey a complete representation of the Twickenham Rugby ground, complete with grandstands and goalposts. The tiers all bore devices either Heraldic in character, or depicting instruments used by architects. Weighing a hundred-weight and a half, the cake was made by the Red House to the bride's own design.[8]

After Gerrard departed on honeymoon, Bath confronted a strong Gloucester side 24 hours later on the Rec. With time running out, Peter Moon urged his pack to one more big effort and the deadlock was broken when right wing John Bartlett sprinted from halfway for the winning try. Frustratingly, this performance was followed by a succession of indifferent displays and there was further disappointment when Bertie Buse gave up rugby in February 1938 to prepare for the cricket season with Somerset. In eight years, 'Buzzer' had made 137 appearances, 125 at full-back and 12 at threequarter.

For the visit of Bristol on 5 March 1938, there was brilliant sunshine and not a breath of wind. A masterstroke was Bath's decision to bring Harry Oak out of retirement to hook and Bristol never really recovered from the loss through injury of Percy Redwood. A telling break by Bartlett provided a try for Lance Wardle on 13 minutes and an 8-0 win was sealed by a penalty from Harris early in the second half.

Gerrard missed the game through injury and appeared in only six matches during the season, fuelling rumours that his doctors were advising him to retire because of his troublesome thigh. He still led the points scoring with a tally of 43 from a try, 5 goals (conversions) and 10 penalties but his team's record amounted to just 13 wins from 34 games, with 20 lost and one drawn.

The build up to the 1938/39 season began none too auspiciously when Gerrard resigned from the committee, seemingly convinced that his career was over. Then Roy Harris, having been chosen to succeed him as captain, accepted a teaching post at Taunton School and advised that he would not be available for the early games. Ken Foss took over. Fortunately for Harris, his employer as headmaster was none other than Donald Crichton-Miller, the former Bath and Scotland forward, and his release for most Saturdays was thought to be assured.

'The game of the season', 15 October 1938. Bath 11 Bristol 8.

It was a young team, with teenagers Tommy Hicks and 'Curly' Halse regularly turning out at half-back and 15-year-old Freddie Hayman making his debut on the wing against Devonport Services on 24 September. In Plymouth, preparations for war were obvious everywhere and all the opposition players had brought their uniforms in case of a sudden recall to ship or barracks.

On 1 October, against St Mary's Hospital, Gerrard made a dramatic return, looking every bit his old masterful self as he converted a try by the policeman Bill Gay (father of David and Allen of the 1960s), kicked a penalty and then landed a drop goal to win the game 12-8. Bristol were then defeated 11-5 with tries from the RAF men, A.V. Rogers and Robinson, plus a conversion and penalty from Gerrard.

Even better, they managed a victory at Kingsholm, thanks to Robinson's break and his slick combination with Harris, whose try was converted by Gerrard for a 5-3 win. The double was completed with a 6-5 victory on the Rec on 18 February 1939 but this achievement was in no way reflected in the season's record – just 9 wins from 35, with 20 defeats and 6 draws – and the side appeared to depend too heavily on Harris, whose appearances were, after all, restricted by school duties and injury.

Not surprisingly, finances suffered and showed a deficit of £133 at the end of the season, with F.C. Wills, Joint Honorary Secretary, suggesting that the club could not carry on without donations from businessmen and members. A club appeal was launched and one of the first to contribute was the *Bath and Wilts Chronicle & Herald* with ten guineas. As late as 1 August 1939, arrangements for the club dinner were being finalised and the skipper, W.F. Gay, was outlining plans for pre-season training which was to commence 'on a more scientific basis, and will be less haphazard than of late years'. He couldn't have been more wrong.

Two weeks earlier, the RFU had announced that England was to resume fixtures with France in February 1940; now they were making hurried arrangements to repatriate the Australian tourists before they had even played a match. Twenty-five years after Vincent Coates and Co. left for the fields of Flanders, Bath players were again hanging up their blue-white-and-black hoops and queuing up for khaki.

-11-

Targeted by the Luftwaffe

AS NEVILLE CHAMBERLAIN delivered his ultimatum to Adolf Hitler on Saturday 2 September 1939, Bath rugby players should have been engaged in a final trial. Instead, two of the Territorials among their number, Sappers Norman Halse and Thomas Hicks, were being called to the Colours, passed fit for service to King and Country at the local TA drill hall by none other than the rugby club's president, Dr Scott-Reid.

The *Chronicle's* rugby correspondent, A.S. Matthews, reflected in his column, 'The Captain's Notebook', in that night's paper:

How can one talk about rugby football and its prospects in an atmosphere as charged with the grim word War, as it was in August 1914? The idea of 'Business as usual' in a football sense seems an anachronism. What is going to happen? No one knows. I am writing on Friday afternoon, as much in the dark as anyone else. I only know that the trial is off, and that for the rest we don't know... If War stalks the earth again, then football will cease as an organised pastime like it did in the last war; and the boys you and I know and admire will be playing another game, with a firm lip and that determination to 'break through' which our backs so often show us.[1]

The declaration of a state of war the following morning merely confirmed the inevitable. The first casualty in a rugby sense was the opening game against Llanelly six days later, as the RFU followed the Welsh Union's lead by cancelling all fixtures until further notice, with the exception of schoolboy matches. Meanwhile the Management Committee, meeting on 19 September, decided to write to all clubs on the 1939/40 fixture list asking if they were prepared to send teams in the event of rugby being resumed. Two days later, however, the club dinner was cancelled.

Halse (Service No. 207 4803) and Hicks (207 6774) were not the only Territorials expecting to be mobilised. Others included Lieutenant Gerrard, of the same Wessex Royal Engineers, as well as fellow-first teamers J.S. Wood, K. Weiss, R.W. James and P. Brown. Among the Regulars in the club were the RAF quartet of Basil Robinson, John Bartlett, A.V. Rogers and Bryan Wallis while Eric Smith was with the Tank Corps at Bovington Camp.

A few were still available for a match against The Admiralty on 7 October when Bath managed to put out a team captained by county three-quarter Geoffrey Foster and

Don't forget the Bath & Admiralty RUGGER DANCE (April 4th, 1940, at The Pump Room, Bath — Dancing 8 till 1 — Tickets 2/6

6 Pts 1 PEN. K. WEISS. 1 TRY. R. HARRIS

BATH & ADMIRALTY R.F.C. Blue White & Black

Full Back
(1) **J. Hodder**

Right Wing	Right Centre	Left Centre	Left Wing
(2) ***A. E. Merrett**	(3) **P. Fortt**	(4) **G. Foster**	(5) **F. Hayman**

Stand Off Half (7)***T. R. Harris** (Capt.) — Scrum Half (6) **S. Beaverstock**

Forwards

(8) **A. Ash**	(9) **L. James**	(10) **L. Phillips**	(11) **W. Barrow**
(12) **A. W. Holden**	(14) **F. L. Gann**	(15) **G. W. A. Keir**	(16) **K. Weiss**

Referee : Mr. G. Goldsworthy, Newport. **Kick Off 3.15 p.m.**

11 Pts 1 TRY IRVINE CONV. PRIDMORE 2 PENS. "

Forwards

(8) **W. R. Jenkins**	(9) **H. Morgan**	(10) **D. Irvine**	(11) **W. A. L. Colhoun**
(12) **E. Tosney**	(15) **R. H. Williams**	(14)***F. H. Coutts**	(13) †**A. M. Rees**

Stand Off Half (6) **C. A. Pridmore** (Capt.) — Scrum Half (7) **G. Ewans**

Left Wing	Left Centre	Right Centre	Right Wing
(5)**W. K. Jones**	(4) **D. W. Williams**	(3)***H. Webber**	(2) **D. J. Randall**

Full Back
(1) **N. Heppenstall**

* COUNTY
† INTERNATIONAL

METROPOLITAN POLICE. Blue

EASTER MONDAY— BATH & ADMIRALTY R.F.C. v. An ARMY XV. -- Kick-off 3.15 p.m.

PRICE 1d. If you have the lucky number you will be given a ticket to admit two, to the ODEON CINEMA, on application at the Supporters' Hut. **NUMBER. 381**

Playing as Bath and Admiralty, 23 March 1940.

including ten with first-team experience. Wallis crossed twice in a 36-0 victory, other tries being scored by Fred Hayman, Jack Arnold, A. Ash, D. Wilson and Leslie Phillips.

It was decided that if rugby was to continue through the hostilities, the Bath club should amalgamate temporarily with The Admiralty which, as the largest military establishment in the city, would be able to supplement any non-combatants left in the club as well as those home on leave. The first match, against Mr McNamara's XV on 14 October, was won 17-15 and Wallis, having cycled five miles in his RAF uniform, was again rewarded with a try.

Bath & Admiralty RFC played a further 19 fixtures in 1939/40, although there was no rugby on the Rec between 16 December and 2 March, purely because of bad weather. Opponents included Bristol Supporters' Club, Stroud, Weston-super-Mare, Gloucester, Cheltenham, Somerset Police, Metropolitan Police and R.A. Gerrard's Army XV, featuring not only the great man himself but also other former Bath players in Scotland trialist Sergeant Jock Minto, Corporal K. Wilcox and Sergeant Ron Ascott.

The matches were welcome social occasions and Major Arnold Ridley was a spectator at the Somerset Police match on 13 April 1940, enjoying a break from his duties as a public relations officer at GHQ in France. It was only a 'Phoney War' for some, however, and news came through of Distinguished Flying Crosses awarded to Basil Robinson and John Bartlett who 'has been in more than one flying crash'.

Only days after the season closed with a 6-3 defeat at Weston, Bath's try scorer in that game, Jack Arnold, enlisted with the RAF as a Flight Mechanic. Geoffrey Foster was waiting for a vacancy in the Royal Armoured Corps and Roy Harris was being gazetted to a commission in the Royal Artillery while the club's Honorary Secretary, Victor Smith, was joining the Royal Army Ordnance Corps. Bert Merrett, captain of the United XV, was also on his way to the Royal Artillery and Leslie Phillips to the ranks of the Somerset Light Infantry.

After Dunkirk and at the height of the Battle of Britain, nearly all the Bath club's players were in the services and the Management Committee resolved on 10 August 1940 that 'activities of the Club be suspended for the time being' although committee members were to remain in their posts, with power to act if necessary.

Eventually, a match was staged at Bath on 19 October between an Empire XV and the West of England, organised by the legendary Len Corbett, of Bristol, in aid of 'Welfare of the Forces'. The home side won 25-8 against a team comprising All Blacks, Welsh, Irish and Scotland trialists, with a smattering of county players.

The next fixture saw a Bath & Admiralty XV defeat an RAF XV 14-6 on 23 November, but there was a tragic aftermath when the home captain, a Civil Service player called Fred Green, collapsed after a social event at the Red House Restaurant, dying later in the Royal United Hospital. Only 30 years old, he had appeared 'in good spirits generally and seemed perfectly well' although he had not played since the previous season and had not trained for what had been a hard match.

It was ironic, since the chief concern of the club had been that casualties might be caused by surprise air raids and they had sought special dispensation to stage matches

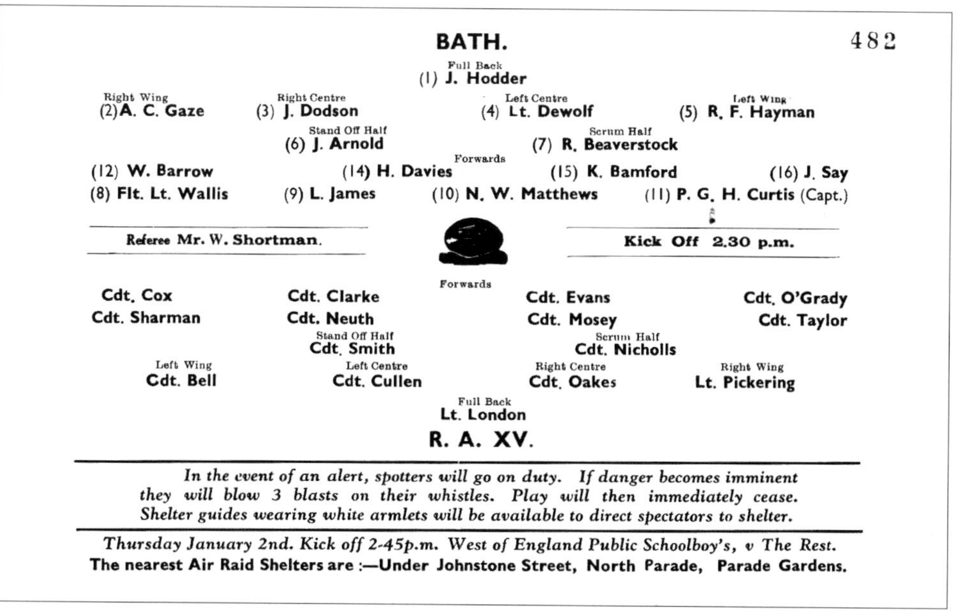

BATH. 482

Full Back
(1) **J. Hodder**

Right Wing (2) **A. C. Gaze** | Right Centre (3) **J. Dodson** | Left Centre (4) **Lt. Dewolf** | Left Wing (5) **R. F. Hayman**

Stand Off Half (6) **J. Arnold** | Scrum Half (7) **R. Beaverstock**

Forwards
(12) **W. Barrow** | (14) **H. Davies** | (15) **K. Bamford** | (16) **J. Say**
(8) **Flt. Lt. Wallis** | (9) **L. James** | (10) **N. W. Matthews** | (11) **P. G. H. Curtis** (Capt.)

Referee **Mr. W. Shortman.** | **Kick Off 2.30 p.m.**

Forwards
Cdt. Cox | **Cdt. Clarke** | **Cdt. Evans** | **Cdt. O'Grady**
Cdt. Sharman | **Cdt. Neuth** | **Cdt. Mosey** | **Cdt. Taylor**

Stand Off Half **Cdt. Smith** | Scrum Half **Cdt. Nicholls**

Left Wing **Cdt. Bell** | Left Centre **Cdt. Cullen** | Right Centre **Cdt. Oakes** | Right Wing **Lt. Pickering**

Full Back
Lt. London

R. A. XV.

In the event of an alert, spotters will go on duty. If danger becomes imminent they will blow 3 blasts on their whistles. Play will then immediately cease. Shelter guides wearing white armlets will be available to direct spectators to shelter.

Thursday January 2nd. Kick off 2-45p.m. West of England Public Schoolboy's, v The Rest.
The nearest Air Raid Shelters are :—Under Johnstone Street, North Parade, Parade Gardens.

'Air Raid Precautions' in a matchday programme, 28 December 1940.

attracting large numbers of spectators. The precautions were outlined by club officials at the end of 1940:

a. Spotters Messrs Jones and Anderson be nominated and in the event of an alert should take their places, one at the North Stand and the other at the Flower pot stand to watch the skies. If danger were impending they should blow three long blasts on powerful whistles and play should cease, the public to be informed of this through the programme and by means of a board to be sent round the ground prior to the kick-off.
b. Shelter guides to be on duty throughout the match.
c. Position of Shelters to be indicated on Club programmes and by notices.
d. Shelter to be available under North and West Stands and in the shelter on the ground.[2]

Although raids on Bath had caused only minor damage in August 1940 to a road junction, a couple of houses in the Twerton district and the Bath City football ground,

Bath 1940/41. From left to right, back row: F.C. Wills, S.L. Amor, B.C. Barber, Dr Scott-Reid, V. Smith (Honorary Secretary), W. Barrow, C. Bailey, J. Bevan Jones, Captain Norfolk, A.E. Anderson, D. Rees, A. Lock, G. Donaldson, J. Tolman. Middle row: J. Townend Piper, C.R. Woodward, L. James, H. Davies, P.G.H. Curtis (captain), J. Hodder, J. De Wolf. Front row: L. Harding, K. Holvey, Capt. Thomas, R.F. Hayman.

Training, 1940s style.

Bristol was heavily bombed by the Luftwaffe from November 1940 and there were constant air raid warnings in Bath. The 400th alert in Bath on 16 January 1941 saw a single bomber jettison its load, causing damage to Englishcombe Lane, Twerton High Street and West Twerton School. Even after the Dolemeads area – not far from the Recreation Ground – was hit by up to four high-explosives on 11 April, a rugby match was played next day.

Meanwhile, Gerrard had been promoted to Major, although he was still 'somewhere in England' leading an unbeaten Army rugby team which included Lieutenant John Wood and Sappers Curly Halse and Tommy Hicks, plus Ron Ascott. For a season that had almost been cancelled, there was plenty of rugby in Bath during 1940/41 and the wartime truce between the codes allowed an Army XV made up almost entirely of Yorkshire Rugby League players to win 22-11 on the Rec. The Somerset Home Guard, with Norman Matthews at their head, also turned out on 14 April to defeat an Army XV 5-0 and later that year were appealing for more fixtures, having 'set up camp' on the Showground at Lambridge. One snag was that they did not have enough clothing coupons for jerseys, shorts and socks and were therefore seeking donations of kit.

On 26 August 1941 came news that John Barlett DFC, having risen to the rank of Wing Commander, had been killed on active service. The son of a former manager of Lloyds Bank in Milsom Street, the wing three-quarter had been educated at Victoria College and was remembered as a 'brave and delightful personality' and 'one of the cleverest runners in Rugby'.

An appeal for funds.

It was a depressing time and the club committee, worried about another deficit of £31 8s 1d from the previous season, again considered winding everything up for the duration of the war. Although an appeal for subscriptions to stand seats raised just £127 – the target had been £250 – it was decided to press on. The fixture list comprised mainly Services sides, including the New Zealand Forestry Company, North Irish Horse and 455 Battery, 68th Searchlight Regiment as well as the usual Army and RAF XVs. Interestingly, wartime security precluded any public disclosure of opponents so spectators often did not know who the opposition were to be until they arrived at the ground. Before the 1 November meeting with a Welsh Army XV the *Chronicle* reported: 'I cannot name the unit coming, but it is famous and football is one of its assets'. The secrecy had other unfortunate consequences, as when two teams – an Army XV and the North Irish Horse – turned up on the same afternoon and the opposition had to be selected by the toss of a coin! North Irish Horse stayed as spectators and their fixture was fulfilled the following weekend.

Young Freddie Hayman, who had developed into a dazzlingly fast wing, joined the Canadian Army later that month but Captain Gerrard returned on 27 December for a

14-3 victory over Bristol, who lost hooker Fred Hill before half-time with a nasty cut over his artificial eye. Hill was to play for England in a Victory International before joining Bath to form a legendary post-war front row with John Roberts and Tom Smith.

On 16 February 1942 it was reported that Chief Petty Officer George 'Joe' Nudds was missing, presumed killed, after the sinking of HMS *Culver*. Nudds, a three-quarter or fly-half described as 'a brilliant and resourceful player', was a contemporary of Considine and had made his debut against Blundells School on 11 October 1922. Although he joined the Royal Navy in 1926, he was still turning out for the club while on leave until December 1929.

The realities of war hit home, literally, on the weekend of 25/26 April 1942 when the Luftwaffe targeted Bath in one of the infamous Baedeker raids (named after the pre-war German guide books to European cities and other places of outstanding cultural interest). Some 400 citizens were killed, including the club's trainer and baggage man, Jack Cutting, and nearly 900 more were injured.

The Recreation Ground took a direct hit, which destroyed the West Stand entirely and left the North Stand severely damaged. Monday's *Chronicle* reported: 'Stands at the football ground are a tangled mass of girders and ironwork. Sheets of corrugated iron were blown away by the tremendous force of the explosion.'

If things had been tough before, now, with no assets except a mass of twisted girders and crumpled corrugated sheeting, it seemed utterly futile to attempt to keep rugby going through the war. But Major Gerrard, now overseas, conveyed through his wife, Molly, a heartfelt plea that they should carry on and when she herself offered to ring round all former subscribers to the club, the management committee decided on 24 October to persevere. As an antidote to anxiety and austerity, rugby still held many advantages, as the *Chronicle* pointed out:

Many will surely rejoice at this courageous policy and resolve to give their regular backing, even if the two stands are heaps of rubble, and the best that can be done is to place flower-pot stands around. The Club, with a legacy of scrap iron and stone that is going for salvage, could not have been blamed for 'packing up' for the duration.[3]

There was more to celebrate in November when the *Chronicle* revealed that Major R.A. Gerrard had played such an important role in the victory over Rommel's Afrika Corps that he had won an immediate Distinguished Service Order. The citation read: 'On the first night of the El Alamein offensive he led the first wave of sappers detailed to clear three lanes through minefields. He moved from lane to lane regardless of his own safety.'

The successful piercing of the enemy minefields in this sector was officially regarded as due to his personal efforts and example, all the while under fire from German machine guns. The mine-clearing effort paved the way for Montgomery's triumphant push which provided the Allies with their first significant victory and turned the tide of the war.

On 26 January 1943 – four days after his 31st birthday – Gerrard joined the roll of the fallen, killed by a mine which exploded under his vehicle in Libya. The War Office telegram arrived two weeks later and was diverted to Captain Stanley Amor, the Bath Club Chairman, who then broke the news to Mrs Gerrard. The *Chronicle*'s obituary read:

So passes a great sportsman and a great soldier who won honour on the field of play and on the field of battle… Major Gerrard addressed himself to all dangerous tasks with utter fearlessness. Now he sleeps on the battlefield in a spot that will be 'for ever England'. One can hear him cry to those who are left: 'Chin up, carry on'.[4]

Two days later, a minute's silence was observed before a match with a strong New Zealand Forces XV; a lone Liberator bomber swept over the Recreation Ground in salute. Plans were already being laid to set up a Gerrard Memorial Fund and his name still lives on in a scholarship awarded to pupils of Taunton School showing exceptional sporting ability.

Another Bath player involved in the desert campaign was Geoffrey Foster, of the Royal Tank Regiment, awarded the Military Cross in April 1943 for 'gallant and

The morning after … The remains of the West Stand, 25 April 1942.

'Business as usual by summer 1942'.

distinguished service', while former Club captain Ian Spence also won the MC for service in the Middle East. RAF bomber pilot Basil Robinson, godfather to Gerrard's baby son, Duncan, was promoted to Group Captain and awarded the AFC and Bar to his DFC and DSO, only to be shot down and killed over Germany in August 1943.

On 15 February 1944 came the news that Captain Peter Moon, an outstanding player and personality in the pre-war years, had lost his life in the 8th Army's invasion of Italy, aged 32. In civilian life a chemist, who practised with his stepfather E.G. Dickenson in George Street, he had seen active service in Syria, North Africa and Italy.

Amid all the heartache, there could be moments of hilarity. During the Allied invasion of France, Corporal 'Curly' Halse was serving with the 43rd Division, Royal Engineers, along with Sergeant Tommy Hicks. Early one morning, Curly's unit was established along a fog-shrouded ridge on Mount Peacon, the highest area in Normandy. A lone figure suddenly emerged from the mist. Rifles were immediately cocked and sighted on 'the enemy' when Curly shouted: 'Hang on, it's one of ours!' Indeed it was – none other than Lance Wardle, a third member of the pre-war Bath team, wandering about in the forward lines. 'Out of position, as usual,' recalled 'Curly' shortly before his death

Wing Commander B.V. Robinson (left) and Major R.A. Gerrard at the christening of Gerrard's son, Duncan. Both men perished on active service.

in 2001. Asked how he recognised his old team-mate, he insisted: 'from the No. 12 on his back, of course!'

A few weeks later Major Wardle was invalided home after being injured by a mortar burst, while Halse was injured in the arm and leg later in 1944, although they were luckier than some of their team-mates. Lance Corporal Leslie Phillips – 'a tearaway forward who never spared himself or his opponents' – had been posted missing as one of the first wave of airborne troops on D-Day and was later confirmed killed in action. It was later learned that he was in an aircraft that crashed at Dives-sur-Mere with the loss of all on board; not long afterwards, his wife gave birth to a baby daughter and named her Lesley in honour of the father.

Lieutenant-Colonel Dick James, 29, second-in-command of the 4th Somerset Light Infantry, also lost his life in the thrust through Normandy in July 1944. Brother-in-law to S.G.U. Considine, he was a fine three-quarter but a knee injury ended his career and he had served on the committee until the outbreak of war.

Some families suffered even more grievously. Private E.W. Holmes, a wing forward who had a few first XV games but played mainly for the United, was killed in action in France having already endured the loss of his wife and two sons in the Bath Blitz of April 1942. I.J. Pitman lost a brother and a sister, who was a ferry pilot.

Tommy Hicks fought on in the advance through France, earning the appreciation of the Commander-in-Chief, Home Forces, after he and another Bath man, Lieutenant D.K. Silvester, worked with fellow sappers to construct a 680ft bridge across the River Seine, all the while under heavy enemy fire. Next day the bridge took a direct hit but it was repaired and opened again within two-and-a-half hours, allowing a stream of armoured vehicles en route to the north of Paris and the Belgian frontier. Hicks was later awarded the Military Medal.

Roy Harris was by this time a Major with the Royal Artillery in Burma and was three times Mentioned in Despatches. In one typically daring episode, he floated a 25-pounder field gun on a barge downriver behind Japanese lines. Post-war, he joined the RAF and reached the rank of Group Captain. According to Arnold Ridley, 'Roy Harris was the finest Bath player never to play for England'.

The following April Jock Minto, having seen service in Italy with the King's Own Scottish Borderers, was posted to Palestine. Major C.P. Morley, a pre-war contemporary of Gerrard in the Bath three-quarter line, was released from a prisoner-of-war camp and then awarded the Military Cross for bravery in the North African campaign.

Back home, thoughts had already turned to the practicalities of the Club resuming when hostilities ceased – whenever that might be. Serious consideration was given to moving from the Rec to the Horse Show Ground at Lambridge along the London Road but the sub-committee set up to deliberate the matter was unequivocally in favour of staying put and their recommendation was unanimously approved by the Management Committee. All present at the meeting on 31 July 1944 were left in no doubt about the difficulties of re-establishing the club, as the minutes recorded:

... it was agreed that the public should be informed that unless financial assistance was forthcoming, the Club was very much in danger of extinction.

Their decision had been influenced by the necessity of restoring covered spectator accommodation, in order to attract first-class clubs, and also a sizeable adverse reaction from the public.

The Club would press forward for Government approval, through the Recreation Ground Company, to carry out temporary repairs to the North Stand and erect some sort of temporary make-do stand on the devastated West side.[5]

With the help of 60 clothing coupons from the RFU, the club ordered 15 jerseys from Messrs John Moore, of Argyle Street. Restrictions on multi-colour clothing forced them to choose a set of white shirts.

When a general meeting was held at the Red House on 4 September 1944, it was first agreed that the club be reconstituted as in 1939. More significantly, ladies were admitted to membership with full voting powers for the first time and Mrs Molly Gerrard struck a blow for equality by securing one of the 12 vacant places on the Management Committee, to be joined by Captain Amor, Messrs B.C. Barber, R.S. Chaddock, F. Cashnella, R. Fear, H. Davies, H. Slade, H. Vowles, G.B. Jones, H. Crane and J. Tolman. Frank Cashnella, having resigned in 1932, thus renewed his remarkable association with the club he first represented as a teenager in 1898.

While repairs to the West Stand were being delayed by wrangling with the War Damage Commission, Cashnella suggested at their first Management Committee meeting a realignment of the pitch east-to-west, although this was vetoed by the Recreation Ground Company. Nevertheless, with a new set of shirts and two balls provided by the RFU, the Bath club was ready to resume. The only other club in Somerset to have carried on throughout the war was Bridgwater.

First opponents, on 17 October 1944, were the RAF who were beaten 16-0 by a team with seven newcomers. With fly-half Danny Evans, the former Wales international, as *de facto* captain for the remainder of the season, interest and enthusiasm grew week by week until 2,300 spectators turned up to watch Bath beat St Mary's Hospital 15-13 on 3 February 1945. Evans, due to be posted away from Bath, played his last game on 2 April in a 5-3 victory over Leicester Barbarians, kicking the winning conversion.

The annual general meeting of the club convened on 8 June 1945 when the president, Dr Scott-Reid pointed out that, in carrying on during the war years, the club had given sport and enjoyment to many service players.

He then paid tribute to those old Bath players who had lost their lives during the war and to whom the Bath club owed a great debt of gratitude. Mr. Scott Reid continued by asking the meeting to rise and stand in silence as a tribute to these men.[7]

On 8 September, proper rugby resumed with the fixture that was cancelled six years earlier – the Rag Doll match at home to Llanelly – but only back row forward Kenneth Weiss remained from the team that finished in 1939. The Scarlets won 16-0 but the overwhelming feeling must have been relief that life was returning to some semblance of normality.

The Bath team, captained by Austin Higgins, included back-row forward Tom Smith who had made his debut as a 16-year-old City of Bath schoolboy almost a year earlier against the RAF. After 20 appearances he was claimed by the military for National Service, returning in 1948 to pursue a lengthy career in the front row.

A temporary stand had been erected in front of the bomb-damaged West Stand. Built at a cost of £100 with steel scaffolding and corrugated sheeting, it was 120ft long and 10ft deep, accommodating 300 in three rows, one of which was seated. The teams assembled and changed at the Cross Baths. The 2,000 who attended included a Mr A.E. Ley, from the Bristol area, who cycled his customary 26 miles.

That was nothing compared to the journey undertaken by Sgt-Major Jock Minto, who arrived home on leave after a hazardous 20-day journey by boat and train via Haifa and Toulon, in time to face Haydn Tanner's London Welsh, although Bath lost 16-8. That was all forgotten a week later, however, as the Rec filled up for the first post-war derby and Bristol were beaten 6-3, Tom Smith missing the game with an eye injury after being knocked down by an errant cyclist.

For the visit of London Scottish on 1 December 1945, the club had finally received permission from the planning authorities to erect a temporary pre-fab grandstand

'Scotsman's gallery'. A free vantage point on North Parade.

providing cover for 600, half of them seated. The stark tubular steel frame clad in corrugated iron sheeting matched the mood of austerity which required that any playing kit ripped beyond repair could only be replaced by coupon clothing. Ever on cue, Arnold Ridley handed in some clothing coupons at the subsequent Management Committee meeting but the problem persisted and such was the state of the kit by the end of the season that they had to borrow a set of black and amber jerseys from HMS *Royal Arthur* at nearby Corsham.

On the field, the now-demobbed Roy Harris made a welcome return over Weston-super-Mare, scoring a try in a 13-3 home win in which Leslie Moores, Fred Hayman and Joe Bailey also excelled. After a 23-0 Boxing Day victory over Old Blues, the team achieved a hugely satisfying 3-3 draw at Llanelly, reckoned to be Bath's best-ever performance in Wales.

Club finances were in a poor state though, with taxation having a crippling effect on income. Out of gate receipts of £553, no less than £329 had 'disappeared' in tax and £135 in travelling expenses.

Ian Lumsden, a speedy centre who had scored after seven minutes of his debut against Northampton, represented a Scottish XV against the touring Kiwis in the New

Year. A fortnight later he scored one of three Bath tries as they maintained their excellent form under the inspirational Higgins with a 13-11 win at Gloucester, the celebrations slightly dampened by the removal to hospital of Harris with a bruised kidney, an injury which kept him out of the Somerset-Gloucestershire side to face the Kiwis the following Saturday.

It was March before the club was able to provide even a cup of tea for the opposition. Faced with the refusal of the men from the Ministry to sanction the necessary permits, well-wishers came forward with canned milk, tea and sugar aplenty, although Cardiff were taking no chances for their visit on 21 March – they brought their own half-time lemons. Despite all the privations, the first post-war season yielded a respectable 16 wins to 19 defeats and a draw.

Some 40 players turned up on the Stothert & Pitt ground at Newton St Loe for the club trial in August 1946, to the satisfaction of new skipper Ian Lumsden, although he missed the opening game, a 3-3 draw at home to Llanelly, because of a knee injury. Nearly 4,000 witnessed a dour contest in which Les Williams scored a late try for the visitors only for C.J. (Cyril) Porter to cancel it out almost immediately with a magnificent penalty kick.

Neither side had the luxury of numbered jerseys and when the Bath committee met to discuss the reintroduction of numbering at the end of September, they were split 6-6 over whether to include a No. 13. Chairman Bill Barber had the casting vote and voted for its elimination in accordance with precedent. The No. 13 was to appear again, however, living up to its baleful reputation by claiming Guy Addenbrooke as its 'victim' in 1950.

Slowly, things were returning to normal and the Ministry of Fuel and Power authorised use of 1,000 watts of lighting for training – allowing four 250w bulbs – which satisfied the club's modest requirements. Clothing coupons were still much sought after, however, and every donation, large and small, was courteously acknowledged by the Honorary Secretary, Victor Smith.

Such privations did not stop Bath enjoying their Cornish tour, on which they won two games out of three and indulged in the obligatory fun and frolic!

More coupons were needed after an exciting 8-6 win over Bristol on 19 October 1946. The visitors appeared to be cruising to victory when Cyril Porter suddenly wrong-footed five defenders to score under the posts, leaving himself an easy conversion. In the celebrations that ensued, Spence Meighan's newly-numbered jersey was torn from his back, as was that of scrum-half H.V. 'Farmer' Bland.

Since the Bath Blitz, the players had continued to change and wash in the small, circular, open-air Cross Bath at the end of Bath Street, known locally as the 'Twopenny Hot'. Fed by natural spring water at a constant temperature it was inviting enough for

Bath lost to Newport 5-20 on 9 March 1946. From left to right, back row: B.C. Barber (committee), C.R. Bailey (committee), H. Davies (Honorary Secretary), Joe Knight, Reg Swaffield (committee), J. Bailey, J. Arnold, D. Rees, Ron Ludlow (masseur), D. Bainbridge, W. Barrow, T. Smith, W.F. Pears, L. Moores, S. Piggins (referee), G. Donaldson (trainer). Middle row: C.R. West, I. Lumsden, A. Higgins (captain), K. Weiss, A. Beasley. Front row: Staff Sgt L. Joseph, F.R. Hayman.

Bath *v.* Llanelly on 7 September 1946: Gerry Jenkins, Bill Barrow and Cyril Porter in a match drawn 3-3.

Tommy Hicks tackles Swansea's Guy Addenbrooke on 21 September 1946. Addenbrooke later joined Bath.

many to consider it worth the trek from the Recreation Ground along Spring Gardens, up the smelly riverside steps (still smelly to this day), along North Parade and down York Street.

Visiting players loved a bathe in the Cross Baths afterwards. So would anyone who had to walk half a mile after playing a game of rugby![8]

Truth to tell, they had little option because the Corporation had refused to grant a licence for the rebuilding of the North Stand, prompting the committee to decide on 16 December 1946 to purchase the temporary West Stand for £548, paying instalments of £100 per month for five months and one instalment of £48.

Cyril Porter, soon to join BOAC as a pilot, was named with Bland as first reserve for England in the final trial at Sunderland but Ian Lumsden went one better, being chosen to make his Scotland debut in Paris on New Year's Day 1947. The French celebrated their return to the Five Nations fold after an absence of 16 years by winning 8-3 but Lumsden won further caps that year against Wales and the Australians.

On 18 January, Bath achieved an 8-5 victory over a Cardiff side containing seven internationals, Bath scoring tries through Joe Bailey and R. Venables Kyrke and making light of the absence of Lumsden, on duty at a Scottish trial. Jack Arnold added a conversion and nearly added a third try on the whistle.

How frustrating then that the country was promptly gripped by the biggest freeze in living memory, colder even than those experienced in the 1800s by Frank Soane and his hardy cohorts. There were no matches until 22 March when Bath managed a 3-3 draw at London Irish and it was 19 weeks before rugby resumed on the Rec with a 7-5 win against Exeter. With the grey-haired club treasurer Charles Burrough an inspiring pack leader, Bath followed up with an exciting 3-0 success over Harlequins on Maundy Thursday and defeated London Scottish 6-3 two days later.

With the permission of The Recreation Grounds Company, the season was extended into May and further successes were achieved against Leicester (12-8), Northampton (16-13) and Moseley (11-0). Bristol won 9-0 at the Memorial Ground but Bath finished off with an 8-3 victory over Gloucester, thanks to a characteristically elusive try by Lumsden. Jack Arnold, now the established placekicker, kicked the rest of the points to secure the 18th win of a 32-match season, with 10 defeats and 4 draws.

That momentum was not maintained in the 1947/48 campaign which began with a string of defeats against Llanelly, Leicester, Swansea and Weston-super-Mare, although new skipper Tommy Hicks could point to the prolonged absence of Lumsden on RAF medical duties. At least work had begun on restoring the blitzed North Stand, but shortages of labour and materials, and bureaucratic wrangles, delayed its reopening until 31 January 1948. With seats for 400 and further cover for 600 standing, the stand also provided showers and dressing rooms for the players. There were a few, however, who still hankered after a good old soak in the hot spring waters of the Cross Baths – particularly as the water in the new showers was often cold!

Tour guide extraordinaire! Cyril Bailey in Cornwall in 1946.

Bill Barrow and Jim Messer booting on against Swansea on 20 September 1947.

Success at the Sevens!

Patchy performances on the field were mirrored by a degree of disharmony among officials. A warning was issued as early as 15 September 1947 'that the Committee views with concern the leakages of Committee Business which continue to take place and if such persist, and the names of offenders become known, they will be named in Committee and suitable action will follow'. Two months later the chairman, J.F.B. Jones, walked out of a committee meeting over their refusal to approve a collection for a Sportsmen's Wedding Gift to HRH Princess Elizabeth, as requested by the Mayor. The committee stood firm on any suggestion of a grant from club funds but did finally agree, with six dissenting, to a voluntary collection at the Gloucester home match, which yielded £8 6s 3d. Shades of republicanism at one of England's oldest rugby clubs?

Things began to look up on the playing side when Bristol were beaten 10-8 on the Rec on 6 March – the first win for two months – and that was followed by a 12-3 win over Taunton. Hicks then returned from a wrist injury to score the winning try against London Irish (6-3), a match that was just as memorable for Curly Halse's reverse pass that created the other try for G.A. Reid. The season tailed off, however, with defeats by Newport (0-25), Leicester (3-16), London Scottish (3-11), Northampton (5-14) and Newbridge (0-16), prompting local builder Cyril Beazer to proclaim at the AGM on 14 June 1948 that the standard of play – 15 wins and 20 defeats from 37 matches – had been the worst seen for many years. One highlight however, was the winning of the Somerset RFU Seven-a-side Tournament.

Encouragingly, it was reported at the meeting that England selector Henry 'Bert' Toft, capped ten times at hooker from 1936-39, had taken over as principal of Bath Technical College and was interested in joining the club, perhaps as coach.

Meanwhile, as a new generation planned the club's resurgence, past heroes slowly slipped away. The previous winter, the club flag flew at half-mast for James Timmins, an outstanding running back of the turn of the century who had done much to transform play from a forward-dominated style. In August 1948, the club mourned the passing of his contemporary, Frank Cashnella, as uncompromising a personality off the field as he was on it. A few days short of his 69th birthday when he died, he had been wholly committed to the game and to the club for more than fifty years.

-12-

Stormy Weather

ALEC ORMONDE LEWIS was already 28 when he made his Bath debut in the back row against Swansea at the Rec on 18 September 1948. Although he came close to scoring, a 14-0 defeat carried little hint of the 10 England caps that were to come his way.

Lewis, a veteran of the Eighth Army's campaign through North Africa, Sicily and Italy, bearing the scars of a run-in with an anti-personnel mine, had reached the rank of Company Sergeant Major when demobbed the previous year. Finding work with Petroleum Board in Wiltshire, he joined Swindon Town FC as an amateur and also had a county trial as a tennis player, but then opted for rugby with the local club. He had played both soccer and rugby as a boarder at the Royal Masonic School before the war, also demonstrating his all-round sporting prowess by representing the Army at fencing. After moving west along the A4 to Bath, to a job with Shell, he scored a try in his second match for the Club, an 11-11 draw in sweltering heat against Devonport Services, and followed that with two more against Penzance and Redruth on the Cornish tour.

Losing 13-3 to Redruth on the Tuesday afternoon was, on the face of it, not the best rehearsal for a visit to Llanelly four days later. Moreover, Bath were without several first teamers, including the injured Jack Arnold and Les Moores, who was on honeymoon. They started confidently though and, hammering away throughout, got the break they deserved just ten minutes from the end when Cyril Porter broke down the right wing and sent Michael Terry in for the winning try. Not only was it Bath's first win at Stradey Park, but it was also their first in a first-class match in Wales.

There was something of a hangover in a 20-9 defeat by St Mary's Hospital, although six players were absent on county duty. Lewis scored again and sampled the derby atmosphere for the first time in a 3-3 draw with Bristol on 16 October 1948, dubbed 'merry and merciless' by one newspaper report. After an 8-0 defeat at Bridgwater, Club captain Dr Allan Todd cracked the whip on training attendance and was rewarded with the first home win of the season, 18-13 against Harlequins. It also marked the return of Ian Lumsden, who twice sent his centre partner, Terry, in for tries. Todd added two more himself before Cornishman Terry completed his hat-trick from an interception.

After a 3-0 home win over Weston-super-Mare on 18 December, 'The Captain' was moved to write in *The Bath Chronicle*:

A. Lewis, best forward on the field, nearly did the trick again. He is a remarkably fine back row forward, and if he does not make International class, it will be surprising.[1]

Ten days later, a shortage of three-quarters persuaded the selectors to pick Lewis in the centre for the home match with Llanelly as Bath sought their first 'double' over the Sospans. Out of position or not, it was a virtuoso performance underlining his strength, pace and safe hands and it was Lewis's extravagant dummy that enabled Williams to tear away for the first try – his eighth of the season. Co-centre Kevin O'Shaughnessy, also profiting from Lewis's presence, scored the second. Forwards Todd, Messer, Reid and Harter were in tremendous form and Les Moores defended stoutly at full-back, successfully protecting the try-line for the third successive game.

Moores had moved to full-back after Jack Arnold had announced his retirement, although he reappeared late in the season for a brief swansong. Arnold continued to devote many years' loyal service to the club – as Team Secretary, touch judge, Club president and life member – as well as contributing countless articles to match programmes, and his Team Secretary notebooks provided invaluable research material for this history. He was also a founder member of the Old Players Association.

As the season moved into 1949, Bath were second best at London Welsh (5-6) and at home to Cardiff (6-9) but an 8-8 draw at Moseley initiated an unbeaten run which included away wins at St Mary's Hospital (11-3) and Newbridge (5-3), a 13-3 victory at home to Gloucester, another draw with Moseley (6-6) and a home win against Wasps (13-8). Next up was the trip to Bristol on 5 March and confidence could not have been higher.

Playing in a snowstorm, Bath attacked throughout 'like a pack of hounds in full cry'. The only score was a magnificent first-half penalty by full-back Paddy Sullivan, who had joined from Bristol earlier in the season.

Six of the last ten games of the season were lost, including Leicester at home 3-8, but the forceful Todd had restored Bath's reputation by finishing in credit with 19 wins from 40 games, with 16 defeats and 5 draws, which made his subsequent mid-summer bust-up with the committee all the more distressing. The dispute centred on Dr Todd's proposal to the AGM of 14 June 1949 'that ultimate responsibility for the selection and training of the first XV shall rest with the captain of the club'. Several members, including Harry Slade, expressed concern that the committee would have no jurisdiction over the composition of the team or playing policy and that the captain would be able to alter the playing structure of the Club without reference to the Management Committee. The minutes of the AGM sum up the captain's viewpoint:

Dr Todd said that he had no directions during the past season, as the committee was selecting the side. He added: 'At the present moment I think it is just a "hotchpotch" of

Left: Tom Smith finds himself in a spot of bother, but Tommy Hicks is there to help out. Cornwall 1948.

Below: Bath RFC, 1948/49. From left to right, back row: K.G. Box, D.S. Watson, G.A. Strong, J. Stockden, J.H. Adams, G. Brown, V. Northam, G. Foster, J. Vaissiere, W. Barrow, T. Lewis. Middle row: J. Griffin, J.H. Bailey, F. Carey, B.D. Brighton, J.W.P. Roberts, C.M. Terry, T. Smith, L. Harter, G.R. Hawkes, A. Lewis, R. Self, M.S. Spark, G. Donaldson. Front row: W.S. Donnelly, T. Hicks, M. Hannah, A. Burcombe, M. Sutton, .W.A. Todd (captain), B.C. Barber (chairman), K.B. Weiss, N. Halse, G.A. Reid, J. Arnold, W. Wilcox, P.H. Adams. Front row: S. Porter, R. Ball.

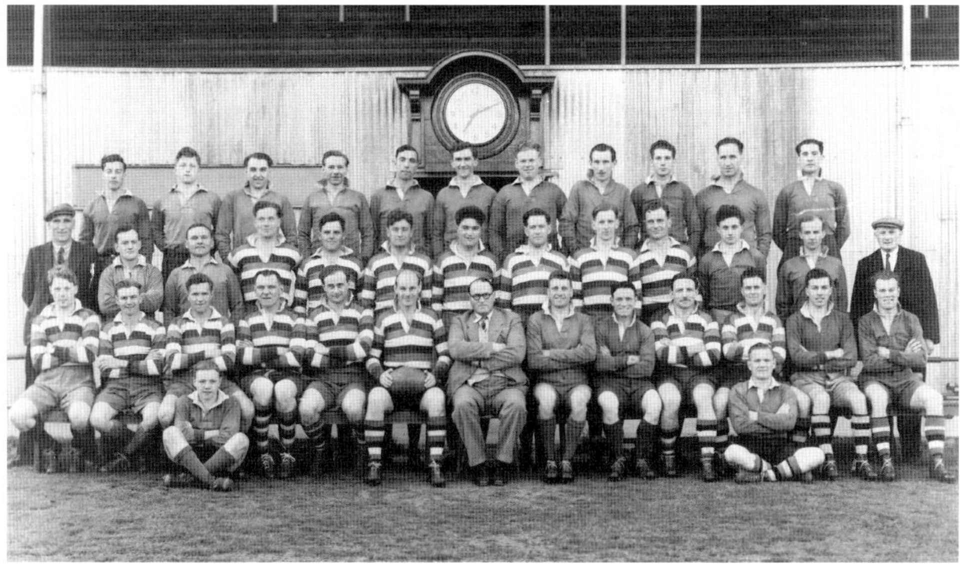

Bob Ball, Bill Donnelly and Alec Lewis ensure 'match on!' April 1949.

Tommy Hicks and Mike Terry make a run for it with Kevin O'Shaughnessy against Leicester on 8 April 1949. The match was won 12-8 by Bath.

ideas, and I think it would be better if the team went on the field with one idea how to play the game. We must pick teams with that defined policy – how they are going to play. There would still be a selection committee, and therefore if the captain did not wish to accept the responsibility, he could leave it to the committee as at present'.[2]

The differences between committee and senior players, which had been evident for some years, were unresolved, beyond a Management Committee decision that the Selection Committee comprise five elected members – initially Messrs Arnold, Barber, Burrough, Davies and Simpkins – together with the captains of the three XVs. The dispute continued to simmer and eventually boiled over at an *ad hoc* selection meeting on 15 September, less than 48 hours before the First XV were due to face Devonport Services.

Feelings ran so high that Todd resigned both the captaincy and his playing membership of the club, a decision which he confirmed by letter the following Monday. After contemplating a 'stand' against the committee and coming perilously close to refusing to play, a deputation of players met the committee to air their grievances. Officialdom's response was to post a notice in the dressing room to the effect that:

...the resolution re the voting powers of the Captains of the United and A teams on selection committee had been rescinded, that no members of the selection committee are ex-officio members, and that any player who could not abide by the rules of the club as constituted was at liberty to tender his resignation which would be accepted by the committee.[3]

The captaincy was offered to Alec Lewis, who thought long and hard before declining. Len Harter was then elected in time to lead the side out at Bristol on 15 October 1949. Bath lost 13-11 and, hardly surprisingly given the turmoil within the club, managed just 3 wins in their first 12 matches.

Sullivan's boot proved decisive in a 14-12 Christmas Eve win over Gloucester but the early months of 1950 were depressing in the extreme as the team went through another bad patch of 10 matches without a win. A time-honoured Bath superstition was reinforced when winger Guy Addenbrooke suffered a bad arm injury wearing the No. 13 jersey against Newport on 18 February and could not play until Christmas the following year. The accursed number was subsequently banished from the Bath playing kit for nearly 50 years.

With 21 defeats and 15 wins from the 39-match programme, everyone was glad to see the back of the 1949/50 season and Alec Lewis's election as captain by the 'regular players' (those with 12 games for the First XV or 20 for the Club in that season) was greeted with acclamation by the June AGM. Within three months, Allan Todd had been restored to playing membership after apologising for his part in the schism of the previous autumn.

Selection committee. From left: Brian Lane, Curly Halse, Jim Vaissiere, Jack Arnold, Charles Burrough, Trevor Lewis and Les Cutler.

Now that relations with the players were on a more cordial basis, the committee could turn their attention to other matters – such as the need to rebuild the West Stand destroyed by enemy action more than eight years earlier. Plans for a new stand had been lodged with the Town & Country Planning Authority in October 1939 but solicitor Lance Wardle reported to the Management Committee on 21 August 1950 that council planners had refused the club's application. Where to turn next? They needed to recruit a powerful ally so James Pitman, former Bath and England rugby player and now Bath's Member of Parliament, was invited to attend a meeting between the Recreation Ground Company and the Planning Committee.

The next meeting of the club's Management Committee was a sombre affair as they stood in silence in memory of the mercurial S.G.U. Considine, who had died on 31 August after a prolonged illness. He was 49.

With the one-eyed wartime international hooker Fred Hill arriving from Bristol and quickly establishing a rapport with props John Roberts and Tom Smith, Bath recovered from opening defeats at Leicester (6-8) and 16-0 at home to Hylton Cleaver's XV to draw 8-8 with Llanelly. Only 2 of the succeeding 11 matches were lost and Bristol were defeated 13-6 at the Rec on 21 October. That match, attended by RFU president Sir Wavell Wakefield, marked the debut of 19-year-old Welshman Glyn John who sealed an outstanding display at fly-half by weaving through for a try under the posts three minutes from time. He was capped from St Luke's College, Exeter, in 1954.

London Irish were beaten on 11 November 1950 by a line-up unusual for the fact that it included another newcomer, Maurice Bailey, as well as his uncle, the former centre, Joe Bailey. Joe had stepped in as a last-minute replacement at wing forward.

Alec Lewis's outstanding form was duly recognised by his selection for the Whites in the England trial at Otley on 2 December, while John Roberts was named as a reserve, but a visit to a freezing Kingsholm at the end of the month provided a reality check when Gloucester triumphed 27-3. Even more sobering was a 39-9 defeat at Newport on

3 February 1951, although 9 points was the most that the unstoppable Black and Ambers had conceded in any match so far!

Confidence was restored with an 8-3 win in the return with Gloucester and, despite a hiccup against Leicester in the following match, Bath then embarked on a winning sequence of 10 wins and 2 draws during which they conceded just 29 points. More significantly, they trumped the 30-year-old club record of 25 wins in a season to set a new mark of 27, with just 10 of their 41 games lost and 4 drawn. Points for totalled 324 with 277 against, with the skipper Lewis leading try scorer with 12 and Paddy Sullivan top points scorer with 80 from 13 conversions, 17 penalties and a dropped goal.

For all the euphoria, there was still deep frustration at the continued refusal of the Ministry of Works to sanction a licence for the rebuilding of the West Stand and that was despite James Pitman's intervention, supported by Sir Wavell Wakefield. Letters to *The Bath Chronicle* echoed a feeling of resentment that the club had been unfairly treated.

'Sir, – I think the most important point in the controversy about the Rugby Club's stand has been forgotten. Rugby is an amateur game and, in many parts of the country, is played chiefly by members of the so-called favoured classes. This fact may have some bearing on the withholding of a licence for the club to rebuild.

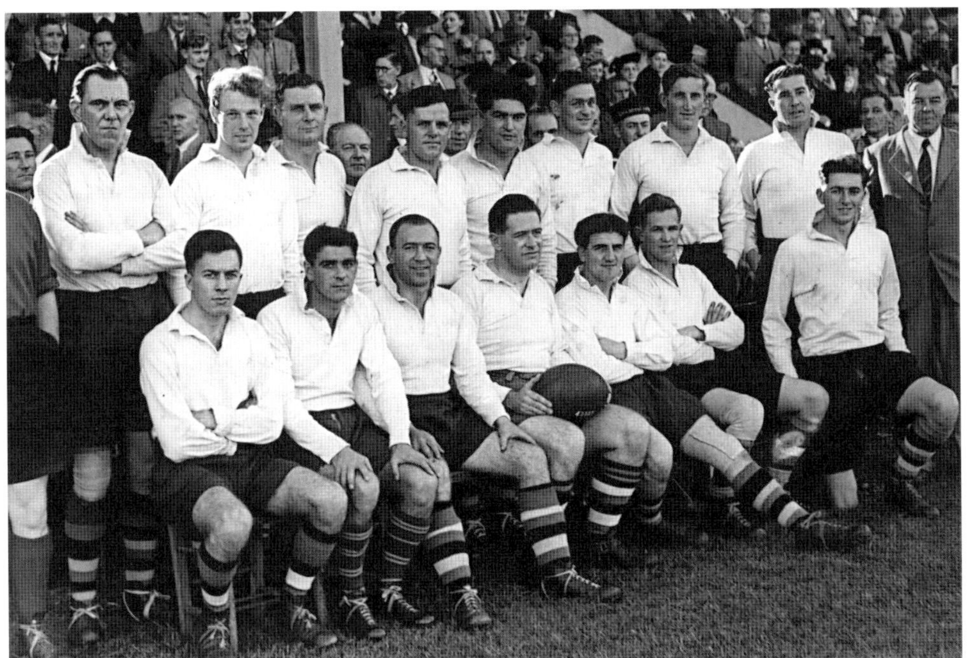

Bath *v.* Bristol (away), 15 October 1949. From left to right, back row: A. Burcombe, W. Donnelly, A.O. Lewis, J.W.P. Roberts, T.H. Smith, G. Addenbrooke, K. O'Shaughnessy, T. Lewis. Front row: K. Wilcox, J. Hopkins, J. Francis, L. Harter (captain), P. Sullivan, M. Hanna, J. Dingle.

I think that the point that should be made is that in the West of England rugby is, and always has been, pre-eminently a working class game, and that the crowd in most West Country areas, and in Bath's also, is largely composed of the working class. I think it would be useful to raise this question.' ...signed BOTH CODES.[4]

The paper's rugby correspondent weighed in too:

The Bath Club, backed by the president of the Rugby Union, Sir Wavell Wakefield MP, and Mr I.J. Pitman, MP for Bath, are not taking the refusal of the Ministry of Works to grant a licence to rebuild the blitzed West Stand, lying down. Why the Minister should discriminate against Bath and in favour of other clubs makes no sense at all. Bath City is only one of the 'favoured' clubs. There are instances both at Bridgwater and Stroud, and the latest is that of the Saracens, where Bath won on Saturday. There they never possessed a stand, but one is in the course of erection for which a licence was, of course, granted.[5]

Officialdom refused to be swayed, however, and the Management Committee meeting on 25 June was dismayed to hear that a rebuilding licence had again been refused. On 7 January 1952 the committee voted to ask the Recreation Ground Company to apply again and word came through the following October that this too had been turned

Bath, 1951/52 (played 38, won 20, lost 15, drawn 3, points for 314, points against 249). From left to right, back row: S. Marsh (United XV baggage man), W.E. Fowles (Joint Honorary Treasurer), D.M. Smith (committee), A.E. Anderson (Honorary Match Secretary), A.L. Cutler (vice chairman), C.A. Burrough (committee), A.F. Foster (Joint Honorary Teasurer), A. Ball (First XV baggage man). Middle row (standing): S. Porter, R.J. Berry, R.B. Owen, J. French, G. Clements, P. Dingle, F.J. Sheppard, G.S. Brown, L.A. Hughes, T. Thorn, P.R. Cobbe, J.W. Francis. Centre row (seated): W.J.F. Arnold (Honorary Team Secretary), A.J. Meek, J.T. Dingle, T.H. Smith, J.W.P. Roberts, A.O. Lewis (captain), J.F. Bevan-Jones (chairman), T. Lewis, J.F. Vaissiere (captain, United XV), F. Carey, D.W. Mattingley, A.J. Polson, E.F. Simpkins (Honorary Secretary). Front row: C.J. Weston, N.P. Halse (captain, 'A' XV), R.A. Ball, G. Adenbrooke, G. Rogers, R.H. Hambly.

Arnold Ridley, club president, 1950-52.

down. It was not to be until August 1953 that a licence was finally granted, ten and a half years after the bombers had done their work.

Meanwhile, at an Old Crocks get-together in April 1951, it was suggested by the Club president Arnold Ridley and J. Bevan-Jones that they form an Old Players' Association. The first meeting was held on 18 May with some 70 people present and by the following year, membership stood at 216 with I.J. Pitman MP as founding president and Alderman W.F. Long as vice-president. Social activities were initially confined to skittles matches.

There was little point looking beyond Alec Lewis as First XV captain for the 1951/52 season. It was too much to expect Bath to exceed or even match the performances of the previous campaign, but for the rangy back row it was one of personal triumph and a well-deserved, if belated, elevation to the international ranks at the age of 31.

His first cap was achieved against Basil Kenyon's Springboks on 5 January 1952 and, although England were beaten 8-3, Lewis remained a fixture on the blindside throughout the Five Nations Championship. A Welsh victory at Twickenham meant that the Bath man did not play on a winning England side until a 19-3 defeat of the Scots at

Cyril Bailey and the Crazy Gang.

Murrayfield but Ireland succumbed 3-0 at Twickenham and the French were beaten 6-3 in Paris.

Bath blooded new players such as centre Len Hughes, second row Angus Meek and back row Peter Hall, who were all destined to succeed Alec Lewis as presidents of the club 40 years and more later. In addition, eventual presidents George Brown, John Roberts, Norman Halse, Geoff Hancock and Roger Berry all stemmed from the ranks of this playing era. It was some time before the team settled down to play in the fashion expected by the Rec faithful. The turning point appeared to be the 120th derby match on 1 March 1952, when 6,000 turned up at the Rec to see Bath beat Bristol 6-3 with tries by T. Thorne and the skipper himself.

At St Helen's the following weekend, Alec Lewis fired over a 40-yard penalty but the Bath players were astounded to see the referee award a try to Swansea after winger Horace Philips appeared to run outside both the touch flag and the corner flag before placing the ball in-goal. When John Roberts encountered Philips many years later, he was greeted with: 'Don't you start on to me about that try, you bugger!'

Undeterred by a 6-3 defeat, Bath reeled off eight victories before losing 17-5 at Moseley and then strung together three more to finish the season with a tally of 21 wins, 15 losses and 3 draws. John Roberts and Tom Smith played in all but two of those matches and they were rewarded for their consistency and commitment with the captaincy and vice-captaincy respectively for 1952/53.

A 'Smoker' was held at the Angel Hotel after the Bristol game and this eminently successful evening saw the coming together of some 165 past and present players. For entertainment the 'Crazy Gang' were in attendance, with Cyril Bailey as leader of the band – dubbed as the 'BCB Seemphoney Orchestra'. Virtuosos such as John Tolman, J. Bevan-Jones, Bert Anderson, Charlie Gough, Stan Bailey, Jack Arnold, Lester Card, Les Matthews, Tommy Hicks and Victor Smith (piano) were to continue for several years as their *dramatis personae*... They made their own fun.

A one-off match against a John Kendall-Carpenter XV at the Rec on 18 September 1952 brought the half-expected announcement from the ten-times capped Oxford Blue that he was joining the club. In his pre-match pep talk, Roberts relayed a message from 'Carps' that he did not wish to displace any Bath regular. The select XV won 10-9.

Quite the most extraordinary 'performance' by the team was witnessed some two weeks later on the quayside at St Ives, the day after a 9-8 defeat at Penzance. The Bath players, some in bed (just!) and others picking over breakfast, were roused by two huge

John Kendall-Carpenter accumulated 23 England caps (1949-54).

bangs as Coastguard maroons shattered the Sunday morning silence. They joined the locals to see HMS *Wave*, a deep sea minesweeper turned fisheries protection vessel, holed and wallowing broadside-on just 30 yards offshore after her anchor cable had parted in heavy seas. Peter Hall takes up the story:

A breeches buoy was strung from the stern to the slip-way and the local men and women were holding on desperately as the ship pitched and rolled. The first off had a particularly bad passage, as at one point the line was taut and dragging the folk down the slippery stonework, only for the ship to whip over and leave the line slack. As a result, the unfortunate mariner was dashed on rocks and came in wet and bloody. Despite this effort, only two thirds of the crew were off by 3.30pm that afternoon.

All this was quite an amazing experience for the tour party, but we were not allowed to spectate for long. Obviously, help was needed and spontaneously, we were all in there hanging on to the 100 yard-long ropes and slithering up and down like a tug-of-war team! I was wearing a brand new overcoat, which was covered in thick dirty brown oil in the struggle. Committee members Jack Arnold, Eddie Simpkins, Arthur Foster, Stan Bailey, Harry Slade, Charles Burrough and Jack Beazer joined the players to add weight to the rescue effort.

Bath *v.* International XV, 18 September 1952. From left to right, back row: L. Cutler (committee), Gwynne Walters (referee), P. Fearis, F. Hill, D. Mattingley, G. Addenbrooke, J. Dingle, F. Thomas, P.G. Hall, P. Stevens, J. Vaissiere, J. Arnold (touch judge). Front row: C. Weston, N. Halse, A.O. Lewis, J.W.P. Roberts, T.H. Smith, P. Hardy, R. Hambly.

Bristol's Peter Storey about to receive the attentions of Frank Thomas, with Fred Hill, John Roberts, John Dingle, John Kendall-Carpenter and Tom Smith on hand to help out, 18 October 1952.

Later the players saw a Greek freighter breaking up on the rocks at nearby Pendeen. Needless to say, the planned fixture at St Ives that afternoon also fell victim to the storm.

Kendall-Carpenter made his Bath debut at Llanelly the following weekend, renewing his partnership with England back row partner Alec Lewis, but they were beaten 23-5. They had more success in their next outing, a 9-3 home win over Bristol on 18 October 1952, which also marked the return of Kevin O'Shaughnessy after two years in Nigeria with the Government Survey Department. Paddy Sullivan punished his former team-mates with three penalties.

By the time the sides met again on 7 March 1953, Kendall-Carpenter and Lewis seemed to be suffering the effects of a tough international campaign as Bristol won 17-0 at a canter. A 15-14 defeat at Neath a fortnight later was viewed far more positively however, with Eddie Simpkins rating it 'the best display ever given in Wales during 40 years as Honorary Secretary'. Llanelly also edged home 6-5 at Stradey Park on 11 April but 12 days later Gloucester were roundly defeated 11-0 as Bath found their form to finish a 41-match programme with 19 wins, 16 defeats and 6 draws.

Having helped England win the Championship, only deprived of a Grand Slam by a 9-9 draw in Dublin, Alec Lewis presented his jersey to the club, prompting the setting up of a sub-committee to plan the erection of a club hut. This was one of England's oldest and most distinguished clubs – still without a clubhouse!

Faces in the crowd, 1952, included David Dolman and his father, Jack Simpkins, Cyril and Eric Beazer, Charlie Mannings and Tommy Hicks.

At the AGM on 12 June 1953, held at Red House Restaurant, scene of so many important meetings and events over the previous 40 years, it was proposed by G. French and seconded by Jim Vaissiere that 'the creation of a clubhouse be approved and the committee be authorised in their discretion to transfer the sum of £846 6s 2d, or part of it, from the Special Fund to a Club House Fund, and to circularise the holders of the existing 4% £1 certificates, with an offer to convert them into £1 Certificates now being issued in connection with the erection of the Club House'.

Ten days later the Management Committee had agreed a set of clubhouse rules and appointed a Grounds Committee comprising Messrs Anderson, C. Bailey, Jones, Smith, Beazer, Dingle and Halse, delegated to control building arrangements. They soon co-opted the architect, Mrs Molly Gerrard, and instructed preparatory site clearance work to go ahead. Meanwhile Cyril Beazer was to lead a deputation to the Ministry of Works following their refusal of a licence for the 'Hut'; there was more bad news from the Ministry, via the RFU, who reported that they saw no hope of approval for the West Stand under prevailing conditions. The suggestion was to re-apply in a year's time to seek approval of a scheme within a £5,000 limit.

Within a month, however, the Gordian knot had suddenly unravelled and the Management Committee was able to send a letter of congratulations to the Recreation Ground Company on their success in obtaining a licence to rebuild the West Stand. The

Club still had to apply for a licence to spend £1,000 of its own funds on the project, with the intention of building a full-length concrete terracing and eventually to erect the stand.

The whole saga had provided plenty of copy for the *Chronicle*'s rugby correspondent, A.S. Matthews, aka 'The Captain', and its resolution coincided with his retirement at the end of 1953, marked by a ceremony in the home dressing room before the Boxing Day fixture with Old Blues, festive visitors to the Rec since 1920.

John Roberts, in a happy little speech, handed to 'The Captain' (Mr. A S Matthews) a handsome pipe and tobacco pouch (well filled) from the players as a tribute of appreciation of his long journalistic association with the club. 'Caught on the wrong foot' by this delightful surprise, he warmly thanked John and all the players for their forethought and kindness and said that, though he will be no longer writing his 'Notebook,' his connection with the Club will continue.[6]

His successor was Peter J. Marshall ('PJM') and by 9 January 1954 he was reporting a little optimistically that following development of the new West Stand over the next eight months, 'the ground will hold at least 12,000, with more than a third of them under cover'. Work was already under way on the new clubhouse which was due to open on 6 February.

The Recreation Ground in the 1950s. Phil Hardy fields a deep one, with Robin Hambly back in support.

John Kendall-Carpenter and Alec Lewis (back row, left and second left) making their final appearances for England, in Paris in 1954.

John Roberts was experiencing mixed fortunes in his second season as captain but again emerged in credit, winning half of the 40 fixtures, losing 16 and drawing 4. There were few highlights, however, beyond a 3-0 win on the first-ever visit to Rosslyn Park on 28 November and an 8-6 victory at London Welsh 9 January. It featured a fine try by the talented Mike Terry but the centre damaged his thigh in scoring and it was his last appearance in a Bath shirt.

A 29-0 thrashing at home to Cardiff the following weekend prompted critical letters in the *Chronicle* but the opening of the new clubhouse on 6 March was celebrated with a 16-6 win over Bristol.

Alec Lewis, now 33 and having been overlooked for the meeting with the All Blacks and the Triple Crown phase of the Five Nations Championship, won his 10th cap in Paris as England sought a Grand Slam. The French triumphed 11-3 though and on 5 April 1954 the 'master' informed Bath's Management Committee that he was retiring from first-class rugby at the end of the season. His innate footballing ability, courage and determination, not to mention his ability to kick goals from 40 yards or more, marked him out as one of the greats. The club accepted his resignation 'with regret'.

Lewis's last appearance alongside John Kendall-Carpenter and Jim Vaissiere was a typically authoritative display against a powerful Harlequins side on 15 April 1954. With a fine sense of theatre, Lewis opened the scoring by collecting a cross-kick to touch down, added another try before half-time and also played his part in defence to secure a 13-10 win. He turned out at full-back against Old Merchant Taylors on Easter Monday, but missed his planned farewell game against Bedford with a heavy cold. That remarkable character, Fred Hill, also called it a day.

At the end of the season, John Roberts led the club on their very first foreign tour, achieving a hat-trick of wins against a Jura-Lyonnaise Select XV (24-3), Givors (9-6 in front of a crowd of 10,000) and Tour du Pin (17-0). The durable prop had appeared in every game and at the annual meeting on 14 June was asked to serve a third season as skipper.

Members stayed on for a special general meeting called to discuss the sale of the Recreation Ground, with construction entrepreneur Cyril Beazer presiding. The following resolution was carried by a large majority:

That having heard the arguments and explanations and being satisfied therewith, we endorse the committee's recommendation not to make an offer for the purchase of the ground.

In retrospect, it seems an opportunity lost but, having only just survived wartime privations and the austerity measures that followed and now committed to rebuilding of the West Stand and a new clubhouse, the members felt they could not take the risk.

The West Stand opening was planned for the visit of Llanelly on 2 October 1954. Members could expect to pay on the following tariff: Gent's Reserved Stand 50s; Lady's Reserved Stand 30s; Gent's unreserved stand 2 guineas; Lady's unreserved stand 1 guinea; Schoolboys – as Ladies; Ground and Enclosure 30s (Including North Stand). Admission prices were: Ground 1s, plus 6d to Enclosure, plus 6d to North Stand. Admission to unreserved West Stand 3s. Lady Helpers to be issued with a ticket on payment of one guinea. 1,001 numbered seats were to be installed in the West Stand, with adequate room for Press.

After the opening ceremony, performed by RFU president W.C. Ramsey, accompanied by I.J. Pitman MP, the big crowd marvelled at the speed and craft of Llanelly, particularly outside-half Carwyn James, who was the inspiration behind their 24-9 victory and was to prove an equally inventive and effective coach to the 1971 Lions in New Zealand.

Alec Lewis came out of retirement to make his very last appearances in early October 1954 – dropping a goal in a 13-8 win at Clifton and signing off for good with a penalty in a 6-6 draw at home to St Mary's Hospital. This was the only match John Roberts missed in two seasons but he returned for the 125th derby match on 16 October 1954, leading Bath to a 5-3 victory in which hooker Brian Lane scored a try converted by Paddy Sullivan.

Only a fortnight later a meeting of the Bath and District Supporters' Club agreed to wind up their organisation, a decision deplored by the Management Committee who put aside the assets handed over (£100) in case the club could be resuscitated at some point in the future. The Bath Rugby Supporters' Club was re-constituted, with slightly different objectives, on 20 January 1997.

At least the new clubhouse was proving a success. In the early days it was guarded by a surprisingly lifelike stuffed wolf, with bared fangs, which had been 'introduced' by first team scrum-half Geo Sidoli and forward Eric Hopton. Unfortunately, it disappeared over Christmas 1954, no doubt liberated by a visiting team. (Sidoli appeared to enjoy an affinity with our four-legged friends and is memorably pictured leading a large boxer dog off the field after it invaded the field during a match against Moseley on 17 April 1954.)

Before too long, the clubhouse had acquired an honours board, courtesy of Cyril Beazer, and a date was set for the consecration of a memorial plaque to players from 'Bath and District' who had died in the two World Wars. The ceremony, performed by the Archdeacon of Bath, was eventually held on the evening of 25 April 1955 and involved a 15-minute service with hymns and prayers and a short address by Reverend Alfred Kitching, wing three-quarter in the powerful Bath side immediately before the First World War.

One of the few with vivid memories of that era was 83-year-old Tommy Davis, perhaps the only man in the Memorial Ground on 5 March 1955 who had witnessed the very first Bath-Bristol derby on 29 October 1888. The only one of the 126 matches he had missed was 'in the middle 20s, when he was ill in bed… When he heard that Bath had won that match…he felt like getting up and celebrating immediately.'

In the meantime, the issue of ownership of the Recreation Ground had been briefly resurrected, prompted by a declaration from Bath City Council of its intention to purchase. The Recreation Ground Company forwarded to the Management Committee meeting of 7 March 1955 a copy of a letter from the Town Clerk:

I shall be glad if you will accept this letter as an assurance on behalf of the Corporation that there is no intention on the Corporation's part if the purchase is completed, to restrict or interfere with the rights and privileges enjoyed by the Bath FC under their existing lease of part of the Recreation Ground.[7]

At the following week's Management Committee meeting it was agreed that the RFU be approached for a loan for possible purchase by the Club. The terms of the Club's lease were also closely examined during March and 'it was quite clear that the Club was entitled to retain possession, subject to continued compliance with the covenants and conditions contained in the lease until September 1982'.

After obtaining support from Somerset for an approach to the RFU, the Committee took further legal advice from local solicitors Cartwright Taylor & Corpe on their rights under the new Landlord & Tenant Act 1954 and their options before and after expiry of

Club stalwarts Jim Vaissiere, John Roberts and Tom Smith.

Fred 'Wonk-eye' Hill, Geo Sidili and John Dingle.

the lease in 1982. The matter was considered by a Management Committee meeting on 25 May 1955 at which, 'after a very full discussion, it was agreed by a majority of 8 to 7 that the Club would not make an offer for the purchase of the Recreation Ground'. The members accepted their recommendation, which settled the matter once and for all.

Even before the city council acquired the Recreation Ground, the Parks Department unveiled a wholly impractical plan in August 1955 to construct a cinder running track around the rugby pitch. Not only would it have entailed moving the pitch a considerable distance away from the newly-built grandstand but it would also have put an end to the county cricket festival. It was some months before the proposal was dropped.

With John Kendall-Carpenter as Club captain, the 1955/56 season yielded few notable successes – 17 victories to set against 18 defeats and 3 draws. Conceding the 'double' to Bristol must have been particularly painful for the 'Prince of Cornerflaggers', all the more so because he had his nose broken in both games! The New Year began with victories over Leicester and at London Welsh but there was little else to shout about. Wing Tony Guest was top try scorer with 18 and John Roberts appeared in 37 games to take his career tally to 268 in just eight seasons. The reward for John Roberts' commitment and consistency was an invitation to lead the club again in 1956/57. He stuck to the task manfully, although it was a relatively lean period in Bath's history.

-13-

Of Jockeys and Silks

THE HISTORY OF Bath and other rugby clubs is full of players who distinguished themselves at other sports. Frank D'Aguilar was a good enough soccer player to impress for Royal Engineers against the all-conquering Crystal Palace team of 1870 while Frank Soane and Frederick Belson were accomplished oarsmen 25 years later. Somerset's Bertie Buse was one of legions of cricketers who were equally adept at fielding a steepling Garryowen.

But few would have been prepared to share the alternative sporting passion of the Marlborough College sixth-former who turned up for training in early December 1956. Ian Balding, a promising steeplechase jockey, must have felt that falling on a loose ball in front of a rampaging Welsh pack was no worse than being tossed among thundering hooves. He made his first-team debut on Boxing Day 1956 in a 20-3 win over Old Blues and after figuring again a fortnight later in a scoreless draw against London Welsh, was virtually ever-present for the rest of the season. Having arrived on the recommendation of another newcomer, Cambridge University skipper Ian Beer, he eventually amassed more than 100 first-team appearances.

Juggling the demands of both sports was no easy matter. The following October Balding just made it to the Rec in time to face Clifton in a Thursday evening game, having ridden The Quiet Man to victory in the 4.00 at Wincanton at odds of 100-8. The winning jockey had not seen fit to tip off his team-mates, however, and John Roberts made pointed reference in his pre-match team talk to 'the Quiet Man in the corner'. They swallowed their disappointment by running in six tries to win 26-0.

The Bath team of the mid-1950s may not have been the most successful of the first 100 years – Roberts' second two-year spell as captain yielded 15 wins in the first season and just 11 in 1957/58 – but they turned out a rather distinguished bunch. Ian Beer followed John Kendall-Carpenter's example by becoming RFU president while Dennis Silk, a goalkicking centre, was to become president of the MCC. And, of course, Balding eventually moved in even more exalted company as the Queen's trainer on the flat and has only recently retired from the turf.

All three figured prominently in a 3-0 home win over Wasps on 23 February 1957, played on a gluepot pitch after a morning downpour. Bath's try came in the first half from Tony Hankins after fellow flanker Beer, who had an outstanding game, beat two men in a determined dash. Much of the credit went to Silk, however, for his generalship in midfield and defensive work against the powerful Wasps captain, John Woodward.

A week later Silk was in equally impressive form against Bristol at the Memorial Ground, but two 45-yard penalties within a minute from the boot of England full-back Bob Challis were enough to earn a 6-0 win. Bath played most of the game with seven forwards after Roberts went off with damaged ribs. The Memorial Ground was not the happiest of hunting grounds at this time.

Silk, another former Cambridge University skipper, stepped in as captain at home to Swansea a week later, kicking the penalty that earned a 3-3 draw. There was another strong performance at Stradey on 16 March when an understrength Bath XV opened the scoring with an early John Dolman penalty but conceded two first-half tries to a Llanelli side featuring seven internationals, including half-backs Onllwyn Brace and Carwyn James.

Fed up with losing gallantly, Bath finally hung on for a 6-3 win at Newbridge on 13 April and followed up five days later on Maundy Thursday with a stirring 6-0 home win over a Harlequins side containing four internationals. Both tries came from five-yard scrums, the first going to scrum-half Paul Dart and the clinching score coming in the final minute as Silk found a gap to touch down at the corner. It was 'Bath's finest hour', trumpeted the *Chronicle*, with more than a touch of hyperbole.

Silk was named Player of the Year, although Beer had been just as valuable an acquisition on the blindside and the back row had been further strengthened by the presence of Bryan Peasley. There were tributes too to prop Tom Smith, calling it a day after 263 first-team appearances since the end of the war. He was soon followed into retirement by another experienced forward, John Dingle, who had been sidelined for 18 months following two head injuries.

At 36 and with 300-plus games under his belt, John Roberts decided he still had one more season in him. Even he must have been surprised though when, after moving house the short distance across the county border to Box, he was immediately capped by Dorset & Wilts under the captaincy of Beer. Meanwhile, scrum-half Gordon 'Titch' Drewett and prop Fred Book were called up by Somerset to play Cornwall and Drewett was later selected by the Western Counties to face the touring Wallabies.

Season 1957/58 was a low-key affair, with just six games won before the New Year, mostly against second-class opposition. The death on 1 February 1958 of Eddie Simpkins, in his 51st year on the Management Committee and his 45th as Honorary Secretary, did nothing to lift spirits.

When a youngster at Bathforum school in the early 1890s, Eddie had collected pennies from his schoolmates to amass the sum of 7s 6d and then trotted off to Messrs Chambers in Walcot Street to buy a rugby ball. Every evening he could be found with his mates down at Lower Common, playing until dark, sparking a love affair with the game that persisted for more than 60 years. His own career began with Fairfield Rovers,

Left: Bertie Buse in 1932 – a great cricketer and a fine full-back.

Below: Ian Balding on 'The Quiet Man', which romped home at 100-8 at Wincanton on 3 October 1957, only hours before he turned out for Bath in an evening fixture against Clifton!

Above left: Ian Beer, who won two England caps in 1955 while with Harlequins. *Above right:* Dennis Silk, later to become president of the MCC.

Eddie Simpkins, Arthur West and an elderly Fred 'Chumpy' Russell checking the score against the 'Downers' on 22 September 1956. Initials on the board correspond with the Old Players' committee at that time.

whom he captained in 1900/01, and he also represented St Luke's College while studying to be a teacher at the Exeter academy. As a 19-year-old he appeared on the wing for the Rest of Bath on 27 March 1902 and represented Walcot later in the season in the return fixture against the Bath club.

By this time Eddie had returned to teach at the school where he had been a pupil and had joined the rugby club at the invitation of Tommy Davis. There were a couple of appearances in trials over the next two seasons before he finally made his first-team debut in a 12-0 defeat at Lydney on 25 November 1905. Most of his appearances were as captain of the 'A' XV before a knee injury ended his playing career at the age of 24 in 1907, the year after he had first joined the committee. In 1911 he was elected joint Honorary Secretary with J.T. Piper.

On completing 25 years as Secretary, he was made an honorary life member, and although ill health forced a temporary retirement shortly before the war, he ended up sharing the duties with his son, Jack. Reminiscing to *The Bath Chronicle* in 1957, Eddie said: 'For many years I was in charge of the team on away trips, and I have seen Bath play on 66 grounds in England and Wales. There are very few home games I have missed in all the years, and there cannot be many who have seen Bath play more times, or even as many, as I have.'

Arnold Ridley, now a vice-president, wrote fondly to the *Chronicle*:

Let us remember him in his lighter moments – moments just as valuable as any. For he was no careless comedian seeking an easy laugh; his jokes pointed morals, his buffooneries had purpose… He was a man of principle, a man of courage, a student of the game in every phase and, above all, a good companion.[1]

Ex-players remember Eddie singing his own version of the Old Players' Anthem, 'We've got a motto, the Bath FC is all right,' in a quavering voice and wearing the most doleful expression:

I'VE GOT A MOTTO ALWAYS MERRY AND BRIGHT
Look around and you will find,
Every cloud is silver lined.
The sun will shine, although the skies are grey now.
Often times to myself I've said:
'Cheer up Eddie – you'll soon be dead!
It's a hard life – but a gay one.'

So passed into memory a man who had shared a committee room with Thomas Gandy, one of the Club's founders. The Simpkins dynasty continued through his son, who held the reins as Club Secretary for another thirty years.

A record 42 fixtures were squeezed into the 1957/58 programme but only five games were won in the second half of the season. Remarkably, one of those was achieved against Llanelly on 15 March when Bryan Peasley and second row Tony Jacob scored the tries in a 10-6 win to ensure that the rag doll stayed at the Rec for the first time in four seasons.

There was a sense of anti-climax, however, when John Roberts made his 354th and last appearance at home to Bedford. Like his debut against Somerset Police ten years earlier, the match ended in a draw, 8-8, but the plaudits flowed thick and fast in recognition of a decade of remarkable commitment, including five seasons as captain.

A year later, he began another 40 years of service as committee man and Club official. When the Management Committee had to seek a successor to Vic Smith as fixtures secretary, Roberts was put forward as the ideal candidate. The story goes that he thought it over for thirty minutes – and then did the job for thirty years!

As durable as the tighthead prop had been, there arrived in the close season a 15-year-old farmer's lad from Tormarton who would eclipse even Roberts' career total, eventually amassing 580 appearances. His name was Phillip Hall and he was already a schoolboy international. Other newcomers in the summer of 1958 included naval officer and second row John Jacobsen, Pete Parfitt, a tighthead prop from Walcot Old Boys earmarked to replace Roberts, and Ray Gazard, an Army sprinter who had represented Wales at long jump but had taken up rugby only that season. He arrived with fellow Welsh champion pole-vaulter Morton Evans, who was destined to enjoy a four-year spell as national pole vault coach to the British Amateur Athletic Board.

Gazard, brought in at short notice to play in a 6-6 draw at Clifton in midweek, showed enough pace and promise to be selected on the following Saturday, 4 October, at home to Llanelly. Bath had lost at Stradey a month earlier but rose to the occasion with a wholly unexpected 8-6 victory in which Gazard scored two sensational tries. A week later he was being watched at Bridgend by a Welsh selector but saw little of the ball as Bath lost 21-0.

Victory seemed possible against Bristol on 18 October until Roy Dash dropped a goal in the dying seconds to conjure a 16-14 victory for the away side in one of the most dramatic climaxes to a derby match. Four victories in the next five games suggested that, under Gordon Drewett's captaincy, Bath were finally getting into their stride but it was a false dawn and they went 12 matches without a win until a 23-11 victory at Devonport Services on 22 February 1959.

That buoyed the spirits to such an extent that they then turned in their best performance of the season in beating Wasps 19-0, despite Ian Beer struggling through the game with a cracked rib. The team's infuriating inconsistency was having an effect on gates, however, and when the home fixture with Swansea clashed with a televised international the 6-6 draw was watched by the smallest crowd that many could

Young Dick Millard retrieves the rag doll.

remember. The incessant rain was undoubtedly a factor and as few as 25 bedraggled spectators were ranged on the 'flowerpots'.

The faithful could not have been impressed by a 14-0 defeat at home to Plymouth Albion in the final match of the season, a sad farewell for Frank Thomas, who retired to his farm at Crewkerne after doing sterling service in the second row for several seasons.

Aware of the need to lay firm foundations for the future, the Club had taken the shrewd decision earlier in the season to acquire for £4,000 the former Horse Show Ground at Lambridge, which had been the home of Bath City FC before their move to Twerton Park. The rugby club, which had earmarked it for 'A' XV matches and training, gratefully accepted an RFU loan of £2,000 at 2 per cent and also decided on 13 April 1959 to grant Walcot Old Boys a seven-year lease of a pitch on the east side of the Lam brook.

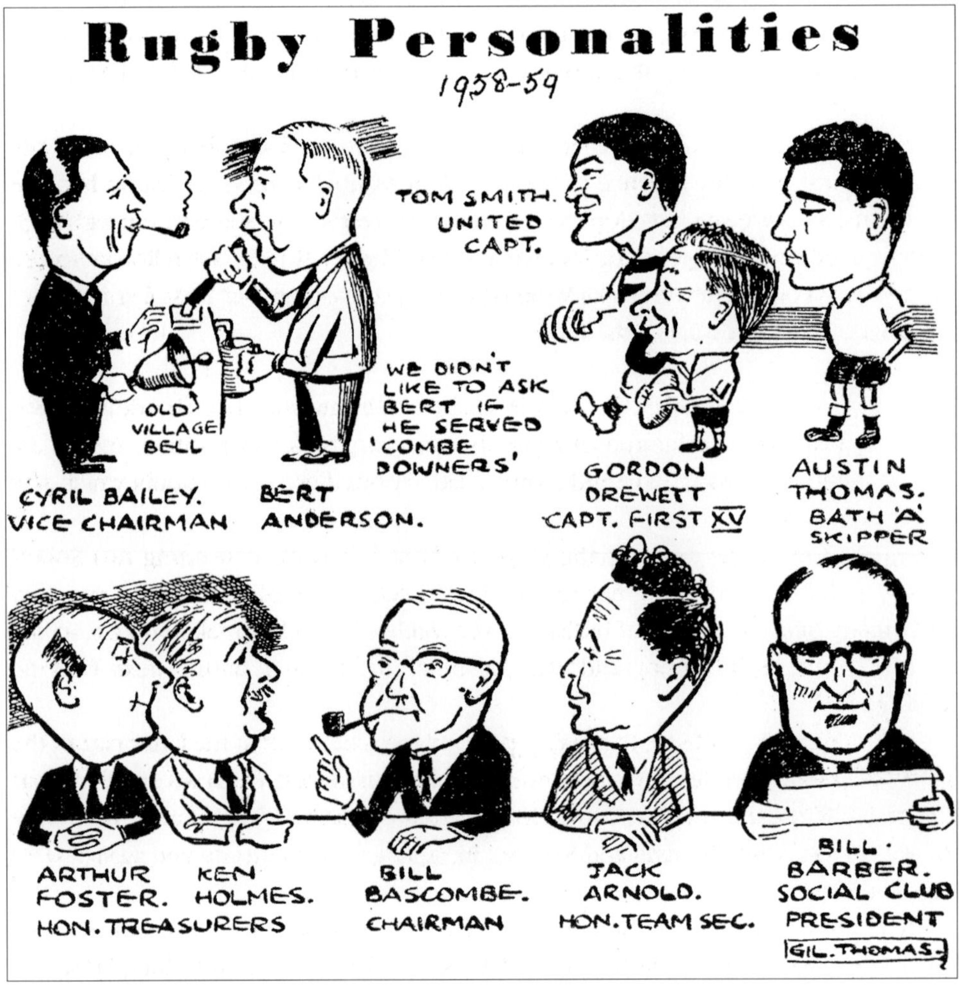

The men who ran the club.

Meanwhile, successful lobbying of the city council resulted in their agreement to improve the drainage on the Recreation Ground. A recent military tattoo had caused considerable damage to the playing surface but the real blame for a notorious bog-like depression in front of the main stand was laid at the door of Herman Goering and the effects of that bomb during the blitz of 1942.

Gordon Drewett was top scorer with 82 points during the 1958/59 season – without scoring a try – and was left to reflect on a record of 12 victories in 39 matches before handing on the captaincy to John Jacobsen. Among the new faces were a strapping 20-year-old ex-Downside schoolboy, Kevin Andrews, and Peter Heindorff, also a forward, who had decided to make the step-up from the Avon club.

There were high hopes of a first win at Welford Road after 40 years but a try two minutes from time earned Leicester a 12-11 victory. Clifton were defeated 21-9 the following Thursday and two days later, on 19 September 1959, Bath fashioned a rare 11-9 victory at Llanelly in front of an estimated 9,000 spectators, scoring tries through Alan Howard-Baker and Roy Farnham, plus a Drewett conversion and a dropped goal from Roger Ford.

Erratic as ever, Bath lost 11-8 at Weston-super-Mare on 3 October and could not entirely blame it on the absence of Drewett, Tony Jacob, Jacobsen and Parfitt because the home side were similarly depleted. Honour was restored to some extent with a 13-13 draw at home to Bridgend the following weekend when flanker Gwyn Robins scored the try that allowed Drewett to kick the equalising conversion, but Bristol cruised to a 27-13 win on the Rec a fortnight later.

A new face in the Bath team that day was Oxford Blue Lawrence Ivor (Laurie) Rimmer, forced to play at full-back rather than in his customary back row position. Before the end he found himself at centre and scored a late try but there was no doubt which side was in command.

Heindorff made his debut in the second row at Plymouth, converting two Robins tries in a 10-8 win, while Rimmer returned at Harlequins on 31 October, scoring a try and pulling off a succession of brilliant cover tackles. He had just taken up a teaching post at Dauntsey's School and was destined to become Bath's next England international.

Frustratingly for Jacobsen, the team's performances tailed off in the latter part of the 1959/60 season, when just 3 victories were achieved in the last 17 games and there was still no joy in the derby fixtures with Bristol. From a 41-match programme, there were 16 wins in total with 20 losses and 5 draws. Intriguingly, the points for and against were equal at 364.

There was a degree of experimentation in the final weeks and two schoolboys showed enough promise to be given first-team debuts. Geoff Frankcom, from King Edward's, blooded in an 8-3 defeat at Exeter, kept his place in the centre for the remainder of the

Bath *v.* Clifton, 17 September 1959. From left to right, back row: Jim Messer (baggage man), Peter Robinson, Alan Howard-Baker, Mike Jones, Richard Marson, Phil Winchcombe, Kevin Andrews, Roger Ford, Jack Arnold (Team Secretary). Middle row: Peter Parfitt, Gordon Drewett, John Jacobsen (captain), Frank Harrison, Barrie Richards. Front row: Brendan O'Mara, Brian Davis, David Lavery.

Skipper John Jacobsen at the annual Remembrance ceremony on 7 November 1959.

season, only missing the trip to Torquay on 28 April. Coincidentally, that game marked the first appearance of fly-half Brendan Perry, and the fleet-footed 17-year-old from St Brendan's College in Bristol marked the occasion with a try in a 19-12 defeat.

Perry, son of Combe Down stalwart Idris Perry, won England Schools caps at all levels and went on to enjoy a long Bath career. While senior England honours eluded him, he eventually took great pride in seeing his son Matt capped by both England and the Lions. Frankcom did not miss out, however, earning his international debut against Wales in January 1965.

The end of the 1959/60 season saw the popular Jack Arnold step down as Team Secretary and also the resignation of former back-row forward Jim Vaissiere to take over as licensee of a local hotel, leaving the club to find a new bar steward. Having successfully acquired the Lambridge Ground and persuaded the River Board to divert the Lam Brook to make room for two pitches rather than one, the committee busied themselves with more mundane matters, such as dealing with a complaint about dirty ditties in the clubhouse.

With Angus Meek assuming the club captaincy and players such as Rimmer and Frankcom providing real hope for the future, there were justifiable grounds for

Jack Arnold, Honorary Team Secretary from 1952 to 1961, was made a life member in 1965 for loyal service as a player and administrator.

optimism when the players gathered for an early season tour to Cheshire in the early weeks of September 1960.

A paltry four victories in the first 14 games set alarm bells ringing, however, particularly after a dismal 6-3 home defeat by Plymouth Albion on 5 November, which merited a long inquest at the management committee meeting the following Monday night. A win, any kind of win, would do at this stage so a scrappy 8-3 victory at home to Saracens was gratefully accepted and confidence was boosted further against a similarly out-of-sorts Cheltenham XV (11-3) before United Services were beaten 8-3 on the heights at Norwood, the Rec being under water.

That was nothing compared to the floods which hit Bath on 4-6 December 1960, the highest in living memory and reported to be the worst since 1882. The water level rose to just underneath the George Roberts Memorial Clock on the North Stand and legend has it that two former players actually rowed a boat across the top of the crossbar! The club's public address equipment was ruined and there was a membership appeal for contributions towards a replacement.

Despite the problems at Bath, representative honours came thick and fast and Pete Parfitt became the fifth player to face the Springboks when selected for the combined Gloucestershire-Somerset team playing as Western Counties. Others already to have faced Avril Malan's tourists were Ian Beer and Derek Wardle (Southern Counties), Laurie Rimmer (North Western Counties) and Cornishman Paddy McGovan (South Western Counties). Parfitt and his Western Counties team-mates went down 42-0 at Kingsholm but Rimmer made exactly the right impression in the North West and was picked for the Twickenham international on 7 January 1961.

England lost 5-0 but Rimmer was ever-present through the Five Nations Championship, continuing Bath's proud international heritage begun by Herbert Fuller in 1882. It was a frustrating campaign for he was on the losing in side in Cardiff (3-6) and Dublin (8-11) before England managed a 5-5 draw in Paris and then defeated the Scots 6-0 at Twickenham.

Meanwhile young Phil Hall, a fearless young flanker in the mould of Soane, had finally been given his Bath first-team debut against Torquay on Christmas Eve and celebrated by scoring a try in a 17-3 victory. The teenager repeated the feat in a 21-3 win over Old Blues on Boxing Day but had a taste of real men's rugby at Franklins Gardens on New Year's Eve when Bath were trounced 32-5 by Northampton. Bath returned to the East Midlands the following Saturday – without England debutant Rimmer – and were beaten 16-3 by Leicester.

Victories over London Welsh, Llanelly and Swansea showed that Bath could compete with the best and, apart from the usual defeats by Gloucester and Bristol, there was little inkling of the humiliation that was to be visited on the team when Harlequins came to the Rec on 30 March 1961. The respective playing records were almost

Cheshire tour party, September 1960.

Bath *v.* New Brighton on the Cheshire tour, 3 September 1960. From left to right, standing: G.P. Frankcom, H.J.F. Simpkins (Honorary General Secretary), G.F. Drewett, I.A. Balding, J.A. Jacob, F.T. Harrison, N. Spinks, J. Jacobsen, L.A. Clark, L.J. Rimmer, P. McGovern, R.A. Ball. Sitting: B.J. O'Mara, P.J. Parfitt, R. Ford (captain), R. Farnham, D.G. Robson.

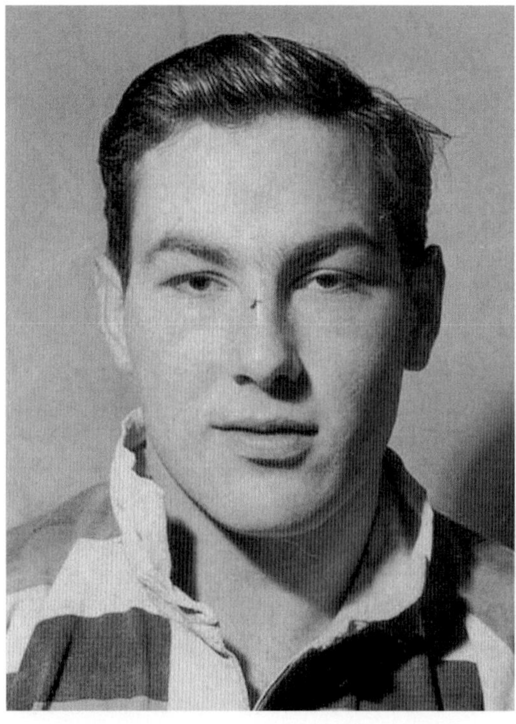

Phil Hall made his debut on Christmas Eve 1960, the first of a remarkable tally of 580 club appearances.

identical but there the similarities ended as Bath were crushed 62-12, a scoreline that stunned Jack Simpkins:

I am still wondering whether Harlequins did beat Bath by the above score on the Recreation Ground on Thursday evening or was it just a nightmarish part of a dream. On second thoughts, however, the painful truth is still vivid in the memory… I hope I never again have to witness the sort of humiliation which a club of Bath's standing had to undergo on what must be the blackest day in their near 100 years of rugby history.[2]

Revelling in the dry conditions, Quins had exploited spineless tackling in midfield to score 13 tries, 10 of them converted. Nevertheless, Angus Meek's team picked themselves up to win the last seven matches of the season and leave their captain a creditable record of 21 wins, 21 defeats and 2 draws. Geoff Frankcom was top try scorer with 12 while Pete Parfitt, whose father and grandfather had worn the Bath jersey, made 38 appearances in the front row.

The captaincy passed to three-quarter Roy Farnham for 1961/62 and he couldn't have wished for a better start! After warming up with a 19-3 win at Stroud, Gordon Drewett's four penalties earned Bath a 12-11 victory at Leicester, only their second success at

Bath 1961/62 saw Roy Farnham as captain.

Stalwarts Brendan Perry, John Donovan and Peter Heindorff.

Welford Road in nearly 40 years. With Brendan Perry proving an inventive fly-half and Geoff Frankcom more than a handful in midfield, Clifton were defeated 18-0 the following Thursday evening in a rehearsal for the visit of Llanelly less than 48 hours later.

It was worth waiting for, as Bath recovered from an early 6-0 deficit to win a thrilling contest 13-6. Thanks to good work by Brian Davis, Kevin Andrews, Peter Parfitt, Paddy Mulligan and Lance Clark in the pack, the Scarlets began to fade and Frankcom scored an interception try before Parfitt broke from a line-out to send Andrews over. Drewett converted both scores.

The scrum-half was in fine kicking form again the following weekend when Bath once more came from behind to beat Bridgend 16-6 on the Rec, thanks to tries by left wing Frank Harrison and Phil Hall. One result was that Brendan Perry, although still only available to Bath when not required by St Brendan's, was selected along with Bob and Lance Clark for an experimental Somerset XV.

A magnificent seven wins in a row – 14, in fact, since 1 April – was completed with victories over St Mary's Hospital and Bridgwater but the sequence ended on 30 September when Harlequins won 13-5 at the Rec. After high-scoring romps at Stroud and against Devonport Services, life became rather tougher, especially without Frankcom once he had begun his studies at Cambridge University. He was feted there, too, after scoring the winning try in the Varsity match; Ian Balding was also on the winning side.

The first of the Bristol derbies on 21 October 1961 was even more eagerly anticipated than usual since it pitted Perry against his schoolteacher and mentor, the celebrated John Blake. The pupil acquitted himself well but a string of unforced errors by others handed Bristol their 15th successive victory over their rivals by 28-0.

Apart from completing their first 'double' over Leicester since 1919 by winning 8-5 on the Rec on 6 January 1962, thanks to a chargedown try by the much-improved Peter Heindorff, the remainder of the season was short on success. Difficulties in establishing a settled side were reflected in the fact that the pairing of Perry and John Spencer against Leicester was the sixth half-back combination in four months. Heindorff was soon to leave for a job in West Germany and to achieve his ambition to play for his national team.

The Club's first experience of playing under lights, at London Welsh on 13 January, ended in a 20-5 defeat and Bath might have earned more than a draw against Gloucester a month later if Gordon Drewett had not missed a penalty in front of the posts. Bristol, mobile up front and inventive behind the scrum, triumphed 16-0 at the Rec on 3 March 1962, but there were enough victories over lesser sides to reward Farnham's policy of open, running rugby with 20 wins, 20 defeats and 3 draws from the 43-match programme. The points total of 470 against 409 conceded was the highest since Philip Hope's side scored 483 in 1921. Fittingly, Farnham was top try scorer with 10, although one of his last duties was to defend his players against Molly Gerrard's accusations of bad behaviour on an away trip to Devonport Services.

Laurie Rimmer, who had failed to add to his 5 England caps in 1961, took over as skipper for 1962/63, a season that was most memorable for the total lack of rugby played between Christmas and the end of February, owing to the 'Big Freeze'. Somehow Bath still got through a 43-match campaign, squeezing in an astonishing 13 fixtures in April alone, including a first tour to Germany.

Rimmer, placing a premium on teamwork and spirit, attempted to advance traditional Bath training methods with a rigorous regime allied to tactical instruction. Once the season got underway, however, it was back to 'crisis management' and he found himself forced to step in at scrum-half at Harlequins after only 13 others turned up. No major scalps were taken in the first half of the season and it was significant that when Somerset lined up against Gloucestershire on 27 October 1962, there was no Bath representation.

The Rec, under a foot of frozen snow at one point, was only just playable for the visit of Wasps on 23 February and the Londoners were quicker into their stride, winning 6-0. Disruption to the County Championship had resulted in the postponement of Gloucestershire's meeting with Oxfordshire and a consequent clash with the Bath *v.* Bristol fixture on 2 March. Even without six county players, Bristol won 29-9, but the expected bumper gate did not materialise and insult was added to injury when the Bath committee had to authorise payment of two guineas to Mr R.J. Nowell for damage to spectacles when he was hit in the face by the ball!

There was no joy either from the next game, settled by a last-gasp try from Swansea's international wing, Dewi Bebb, but a run of seven straight defeats was ended against Neath. Centre Brendan O'Mara scored a first-half try converted by full-back John Hawgood and, with Perry in inspirational form after the break, Bath ran in two more through left wing John Edwards, one of which was converted by Hawgood, to win 13-6. Unfortunately, attendances had fallen away and the Honorary Treasurer, C.D.S. Thomas, pointing out that the Wasps game had yielded just £12 in gate receipts and there had been no matches before that since mid-December, described the trend as 'alarming'.

Geoff Frankcom announced his return to club rugby with the first try in a 17-12 win over Richmond on 23 March 1963 and scored two more in a 24-0 trouncing of Nuneaton a week later. Perhaps the opposition were confused by the presence of two Phil Halls in the pack – second row P.L. Hall having just arrived from Coventry.

There then followed a run of seven defeats until, with characteristic perversity, Bath turned in a rousing display to beat Llanelly 6-3 on the Rec. Magnificently led by veteran

URKUNDE

IN WÜRDIGUNG GROSSER VERDIENSTE
UM DEN RUGBYSPORT WIRD

Herr Peter Heindorff

MIT DER
VERDIENSTNADEL
DES DEUTSCHEN RUGBY-VERBANDES
AUSGEZEICHNET

DIESES BEURKUNDET:
DEUTSCHER RUGBY-VERBAND

HANNOVER,

Left: Pete Heindorff's international credentials with West Germany.

Below: Crowd scene during the match against Cardiff, January 1962.

Right: Laurie Rimmer, capped by England in 1961.

Below: Bath 1962/63, with Laurie Rimmer as captain.

lock Tony Jacob, the Bath eight hounded the Scarlets into the mud and clinched victory with dropped goals from Perry and Hawgood.

At the end of the season though, the overwhelming feeling was one of disappointment, felt just as keenly by Rimmer who had to acknowledge that, for all the optimism the previous September, teamwork and spirit were lacking and there was still a question mark against fitness levels. The record of 16 wins, 25 defeats and a draw told its own story.

Next it was Kevin Andrews' turn to carry the baton of captaincy and although the record improved in 1963/64 to read played 45, won 20, lost 22 and drawn 3, the low points were as low as any experienced in previous seasons. While the squad was bolstered by the presence of former Wales back row Leighton Jenkins, less than a month into the campaign the club was stunned by the resignation of Gordon Drewett after 11 seasons' loyal service. Year after year the diminutive scrum-half had regularly topped the scoring charts with his accurate boot and his absence was quickly felt.

Bristol's dominance continued in the derby fixtures, although it took a very late Mike Lawrence try, converted by Dave Watt, to edge an 8-6 victory on 19 October. Bath players must still have been moping a week later when they lost on the Rec by the same score to Old Cranleighans. The lack of a recognised goalkicker following Drewett's

The Big Freeze. Eight games were cancelled between Boxing Day 1962 and 16 February 1963.

Laurie Rimmer, Brendan O'Mara and Tony Jacob.

departure was proving a considerable handicap, although Perry's tactical kicking proved superior to Clive Rowlands' when Bath edged home 3-0 against Pontypool on 2 November. The youngster also kicked the winning penalty.

Things did look a little brighter after Christmas with wins over Northampton (9-3) and Leicester (11-0) and Bath achieved a rare 14-9 victory at Wasps on 22 February 1964, thanks to tries from wing Nick Bruford (2), scrum-half John Millman and centre John Donovan. Still Bristol proved indomitable though as Bath were defeated 6-3 at the Memorial Ground on 7 March. The visitors gave a debut to one Bill Carling, a member of the Army Air Corps serving in Wiltshire. His son, Will, was born at nearby Bradford-on-Avon 21 months later.

The most influential figure in the Bath side at this time however was Frankcom. When he was playing, the side were competitive, his devastating breaks over 30-40 yards providing the mainspring of the attack; when he was absent, the back line lacked sparkle and penetration. A measure of his influence was provided by the end-of-season statistics which showed he was top try scorer with 16 despite appearing in only 24 of the 45 matches. Best of the rest was John Cousins with 6 while skipper Andrews played the most games, 40.

There is no hiding the fact that these were difficult times for the Club and, although membership figures had been maintained, the accounts showed a loss for the second year in succession. It was a simple equation of escalating overheads against diminishing

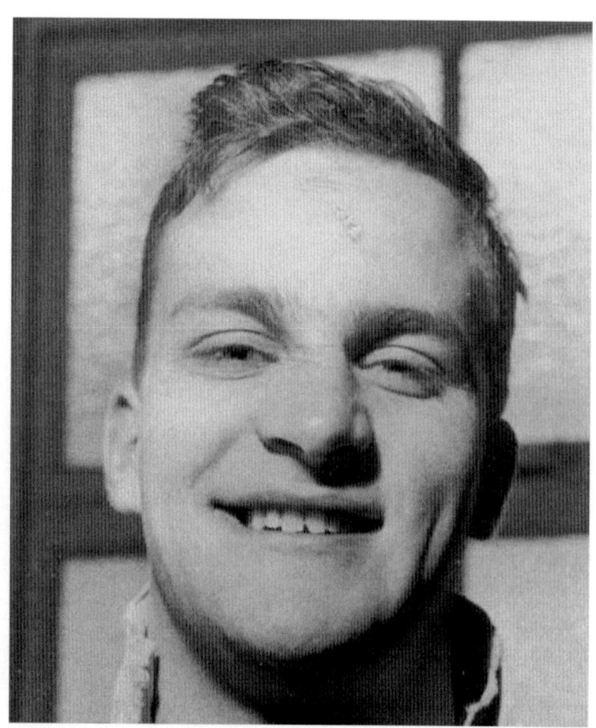

Kevin Andrews, Bath captain in 1963-65, was later president of Leicester.

attendances. As in all rugby clubs, however, there was still much selfless work behind the scenes and the Honorary Treasurer reported to the Management Committee on 4 May 1964 that the 'lady helpers' had served 2,263 meals for players and officials, also banking £228 8s 6d from the sale of tea and sandwiches.

Andrews kept the captaincy for 1964/65 which, on closer examination of what archives remain, appears to have been the 100th season in Bath's history. The centenary was not to be celebrated until the start of the following season, but the management committee was informed at its meeting on 8 August 1964 that plans for a commemorative booklet were well in hand.

There were to be two significant absentees. First Frankcom informed the committee by letter on 23 November that he had obtained a teaching post at Bedford School and would be playing for the local club during term time. He was anxious to retain his Bath playing membership, however, and hoped to be available during vacations.

A fortnight later Andrews announced that he had gained promotion to a post in Burton on Trent that would force his departure by the end of January. His final game, against Metropolitan Police on 16 January 1965, was marked by a 17-15 victory, one of the better performances so far in a disappointing campaign. Andrews was presented with a silver tankard – and also that weekend a baby daughter! Bath's loss was

Leicester's gain as their skipper went on to enjoy many years of loyal service to the Tigers as player and official, eventually being elected president.

Bath, who had won only three games from mid-October to the end of December, turned to centre Gordon Margretts to lead them through the rest of the season. Chastening experiences against John Dawes' exciting London Welsh side and a powerful Northampton line-up inspired by veteran scrum-half Dickie Jeeps prompted the Management Committee to pass a resolution that players who were obviously not First XV material should be asked to return to their junior clubs. It was judged better to lose with young, promising players than with those who had no prospect of improving.

If anyone needed proof of the Club's ability to produce talented players, they only had to look at Frankcom. It must therefore have been a bitter-sweet experience for all associated with the Bath club when, a matter of weeks after joining Bedford, the former King Edward's boy was awarded his first cap for England in Cardiff on 16 January 1965. The congratulations were heartfelt though and Frankcom himself maintained his Bath playing membership, ensuring that his portrait joined the former internationals adorning the clubhouse at the Recreation Ground.

As for his international outings, England went down 14-3 to Wales and also lost 5-0 in Dublin. France were defeated 9-6 at Twickenham but Frankcom and Co. could manage

Geoff Frankcom won four England caps in 1965. He made his debut for Bath as a schoolboy on 9 April 1960.

only a draw against the Scots. For all his talent, the England selectors never called on Frankcom's services again. Back at Bath, in a serious attempt to make better use of the talent available, John Roberts suggested at a committee meeting on 22 February 1965 that they engage a Club Coach and Mr Roger Whyte later agreed to attend Tuesday evening training sessions.

Ian Balding was soon to depart to take up training duties at the start of the flat season so young Allen Gay, son of Police Sergeant Bill Gay, who had been a regular at wing forward in 1930s and would have been captain in 1939/40 but for the outbreak of war, took over at full-back for the last six weeks of the season.

When Bristol arrived at the Rec on Monday evening, 5 April, for the 145th derby match, Bath had still won only one game in the previous eleven. A fixture which had originally been scheduled for 6 March, when the Rec had been snowbound, now coincided with Geoff Frankcom's 23rd birthday. There was only one place that the England centre wanted to be that evening and Margretts was more than happy to switch to the wing to accommodate him.

Frankcom responded with an outstanding performance, matched by fly-half Brendan Perry and his half-back partner Jim Galley, a product of Bristol Cathedral School where Bristol scrum-half Eric Blackman was a teacher.

Despite falling behind to a Mike Ellery try after 20 minutes, Bath responded with a 40-yard penalty from lock Clive Armstrong before Frankcom snapped up a Bristol fumble and kicked ahead to create a try for flanker Tom Martland. Bath, on top in all departments, scored further tries through Bruford (2) and Frankcom, Martland adding a conversion. For the first time in more than ten years they had beaten Bristol.

John Stevens, *The Bath Chronicle*'s rugby correspondent, summed it up as follows:

Geoff Frankcom who was celebrating his birthday, played a vital part in the victory perhaps, but he was for once, only an integral part of a fighting effort from everyone, from hooker Clive Buckle to full-back Allen Gay. The forwards were in tremendous form and undoubtedly laid the foundations for success by their first-class backing up. In the set scrums John Pullin did gain Bristol an edge, winning the loose head 6-3, yet so tigerishly did Bath struggle for the ball in the loose, that extra possession did Bristol little good. Props Peter Parfitt and Peter Jenkins worked their hearts out and their locks, Richard Marson and Clive Armstrong, jumped and scrummaged as if their very lives depended on it.[3]

With eight matches in 22 days during the rest of April, Bath tended to blow hot and cold, reserving their best for the visit of Llanelly on Easter Tuesday. The 19-6 margin gave them their first win against a Welsh club.

Above left: Allen Gay. *Above right:* Tom Martland played his first game for Bath on 1 October 1963 and went on to become Club captain in 1969/70.

Even without Frankcom, they ran in three tries through O'Mara, Margretts and Parfitt, while both Perry and Martland dropped goals, Perry also adding a conversion. The plaudits went to the pack: Parfitt and his front row partners Clive Buckle and Dave Robson, the second row partnership of Richard Marson and John Parsons and, most of all, to No. 8 Heindorff and flankers Phil Hall and John Ziupa.

This traditional 'Rag Doll' game was marred, however, by an unfortunate degree of niggle. The *Sunday Mirror* reported on the collapse of Gwyn Williams on his way home while prop Cedric Jones had allegedly suffered a kick on the forehead. Welsh centre Ken Jones added fuel to the fire by declaring: 'Even the toughest games between keen Welsh rivals are like Sunday School outings compared with the Bath match.' Bath Secretary Jack Simpkins' uncompromising response was to dismiss Llanelly's complaint as 'a lot of nonsense', a view which won support from referee Jack Luscom, who expressed surprise at a threat from Llanelly to discontinue fixtures.

The campaign was wrapped up on 29 April with a 33-0 defeat at Coventry, bringing Bath's points against total to a whopping 690. Points For totalled 563, including 141 tries, of which John Donovan scored 18.

In the days before people became so obsessed with centenaries, jubilees and sundry other anniversaries, activities planned to mark the 100th year of the Club's existence were relatively low key. A series of commemorative matches was organised, against an Alec Lewis XV on 16 September 1965 and against the Royal Navy a week later, no doubt in recognition of the prominent role played by the Admiralty in the life of the city and the Club, particularly during the war years.

A special centenary tie was produced – to be worn only by committee and players – and the *Bath Football Club (RFU) Centenary Book* went on sale priced 12s 6d on the day the team met Alec Lewis's selection. Bath played gallantly in losing 18-12 to a side boasting 13 internationals, the contest refereed by Air Marshal Sir Augustus Walker KCB, CBE, DSO, DFC, AFC, RAF, who for good measure was also President of the RFU.

For the Royal Navy match, the visiting dignitary must have been relieved to hear that she only had to be introduced to the teams. Among the line-up meeting Bath's Mayor, Mrs Elsie Hannah, was Pete Parfitt, veteran of more than 250 first-team appearances and a man who could trace his family's associations with the Club back to his grandfather George Parfitt (1899-1913). His father and uncles had also played in the Bath shirt.

Inevitably, however, there were newcomers such as Peter Sibley, making only his fifth appearance, who could be forgiven for wondering what all the fuss was about. Already 30 years old, he had just arrived from Blackheath to take up a teaching post at Monkton

Prop Dave Robson later became chief scout during Jack Rowell's tenure as head coach.

Above left: Pete Parfitt's first game was on 6 September 1958 and he made 407 appearances before hanging up his boots on 12 April 1971. *Above right:* Peter Sibley.

Combe School. Yet his influence on the Club's development as an advocate of running rugby was to be profound. As player, captain and coach, he shaped a style that anticipated perfectly law changes which soon outlawed kicking direct to touch from outside the 25.

-14-

Best of the First

MEANDERING THROUGH THE mass of match reports and committee minutes that chronicle the first 100 years of the Bath Football Club, there are a host of personalities who elbow their way through the mere statistics.

Inevitably, the temptation is to ponder how the players of the early years of the game would have fared against their counterparts in the twentieth century. Who was the most inspiring captain, the best scrum-half or loose forward? Where would you play Herbert Fuller, who was equally proficient at half-back (scrum-half) or forward during the 1880s? By what yardstick do you measure Frank Soane against Alec Lewis, particularly when they played under different laws?

Fifteen-a-side games began to replace twenty during the 1870s but they generally comprised ten forwards, two attacking half-backs and three mainly defensive backs until a decade or so later when Bath and other clubs began to adopt the four three-quarter system.

When W.A. (Bill) England, a Bath forward of the early 1890s, was interviewed in 1921, his recollections demonstrated how much the game had changed:

When I first started playing it was a good, old fashioned Rugger game, when a man had to be fit and strong, and it was practically more brute force and ignorance in the forwards than ability.

At that time, if you collared a man over the line with the ball you had a maul which lasted just over a minute. You had to try to take the ball away from your opponent, and, if there was a possible chance, to kick it out again. Every time you touched down you gave your opponents a point, which I consider was a very fair way of playing football, and it should never have been done away with.[1]

Until some forwards began to develop specialist skills, the scrummage formation depended very much on who got their first.

The great players, however, stand out as big characters. These are men you would have wanted alongside you for their match-winning qualities, whether fleet-footed geniuses like Considine or bloody-minded scrappers, such as Fred 'Chumpy' Russell.

Who, then, are the contenders in each position?

FULL-BACK

Perhaps the first recognised specialist full-back at Bath was Dr A.E. Hayward Pinch (1888-94), who combined his on-the-field duties with those of Club Secretary. Clarence Whittaker (1912-21) was one of the few players from the powerful pre-Great War side who returned after that dreadful conflict to relaunch the club and was followed by the dependable Bert Comm (1921-24). Jack Arnold (1938-49), quick-witted, fast and versatile, was one of the cleverest players to appear for the club; he gave way to Paddy Sullivan (1949-57), fearless in defence and a prodigious goal-kicker.

RIGHT WING

C.J.B. Moneypenny (1887-92) was a fine athlete and the first Bath player to be invited to play for the Barbarians while W. Pattinson (1889-1894) was a sound defensive player as well as having an eye for a score – 'a man for a stiff and fierce struggle'. But one player demands inclusion on the right wing in the best Bath XV of the first 100 years. Vincent Coates (1910-14), immensely strong and quick, not only inspired Bath's first win over Bristol in fifteen years but, when called to England colours, scored six tries in five games in the early months of 1913.

CENTRE

The task of picking a pair of centres is complicated by the scant information available from the early decades but the reputation of certain individuals thrusts them into the reckoning, notably A.E. 'Titch' Fry (1894-98) and J.T. (James) Timmins (1897-1910) while former Welsh international Norman Biggs (1896-97) shone briefly in a Bath shirt.

Norman Coates (1910-1914) provided the bullets for his brother, Vincent, and Harry Richardson (1919-25) was an influential figure in the back line in the years immediately after the Great War. Jim Pitman (1919-28), capped from Oxford University in 1922, was all pace and class until suffering a serious leg injury; Ralph Banks (1924-39) took his chance as a teenager; Ian Lumsden (1946-49) and Dennis Silk (1956-57) impressed in the post-war years.

The outstanding centre in the first 100 years, however, was R.A. (Ronnie) Gerrard (1930-41). Capped as a 19-year-old, he would have made even more than 14 appearances for England but for injury problems. His power and footballing ability would have been wonderfully complemented by the pace and elusiveness of Geoff Frankcom (1960-65).

LEFT WING

The forward-orientated game of the late 1800s left little opportunity for the speedsters to shine but Dr Dick Meister (1900-11) was an early favourite before the emergence of the seriously quick Alfred Kitching (1907-19), who profited from the attention defences gave to his team-mate, Vincent Coates.

Bill Hancock (1926-37) was a prolific finisher outside Gerrard but loses out because a place in the back line simply has to be found for S.G.U. (Ulick) Considine (1919-25). After some dazzling but individualistic performances at fly-half he moved to the left wing where his virtuoso skills could be given full rein and that is where he gained his one and only cap. Arnold Ridley called him a 'genius'.

FLY-HALF

Even 120 years on, the match-winning ability of T.N. (Tommy) Parham (1886-94) is not in doubt. Pugnacious and quick on his feet, he is a serious contender. Others from the early years worthy of mention include G.G. (George) Vincent (1891-1900) and Tom White (1902-05), a wonderfully gifted playmaker and place-kicker who 'went North'.

Harry Slade (1919-31) formed a useful partnership with Harry Vowles and Tommy Hicks (1937-49), might have earned legendary status but for the war. Brendan Perry (1960-73) burst spectacularly on to the scene as a St Brendan's College schoolboy but was another whose career was hampered by injury. Yet Roy Harris (1936-46) – said to be the best Bath player never to be selected by England – edges ahead of Parham.

SCRUM-HALF

Herbert Fuller (1881-88) stakes a claim for the pioneers and, although capped by England in the pack, was as much a scrum-half as a forward. Billy Fear (1899-1900, 1908-1913) and Alby Hatherill (1906-1919) were influential characters in the years leading up to the Great War, as was the combative Fred 'Chumpy' Russell (1901-21). No-one, however, quite fulfilled their promise as did Harry Vowles (1911-26), who emerged at that time as a precocious schoolboy talent and afterwards formed an outstanding half-back partnership with Considine. Gordon Drewett (1952-63) deserves honourable mention, however, for his loyalty and match-winning qualities.

PROPS

J.B.S. D'Aguilar (1892-97) came into the side as a 16-year-old, was capped by Somerset the following year and was ever-present until emigrating to Ceylon. R.J. Rogers (1903-04) earned distinction as a Great Britain tourist to Australia and New Zealand while Arthur Ford (1906-14) came to the fore as 'a genuine scrummager' and an inspiring captain.

The same could be said for John Roberts (1948-58), who made 355 appearances and formed such an effective and durable partnership with Tom Smith (1944-1957). Roberts' record was to be eclipsed by Pete Parfitt (1958-71), with over 400 games in the Bath shirt, but he deserves a place in the front row alongside the outstanding figure from the first half-century, Frederick Belson (1894-99), remembered by his contemporaries as 'a tall, well-built scrimmager'. He was also the club's first overseas tourist, travelling with Revd Mullineux's party to Australia in 1899 and playing in the Sydney Test.

HOOKER

It was not until the 1880s that teams began deliberately to heel the ball from scrums and the hooking position developed out of all recognition during the twentieth century. Norman Matthews (1926-38), who came within 15 minutes of winning a cap in Cardiff in 1930, gets the vote ahead of Gordon Gregory (1938-39) and the one-eyed Fred Hill (1950), two players who did wear the England shirt while with Bristol.

SECOND ROW

T.B. Timmins (1896-1907) and George Ruddick (1897-1903) were prominent figures in the early years but were quickly overshadowed by the remarkable Frank Cashnella (1899-1921). A vigorous scrummager and hard-running forward in the loose, who scored a good number of tries direct from line-outs, 'Cash' was the kind of forceful personality who would have demanded inclusion in any era.

Who should be his partner, though? W.H. Thomas (1909-12) had to decline a place on the British Isles tour to South Africa in 1910 and later impressed for Cardiff. After the Great War, Dick Chaddock (1919-27) supplied the possession for Considine and Co. to work their magic while George Haydon (1929-31) finished one season as top try scorer from the lock position. In the same era, Mervyn Shaw (1929-34) proved a great leader during his 'exile' from Bristol. Later there came the quiet farmer from Somerset, Frank Thomas (1952-59), and then Kevin Andrews (1958-65), a powerful personality on and off the field. Shaw is the choice, though.

WING FORWARD

'The principal reason in the past why Bath have been able to hold and very often eclipse sides very much more superior on paper has been the excellence of the side's back-row players.' So wrote *Football Herald & Chronicle's* Ian Todd on 28 September 1957. The first 100 years of Bath Football Club certainly provides a surfeit of talent from which to choose. For instance, 'Chumpy' Russell would be in contention for a wing forward spot if he wasn't already bracketed at scrum-half.

On the blind side, it says much for the excellence of Alec Lewis (1948-54) that he is able comfortably to resist the claims of Derrick Wilson (1930-39) and Ian Beer (1957-62).

Phil Hall (1960-76), all aggression on the open side, stakes a strong claim but loses out to the one player whose qualities declare themselves down the decades. Frank Soane (1881-98) would be ideally suited to the breakaway role. Renowned for his tackling, seemingly impervious to pain, he was also a creative influence, just as comfortable playing in the back line. One can imagine him revelling in the modern game.

NUMBER 8

Would this have been the position for Frank D'Aguilar? How to assess his talent – and others from the earliest years – is the most difficult task in this whimsical exercise. We know that D'Aguilar was a forward but also that he scored a try in his only England international, which suggests he at least had the ball in his hands! Consider also that he was a fine cricketer and soccer player, which suggests above-average hand-eye co-ordination. Sentiment should have some place in this selection so he gets the vote ahead of the sensible choice, John Kendall-Carpenter (1952-56), who also faces competition from Donald Crichton-Miller (1931-33) and Austin Higgins (1943-48).

CAPTAIN

Frank Cashnella, Norman Matthews, Mervyn Shaw and John Roberts stand out as leaders of men, sometimes as much in adversity as in victory. Yet Frank Soane's credentials are the most compelling, not least because this remarkable individual played his best rugby more than a century ago and yet the force of his personality is in no way diminished. Let's not forget either that he was the man responsible for bringing rugby to the Recreation Ground.

SELECT XV

16	P. (Paddy) Sullivan	(1938-49)
15	V.M.H. (Vincent) Coates	(1910-14)
14	R.A. (Ronnie) Gerrard	(1930-41)
12	G.P. (Geoff) Frankcom	(1960-65)
11	S.G.U. (Ulick) Considine	(1919-25)
10	T.R. (Roy) Harris	(1936-46)
9	H.J. (Harry) Vowles	(1911-26)
1	F.C. (Frederick) Belson	(1894-99)
2	N. (Norman Matthews	(1926-38)
3	J.P. (John) Roberts	(1948-58)
4	F.J. (Frank) Cashnella	(1899-1921)
5	M.V. (Mervyn) Shaw	(1929-34)
6	A.O. (Alec) Lewis	(1948-54)
7	F. (Frank) Soane	(1881-98)
8	F.B.G. (Frank) D'Aguilar	(1865-70)

Captain: Frank Soane.

In this first of two volumes, we have set out to encapsulate activity over the first 100 years – the bedrock upon which this great club was founded; a period rich in personalities and incident – whilst variable in performance.

We conclude at a time when emerging individual talent suggested promise of greater things to come.

Bath Players

Kevin Andrews

Jack Arnold

Ralph Banks

Frederick Belson

Frank Cashnella

R.S. Chaddock

A.E. Cleall

Vincent Coates

H.J. Comm

Ulick Considine

Donald Crichton-Miller

J.B.S. D'Aguilar

Bath Players

Gordon Drewett

W. England

Geoff Frankcom

Arthur Ford

E. 'Titch' Fry

Ronnie Gerrard

Phillip Hall

Bill Hancock

Roy Harris

Albie Hatherill

George Haydon

Tommy Hicks

Bath Players

Austin Higgins

Fred Hill

John Kendall-Carpenter

A.F. Kitching

Alec Lewis

Norman Matthews

Dick Meister

Peter Parfitt

W. Pattison

Brendan Perry

Dr A.E. Pinch

Harry Richardson

John Roberts

Bath Players

J. and G. Ruddick

Fred 'Chumpy' Russell

Mervyn Shaw

Harry Slade

Frank Soane

J.V. Soane

Paddy Sullivan

Frank Thomas

William 'Billy' Thomas

T.B. Timmins

George Vincent

Harry Vowles

'Shammer' Weeks

Reference Notes

CHAPTER ONE

1 *Bath Sports Herald*, 5 October, 1921
2 Ibid
3 Attributed to A.G. Guillemard, former Honorary Secretary, Treasurer and President of the Rugby Union
4 *The Bath Chronicle*, January 1882
5 Ibid, February 1882
6 Ibid, 28 December 1882
7 Bath FC archive

CHAPTER TWO

1 Somerset RFU County handbook (1894)
2 *The Bath Chronicle*, February 1886
3 *Bath Sports Herald*, 26 August 1922 (Chats About Old Rugby Players)
4 *The Bath Chronicle*, December 1886
5 *Bath Sports Herald*, 26 August 1922 (Chats About Old Rugby Players)
6 *The Bath Chronicle*, January 1888
7 Barbarian Records 1890-1932 (compiled by Emile de Lissa; Ivor Nicholson & Watson Ltd)

CHAPTER THREE

1 *Bath Sports Herald*, 29 October 1888
2 *Western Daily Press*, 4 February 1889
3 Bath FC General Committee minutes, 26 March 1889
4 *The Bath Chronicle*, 19 July 1889
5 Ibid
6 Bath FC rulebook, May 1893
7 Bath FC General Committee minutes, 12 December 1889
8 Ibid
9 *The Bath Chronicle*, 3 February 1890
10 Ibid, 17 November 1890

CHAPTER FOUR

1 *The Bath Chronicle* (undated, 1892)
2 *Bath Sports Herald*, 12 September 1892
3 Ibid, 11 November 1892
4 Ibid, 27 January 1893
5 *The Bath Chronicle*, 23 March 1893

6 *Bath Sports Herald*, 6 April 1893
7 Ibid, 28 October 1893
8 *The Bath Chronicle*, 12 February 1894
9 Ibid, 20 September, 1894
10 Ibid, 24 September 1894

CHAPTER FIVE

1 *The Bath Chronicle*, 8 October 1894
2 Ibid, 11 October 1894
3 Ibid
4 Ibid, 14 November 1894
5 Bath FC annual general meeting, 13 June 1895
6 *The Bath Chronicle*, 2 January 1896
7 Ibid, 9 March 1896
8 The anglicised spelling, Llanelly, was in common use throughout the period of this history
9 Ibid, September 1896
10 Ibid, 22 October 1896
11 Ibid, February 1928 ('In the Nature of an Obituary for Norman Biggs')
12 Ibid, 29 February 1897
13 Ibid, 10 March 1897
14 Ibid, 2 April 1897
15 Ibid, 14 March 1898
16 Ibid, 3 October 1898
17 Ibid, 5 January 1899
18 Ibid, 18 January 1899
19 Ibid, 20 February 1899
20 Ibid, 10 April 1899
21 Ibid, 17 April 1899
22 Ibid, 30 September 1899
23 Ibid, 19 October 1903

CHAPTER SIX

1 Sydney Arrow (no date)
2 Bath FC Committee note of condolence, 17 January 1900
3 *The Bath Chronicle*, 13 January 1900
4 Ibid, 21 May 1900
5 Ibid, 9 February 1901
6 Ibid, 27 April 1901
7 Ibid, 11 January 1902
8 Ibid, 17 March 1902
9 Ibid, 23 February 1903
10 Ibid, 23 March 1903
11 Ibid, 30 March 1903

12 Ibid, 21 September 1903
13 Ibid, 14 December 1903
14 Ibid, 29 June 1903
15 *New Zealand Herald*, 8 August 1904

CHAPTER SEVEN

1 *The Bath Chronicle*, 28 November 1903
2 Ibid, 21 November 1904
3 Ibid, 5 December 1904
4 Ibid, 24 February 1905
5 Ibid, 25 February 1905 ('Football Notes')
6 Ibid, 2 November 1906
7 Ibid, 22 February 1909
8 Ibid, 29 May 1909
9 Ibid, 14 February 1910
10 Ibid, 14 March 1910

CHAPTER EIGHT

1 *The Bath Chronicle*, 7 April 1911
2 Ibid
3 Ibid, 8 April 1911
4 Bath FC annual general meeting minutes, 15 July 1911
5 *The Bath Chronicle*, 25 November 1911
6 Ibid, 2 March 1912
7 Ibid, 26 October 1912
8 Ibid, 8 September 1913
9 Ibid, 13 June 1914
10 Ibid, 1 September 1914
11 Bath FC Management Committee minute, 1 September 1914
12 *The Bath Chronicle*, 22 January, 1915
13 Bath FC Management Committee minute, 23 October 1916
14 *The Bath Chronicle*, 30 September 1916

CHAPTER NINE

1 *The Bath Chronicle* (no date)
2 Ibid, 6 September 1919
3 Ibid, 29 December 1919
4 *Sunday Times*, 4 January 1920
5 Bath FC Management Committee minute, 12 February 1924
6 *The Bath Chronicle*, 16 August 1924
7 Ibid, 6 October 1924
8 *Cardiff Evening Express*, 27 December 1924
9 *Bath Sports Herald*, 15 April 1925

CHAPTER TEN

1 *The Bath Chronicle*, 23 November 1925
2 Ibid, 17 September 1927
3 Ibid, 28 July 1928
4 Bath FC Management Committee minute, 28 October 1929
5 *The Bath Chronicle*, 4 January 1932
6 Ibid, 12 October 1936
7 Ibid, 1 November 1937
8 Ibid, 19 November 1937

CHAPTER ELEVEN

1 *The Bath Chronicle*, 2 September 1939
2 Bath FC Management Committee minute, 9 December 1940
3 *The Bath Chronicle*, October 1942
4 Ibid, 11 February 1943
5 Bath FC Management Committee minute, 9 December 1940
6 Ibid, 31 July 1944
7 Bath FC annual general meeting minute, 8 June 1945
8 *The Bath Chronicle*, 14 December 1946

CHAPTER TWELVE

1 *The Bath Chronicle*, 20 December 1948
2 Bath FC annual general meeting minute, 18 June 1949
3 Bath FC Management Committee minute, 19 September 1949
4 *The Bath Chronicle*, 26 March 1951
5 Ibid, 7 April, 1951
6 Ibid, 28 December 1953
7 Bath FC Management Committee minute, 7 March 1955

CHAPTER THIRTEEN

1 *The Bath Chronicle*, 10 February 1958
2 Ibid, 1 April 1961
3 Ibid, 6 April 1965

CHAPTER FOURTEEN

1 *Bath Football Herald*, 19 November 1921

Bibliography

The Oxford Compendium to Sports and Games (John Arlott; Paladin, 1977)

The Rise and Fall of the British Empire (Lawrence James; Abacus, 1995)

The Wisden Book of Obituaries 1892-1985 (Queen Anne Press)

Men In Black, 75 Years of New Zealand Rugby
(R.H. Chester/N.A.C. McMillan; Pelham Books)

Walcot Old Boys Centenary 1882-1982 (Walcot RFC)

Avonvale RFC Centenary 1883-1983 (Avonvale RFC)

The History of the Rugby Football Union (Owen; Playfair Books 1955)

Rothmans Rugby Union Yearbook Series (Queen Anne Press)

The Complete Who's Who of England Rugby Union Internationals
(Maule; Breedon Books, 1992)

Gladiators of a Roman City – A History of Bath Football Club
(Harry W Barstow; Bath FC and Corsham Publishing)

Bath, Ace of Clubs (Jones; Breedon Books, 1993).